go FISH

FRESH IDEAS FOR AMERICAN SEAFOOD

LAURENT TOURONDEL
and Andrew Friedman

WILEY

JOHN WILEY & SONS, INC.

TO MY FAMILY,
WHO FIRST TAUGHT ME TO COOK,
AND,
ESPECIALLY,
TO MY DAUGHTER,
ADELYNN

AND IN MEMORY OF KONÉ ABDOULAYE,
LOST ON SEPTEMBER 11, 2001

CONTENTS

FOREWORD

BY DANIEL BOULUD

I have been a fan of Laurent's talent since the early nineties. The fact that, as well as being a gifted chef, he is an all-round genuinely nice person has certainly not hindered the development of our friendship. I feel honored that he has asked me to write this introduction.

Not only do Laurent and I share a common culinary background deeply grounded in traditional French gastronomy, but also the inspiration for both our cuisines is based on seasonal ingredients. In addition, very important, both of us credit our grandmothers with being our first culinary inspirations. In view of that, it seems rather obvious from Laurent's favorite ingredients that his grandmother must have liked fish.

Laurent has worked with many chefs with world-class reputations—Jacques Maximin, Pierre Troisgros, his son Claude, and Joel Robuchon, to name a few. All that he learned from these illustrious mentors shows up as a classical cuisine subtext in each of his dishes, while the actual dish is always intensely personal and creative. Many French chefs who move to a new country remain rather insular in their use of ingredients and techniques: they cook what they were trained to cook (which is delicious but remains traditional) and are not always particularly open to new culinary concepts.

Laurent, on the other hand, has always embraced what he has discovered on his travels and incorporates flavors from around the world into many of his dishes. I find (and I'm sure his many fans concur) that this dichotomy between the time-tried and the innovative makes for great cuisine. The food press obviously agrees, since Laurent has garnered many awards and accolades throughout his years as a chef—not the least of these being three stars from the *New York Times* for his restaurant Cello and the title of Best New Chef 1998 from *Food & Wine* magazine.

While I have eaten meat or selections from Laurent's menus, he is particularly renowned for his instinctive knowledge of the best way to prepare all fish and shellfish. Be it raw with the perfect dosage of spices to make it melt on the palate, or flavored inventively and cooked to perfect doneness, Laurent is a master. This cookbook reflects both his passion and this talent.

Luckily for the home cook, Laurent has been able to translate his dishes onto paper and make them accessible to nonprofessional cooks. I admire the fact that he has taken many of his wonderful, complex dishes and written recipes that don't overwhelm or frighten—people will actually enjoy re-creating them at home. This cookbook will not become one of the pristine coffee-table cookbooks that one looks at, sighs over, and

never cooks from because the recipes are too difficult. I predict that every copy of *Go Fish* sold will soon be dog-eared and stained on each of the many pages where a favorite recipe has been used and reused.

This is unquestionably a cookbook for the passionate cook: a celebration of fish in all its incarnations (and, as an added bonus, some other wonderful recipes for side dishes and desserts). These recipes don't deal with food that is oversophisticated in preparation, though the completed dishes will certainly taste sophisticated; you will be able to make them with complete confidence in your own kitchen (much to the delight of your family and friends).

This year Laurent has not only written this book but also opened a new restaurant, BLT Steak (Bistro Laurent Tourondel), in New York City. With these ventures, I know that he will remain—as he should—one of the big fish in New York City's big pond, which, with Laurent's penchant for seafood, somehow seems a very fitting thing.

ACKNOWLEDGMENTS

I'd like to express my hearfelt gratitude to the following people, all of whom made invaluable contributions to this book:

My editors, Susan Wyler, for her belief and support, and Pam Chirls, for helping us down the home stretch;

My co-writer, Andrew Friedman, for guiding me through my first book;

Quentin Bacon, for his beautiful photography and keen eye;

My agent, Judith Weber, for her early efforts and advice;

Denise Canter, our talented prop stylist;

F. Rozzo & Sons, Inc. and Pisacane, fish purveyors *extraordinaire,* for their help securing the fish;

Rod Mitchell of Browne Trading Company, for his consultation on the fish descriptions;

Fred Dexheimer, for the wine pairings;

Jean-Francois Bonnet and Johnny Léon, two of the best pastry chefs I know, for some of the dessert recipes;

Jennifer Baum, for her wisdom and encouragement;

Jimmy Haber, my partner in BLT Steak and BLT Fish (Bistro Laurent Tourondel);

My sous chefs from over the years, especially Tina Bourbeau, Bertrand Chemel, Matt Evers, Michaël Kanter, Mathieu Palombino, Eric Meurier, John Rondazzo, and Olivier Valleau;

Christopher Pappas at Dairyland for help securing ingredients;

And to the journalists who have written so positively about me, and the food lovers in New York and Las Vegas who have given me my career. It's my great honor to cook for you all.

INTRODUCTION

COOKING FISH AT HOME

I've always wanted to write a cookbook, not only because I love to cook and teach about cooking but also to honor my grandmother and great-grandmother, the two best home cooks I ever knew. As a child, in the small French towns of Montluçon, where I lived, and Creuse, where my great-grandmother lived, these two women taught me how to cook in a home setting. When I was a little kid, I spent countless days picking the fruits and vegetables that grew in the garden behind my family's house. Then I'd watch *Mamy*, the grandmother who lived with us, work her magic with Swiss chard, carrots, potatoes, strawberries, and the other fruits and vegetables we grew. Often she didn't decide what she would use until the lunch or dinner hour was at hand. Because she cooked with such economy, she taught me to make every ingredient count.

When I was old enough to help, she began teaching me to make dishes like *saumonette à la moutarde* (a fish exclusive to European waters, served with mustard sauce), *skate au beurre noir* (skate with brown butter sauce), and my favorite, *sole au persil et citron* (sole with parsley and lemon). We didn't only cook seafood, but those are the dishes I remember most fondly, perhaps because my grandmother loved fish so much. And my grandfather loved *to* fish. When we vacationed by the sea, he actually caught the fish we ate for dinner. I can still remember, when I was five or six years old, getting up at four-thirty in the morning, crawling into a fishing boat, and venturing out beyond the coast with fish nets and crab traps.

There's one more reason I love cooking with fish and shellfish: I've found that it's easier to achieve great flavor with fewer ingredients in less time with fish and shellfish than with any other type of food.

We ate very well every day of the week. But there was one day when we ate even better. On Sunday mornings, my grandparents and I would get in my grandfather's Peugeot and make a one-hour pilgrimage to my great-grandmother's house in Creuse. As we walked up the path to her little stone cottage, we were met by the aroma of the meal she had been preparing all morning. My favorite dish was potato pie: First, she lined a baking dish with her secret dough, then filled it with layers of slivered potatoes, parsley, and onion. She covered this with another layer of dough and baked it. When the pie came out of the oven, she poured cream over the top and let it seep in, infusing the potatoes with flavor. When we arrived at the house, the finished pie would be sitting on the opened oven door, covered with a linen tablecloth, keeping it just warm enough.

The main course was usually *hare civet* (rabbit in red-wine sauce) or oven-roasted *pintade* (guinea hen), both of which were cooked in the wood oven that also heated her small home in the winter. For dessert, there was a *flognarde*, a cross between a beignet and a crepe, which she topped with sliced apples and sugar. We savored this meal sitting on a wooden bench at a wood table in her kitchen, the food warming us from within and the stove warming us from the outside.

I hadn't yet discovered the pleasures of brandy or cigars, so there was only one thing to do after a meal like that: take a nap. I still remember wrapping myself in my great-grandmother's old down comforter, sinking into its plush depths and nodding off, warmed by bricks that she heated in the oven and tucked into the comforter, down by my feet.

When I woke, if the sun was still in the sky and if I still had room in my belly, and if it wasn't too close to dinnertime, my grandparents would walk me across the street to a little *glacier*, where the owners made their own ice cream. My favorites were pistachio and strawberry. If they had those flavors, it was a truly perfect day.

I suppose I should tell you a little about myself, in case you've never dined in one of my restaurants.

In a lot of ways, it's a miracle that I ever became a restaurant chef. Ironically, although my grandmothers were great role models for a home cook, one of my great-grandfathers, a chef in a nearby town, seemed to hate his life in what would become my profession. He had a limited schedule, to say the least: During the week, he opened his bistro for friends to hang out, drink pastis, smoke cigarettes, and play cards. On the weekend, he booked the place out for private affairs like weddings and baptisms. But even then, if you showed up late from the church, you'd find the place locked, with my grandfather scolding you through the window.

Nevertheless, when I was eleven years old, my father got me a weekend job working in Le Grenier à Sel, his friend's one-star Michelin restaurant. When I showed up for work, what I saw was fascinating, but had little to do with what I knew and loved about my grandmother's and great-grandmother's kitchens. There were things going on that baffled me. Bones and vegetables were covered with simmering water to produce what they called *fond* (stock), something I had never seen or even heard of at home. What did they need it for, I wondered? My grandmother's food seemed just fine without it. They were also doing things that made no sense to me, like peeling tomatoes. In time, I learned to do this, but when I became my own boss, I stopped. I never peel tomatoes, not even in the three-star restaurants where I've been the chef.

There were other differences between the home kitchen and the restaurant that bothered me: the fruits and vegetables were stored in baskets and crates. They weren't picked from the restaurant's garden because there wasn't any garden at the restaurant. They were grown elsewhere and delivered to our town, which distanced me from the food even more.

I was also struck by how serious the cooks were, each one joylessly engaged in his little piece of the process. And by how many of them there were. My grandmother cooked dinner for five people every night with just me to help.

After that first kitchen job, I went on to work at a number of restaurants, including a nearby Spanish place called Don Quichotte. I decided to make cooking my career and went to Saint Vincent Ecole de Cuisine in my hometown, graduating with a *certificate d'Aptitude Professionnelle de Cuisinier.* After school, I spent two years as *tournant* (a "floater," or cook who works all stations) of a kitchen brigade that cooked for military personnel at the Hotel des Officiers Mariniers in Toulon, France.

One of the facts of my life has been that I have a serious case of wanderlust; I love to travel and explore. And I'm a lucky guy because it turns out that this is a good longing for a chef to have. In this book you'll see influences from just about every place I've lived, worked in, or visited since the mid-1980s. I've been all over the globe, from Europe to South America to the Far East. I even spent a year knocking around the United States. And in New York there's no end to the culinary experimenting you can do.

One of my first relocations was to London, where I joined the kitchen brigade of Boodle's Gentlemen's Club on St. James Street, home of the famous gin. At Boodle's, I met my first professional mentor, Chef Keith Podmore, who taught me a lot about discipline and respect, and who really motivated me to work as hard as possible. I spent three years there, moving up the ladder, rung by rung.

Then I took some time off to travel around the United States, eating and learning about new foods. I ate barbecue in Texas, chowder in New England, deep-dish pizza in Chicago, and sushi in the Pacific Northwest. In New York, I had my first taste of what would become my future home, when I came here to cook at Beau Geste restaurant under Chef Bruno Tison, who had been the chef at the Plaza Hotel. Here I worked in an area I would become very familiar with during my career: the fish station.

I loved New York City: a great, big, in-your-face city with people from all over the world. It was, and still is, an exciting place to live and cook. Even though I soon decided to return to France, I knew I'd be back.

Bruno gave me a list of chefs to call on for a job back in France One of them was a living legend, Jacques Maximin, who hired me to work at his three-star restaurant, Ledoyen, on the Champs Elysée. Another big influence was Philippe Dorange, who oversaw Ledoyen's kitchen for Maximin. This was my first experience with a big brigade, working as *chef garde-manger.* I learned a great deal about management (I had a staff of twelve people working under me) and ordering, not to mention the chance I got to hone my talents for making pâté, terrine, and ballotine, working as both the *entremetier* (preparer of vegetables and legumes) and *saucier* (preparer of sauces, a very important role in a classically organized French kitchen). I also developed my skills at butchering and at cooking for big, formal buffets, such as the catering we did at the Roland-Garros tennis championship. It was almost like another year of school. It was also great fun. Often, on just a few hours' notice, we found ourselves cooking for a big movie opening or other star-studded affair, like the night that *Batman* premiered in Paris and the whole cast, including Jack Nicholson, showed up.

My next stop was Moscow. I don't know many people who have cooked in Russia, especially back when I did. But it was that old wanderlust again; how could I resist the opportunity? I became *second de cuisine* at Potel & Chabot's Restaurant Mercury in the Hotel Inter-Continental. Moscow had always been a mystery to me, and it was not easy to get there, let alone snag a job. I found everything about Russia fascinating. I learned some of the language and developed an understanding of the cuisine, much of which was developed generations earlier by French chefs who were transplanted there to cook for the czars. I got to cook for the leader of the Communist Party, and I saw a little of the "old" Russia in Mishka, the "undercover" KGB agent who worked in the kitchen. We all knew he was KGB because even though he wore whites, he never cooked!

Then the opportunity of a lifetime came my way and I returned to France to work with the legendary Troisgros family at their eponymous restaurant in Roanne, where I was first assigned to be *garde-manger,* the cook who makes salads and other cold dishes, and later to the fish station. I learned even more discipline and respect for technique, deepened my appreciation for in-season ingredients and how to tell good from bad, and learned an amazing amount about cheese. I also incorporated into my own cooking the Troisgros penchant for using acidic ingredients like vinegar and citrus to balance their food. I even got to work directly with Pierre Troisgros, who supervised me at the *garde-manger* station, and with Michel Troisgros, who oversaw *entremetier* and *poissonier* (fish station), not to mention Claude, with whom I would reunite a few years later in New York. You don't leave that restaurant, which had enjoyed a three-star Michelin rating for more than thirty years, without coming away thinking that it's simply the best. They even had the best staff meals I've ever known.

In 1993, I returned to New York City to become the executive chef of Potel & Chabot's catering operation there. Regular clients included Woody Allen, Paul Simon, and Michael Douglas, to name just a few. Through Potel & Chabot, I was also the private chef for the Kennedy family boat, *Honey Fitz.* This was a real New York job: I got to meet different people every day, rub elbows with superstars, and cook in some of the great landmark buildings of the city, like the Metropolitan Museum of Art, the Museum of Modern Art, the Guggenheim, and the Morgan Library, not to mention creating menus for a slew of Broadway openings.

In 1994, Claude Troisgros hired me to become the executive chef of his new restaurant in New York City, C.T. This was a big job for me and I made the most of it, collaborating with Claude to bring a lot of exotic flavors to the menu, crossing French food with Brazilian. We had thirty-two employees in the kitchen alone. The restaurant was a big critical success: the *New York Times* gave us three stars.

In addition to giving me my first opportunity to work as *chef de cuisine* (the hands-on chef who supervises most of the actual cooking), Claude was a wonderful teacher: he taught me a lot about building a menu, combining international influences, using public relations to promote the restaurant, and how to please a demanding, often star-studded clientele.

After this job, I had another chance to learn from one of the world's great chefs. Even though I had run my own kitchen and become a chef, I went back to France in 1995 to work a *stage* for Joël Robuchon. It was a great chance, and I was glad that I was still sticking to my personal policy of going wherever I had to in order to improve my skills.

Then, in 1996, I moved to a whole new world, Las Vegas, Nevada, when Gamal Aziz recruited me to become the executive chef of the Palace Court restaurant at Caesar's Palace Hotel & Casino. Las Vegas wasn't the restaurant city it is today—I still hear Elvis Presley's song "Viva Las Vegas" when I think of it—so this was another completely different environment for me, a high-roller restaurant where we served American classics like bananas Foster, surf and turf, and cherries jubilee. While working there, *Food & Wine* magazine named me one of the Best New American Chefs of 1998. You can't imagine how important this can be for a young chef. I got a ton of phone calls and many job offers.

In 1999, I returned to New York City to open Cello, an upscale seafood restaurant. It was a big success. We swiftly earned three stars from the *New York Times* and additional attention from coast to coast. *New York* magazine named me one of "99 People to Watch in 1999." We got raves in the *Zagat* guide, a James Beard Foundation nomination as Best New Restaurant, and *Condé Nast Traveler* magazine called it one of the sixty best restaurants in the world. We also served a real who's who of Hollywood, sports, and politics: regulars included Sean Connery, Warren Beatty and Annette Benning, Sigourney Weaver, Danny DeVito, B. B. King, Henry Kissinger, Rudy Giuliani, Ron Howard, Pelé, Ralph Lauren, Paul Newman, Susan Sarandon, Jeff Goldblum, Dan Ackroyd, Joan Collins, Catherine Zeta-Jones, Tony Bennett, Barbara Walters, and members of the Rockefeller family.

During 2004 as this book was being completed, I've opened a new restaurant, BLT Steak (Bistro Laurent Tourondel)—a bistro where we serve my version of classic steakhouse food. There are a number of fish dishes on the menu, many available with the sauces featured in this book, and several side dishes that you'll find in these pages. If you're ever in our neighborhood in midtown Manhattan, I hope you'll drop by and enjoy these in person.

Obviously, I've come a long way since the day I walked into my first professional kitchen all those years ago, and I've learned a lot about the restaurant business. But there's something I realized way back then that has never changed: restaurant cooking has little or nothing to do with home cooking. I may be a restaurant chef, but in this book I want to share my love of cooking fish and shellfish at home, in a way that you will find useful, sharing recipes you can make using ingredients you can find, afford, and enjoy.

The difference between my grandmother's kitchen and the restaurant one I discovered on that Saturday morning all those years ago foreshadowed the double life I lead when it comes to cooking today. In my restaurants, we cook fish from all over the world in very elaborate recipes. The kitchens are twice as big as the one in that restaurant in my hometown, and the cooks look just as serious as those guys back home. They better be serious. We've got a lot of work to do. And that's what it is for us. Work.

But when I cook at home, it's a different story. If you think you don't like to cook complicated recipes, imagine how you'd feel about it if you'd worked all week doing exactly that. Don't get me wrong; I love my job. But it's a myth that restaurant chefs cook the same way for themselves at home as they do for guests in their restaurants. In reality, we cook recipes that are no more or less complicated than the ones you probably cook at home. But we bring a knowledge of ingredients, combinations, and techniques that make our food very special, even if it doesn't take too much time to make.

At home, I cook dishes that don't require very much trouble. I keep things simple by keeping recipe lists short. Every ingredient makes an impact. And I select dishes that are enjoyable to prepare. In the following recipes, I'm going to share my passion with recipes designed especially for you, the American home cook. In fact, I'm only going to use seafood that comes from American waters, in recipes that don't use too many ingredients or take too much time.

With the exception of the vegetables, side dishes, and a few of my favorite desserts, all of the recipes in the book feature fish or shellfish. The vegetables and side dishes don't because they are meant to accompany the dishes that do. And I just had to include a few desserts because they're based on those dishes my grandmothers made for me all those years ago, where I first learned how surprisingly simple great food can be.

Laurent Tourondel
NEW YORK CITY
SEPTEMBER 2004

GREAT AMERICAN FISH AND SHELLFISH

When I do a cooking demonstration for home cooks, the first question they ask is always the same: "Why fish?" I love the variety of fish and shellfish, and what you can do with them: their mildness makes them wonderful vehicles for almost any flavor, and seafood marries well with spices and herbs from all over the world.

And there's another reason: fish is very easy to cook. You might think it's difficult, but it's not. Most fish cooks very quickly, and once you understand how to judge cooking temperatures and carry-over heat (don't worry; I'll explain them both), it couldn't be simpler.

Because this book is meant for American home cooks, it uses only fish that come from American waters. In the restaurants where I've been the chef, we've cooked everything from langoustine to turbot to Dover sole, and other imported treasures of the sea. Sure, you can obtain these ingredients in some American cities or by mail order—for a pretty penny, I might add—but I believe that part of keeping home cooking simple is relying on locally available ingredients.

One of the things that fascinates me about fish is that each type has a story to tell, whether it's the way it matures, how it came to be fished, or even how it got its name. Just as deep oceans are full of surprises and mystery, fish and shellfish you might think you know still have secrets to reveal.

Many of these fish will be familiar to you. For example, we're about to talk a little about salmon, tuna, lobster, crayfish, snapper, mackerel, striped bass, and shrimp. But there are also a number here that you might not know. For instance, hake is one of my favorite fish. Its texture and flavor are more satisfying than, say, halibut, and it's less expensive. It's readily available, but most Americans have never tasted or even heard of it. I hope I have the pleasure of introducing it to your table.

So, let's put on our masks and snorkels and take a look at what goes on under the surface of American waters:

anchovy

water Pacific Coast, mostly in the waters off California.

appearance Very small, herring-like fish with a blue to light green back.

size Up to 1 foot long.

my notes To me, white anchovies, a species from Spain that you might obtain in some specialty stores or by mail order, are the ultimate anchovy, with a very fine, understated flavor; they are lightly cured and marinated in white wine vinegar.

arctic char

water Mostly farm-raised. Also fished in the waters off Canada, just north of New England. Primarily a freshwater fish, but also flourishes in salt water.

appearance Fin fish with a flesh that ranges in color from white to red.

size Farm-raised arctic char are usually about 4 pounds; in the wild, it's not unusual to find them up to 10 pounds.

my notes Arctic char is a close relative of salmon and trout, but it has a finer, milder flavor. I especially love cooking char *en papillote,* as I do on page 170. If you want to try other ways, substitute it for salmon or trout in recipes that use those fish.

bass, black sea (black will, chub, sea bass)

water This saltwater fish is caught all along the East Coast, from Maine to Florida.

appearance Fin fish with predominantly black scales and delicate white flesh underneath.

size 1 to 8 pounds, but most commonly available between 2 and 3 pounds.

my notes I enjoy eating this fish raw, when its flavor is more gentle, almost like that of a shellfish. Sea bass is especially perishable, so keep it cool on the trip from the market to your house, and never let it stay unrefrigerated for more than a few minutes.

bass, striped and wild striped

water These fish are caught in cold waters up and down the East Coast of the United States.

appearance Fin fish with shimmering silver scales and black stripes.

size Up to 50 pounds and sometimes larger, but the best are 5 to 6 pounds. (If you're a chef, with direct access to a purveyor, 15 to 20 pounds are ideal.)

my notes Striped bass and wild striped bass have a fine taste and texture. Be sure to always err on the side of undercooking or it will toughen up. I don't care for farmed striped bass, which is actually a hybrid of wild striped bass and white bass.

black cod (sablefish)

water Pacific Coast from California to Alaska.

appearance Rough black skin that resembles sable fur.

size Up to 40 pounds, but usually fished at 3 to 10 pounds.

my notes Actually not related to cod; it's a member of the skilfish family. The best comes from Alaska.

caviar, american

water American caviar is the roe of American fish, primarily paddlefish (also known as spoonbill), trout, and white sturgeon, all of which are generally fished in the waters of California, Louisiana, and Oregon. It once came from Atlantic sturgeon, but since this is an endangered species it is currently forbidden to fish them. There are, however, a few California purveyors who farm-raise Atlantic sturgeon.

appearance Small, black, grainlike.

size Almost imperceptibly small.

my notes American caviar is far less expensive than the more famous Caspian caviar. You might be surprised at its quality. Note that only sturgeon eggs can be referred to as caviar; if the roe comes from another species of fish, this must be noted in its name on the label.

   The most popular caviar in the world is processed by Russia and Iran from Beluga (the largest), Sevruga (the smallest), and Osetra sturgeon, all of which produce gray to black eggs. The sturgeon that produce Iranian caviar are fished from the same sea as those that produce Russian caviar, but Iranian production uses less salt and no alloys to process it.

clams, cherrystone

water Atlantic Coast.

appearance Medium size with a hard shell.

size 2 to 3 ounces each (5 to 7 per pound).

my notes In addition to its size, I like this clam for its relatively low price.

clams, littleneck

water Atlantic Coast.

appearance Among the smallest clams sold, though not as tiny as butter clams.

size Approximately 2 ounces each (7 to 10 per pound).

my notes These quick-cooking clams are ideal for soups and stews because you can poach them in the liquid at the last second.

clams, razor

water Atlantic Coast.

appearance Long and thin with a bamboo-like shell.

size Approximately 2 ounces each (8 per pound).

my notes If you have a hard time finding these clams, look in Chinese markets.

clams, manila

water Pacific Coast, and—to a lesser extent—Atlantic Coast.

appearance Very thin with a coral-colored shell.

size They can grow quite big, but ideally shouldn't be larger than 1 inch in diameter.

my notes: I like Manila clams in pasta sauces; often their shells can be left on for dramatic presentation.

cod, atlantic

water Atlantic Coast, from North Carolina northward.

appearance Lean fin fish with flaky white flesh.

size Average weight is 10 pounds, though you'll probably find smaller specimens in your fish store.

my notes The Atlantic cod, a completely different species from the Pacific cod, is by far the better of the two. This is one of my favorite fish with a large flake and mild flavor. It's available fresh, smoked, salted, or dried. I especially like the cheeks. Cod is a diverse family that includes one of my favorite fish, hake (pages 7–8). If possible, seek out line-caught cod rather than those captured by net, which often unnecessarily kill other oceanic life forms.

cod, pacific

water West Coast, from Oregon and points north.

appearance Lean, with flaky white flesh. Distinguished from the Atlantic cod by its pale gray coloring.

size 5 to 10 pounds.

my notes The Pacific cod looks very much like its Atlantic counterpart, but is by far the lesser of the two.

cod, salt (bacalao)

water The best salt cod comes from Portugal.

appearance When shopping for salt cod, look for a nice white flesh.

size A preserved fish, it is available as fillets.

my notes The key thing about salt cod is that it has to be soaked before cooking to draw out the excess salt: put the cod in a bowl, cover it with cold water, cover the bowl, and soak in the refrigerator for 24 hours, changing the water three or four times.

crab, blue

water Saltwaters along the Atlantic Coast, from Massachusetts to the Bahamas; most plentiful off Virginia and in Maryland's Chesapeake Bay.

appearance The classic crab shape: low, round body with pincers.

size About 5 inches across.

my notes There are three grades of crabmeat. For this book's purposes, we are mostly interested in lump (also known as jumbo or backfin), which is large pieces from the crab's body. Smaller but acceptable pieces are known as "flake." Stay away from blue crab claw meat, which has an unattractive brown color and is far inferior in quality. You should also seek out unpasteurized crabmeat, which has a more delicate flavor than pasteurized. (Crab is often pasteurized to grant it a long shelf life.)

crab, dungeness (california crab, market crab)

water Most plentiful between Oregon and Washington. Also found in the Pacific Ocean from Mexico to Alaska.

appearance Large, almost heart-shaped shell.

size 1 to 3 pounds, though they grow much larger. You can also buy picked Dungeness crabmeat from many fish stores; it is generally sold in 1-pound plastic containers.

my notes One of the most flavorful crabs.

crab, peekytoe (bay crab, maine rock crab, sand crab)

water 20- to 40-foot deep waters off the coast of New England

appearance "Peekytoe" is *not* a species of crab; because the crabs from which this meat comes have an inward-turning point at the end of its legs, they are known as "picked toe," or "peekytoe."

size N/A (you only buy this as picked meat).

my notes Rod Mitchell, the proprietor of the Browne Trading Company, and the fish purveyor who consulted on these descriptions, is based in Portland, Maine, where lobster fishermen call these crabs "peekytoe." He's the one who started marketing them by that charming name. Fine and sweet.

crab, soft-shell (See Crab, Blue)

Soft-shell crabs are blue crabs caught just after molting, or shedding their tough outer shells. A real delicacy from May to September.

crab, stone

water More than 900 species exist, but I use only the Florida stone crab.

appearance All you'll ever buy is a claw (see My Notes).

size N/A.

my notes The only portion of the stone crab that's of interest is the claw. Fishermen remove one, then return the crabs to the sea, where they regenerate the claw and are fished again. They're just as good cooked and chilled as they are hot.

crayfish (crawfish)

water Freshwater streams, mostly in Louisiana, but also in the Pacific Northwest.

appearance They look almost like tiny lobsters.

size 5 to 6 inches long.

my notes I use these only for New Orleans–style cooking, like the recipe on page 180. By the way, the best are the Signal, or White, crayfish from the Sacramento River.

cuttlefish

water This cephalopod may be fished off the East Coast of the United States (see My Notes).

appearance Similar to a squid, but with an internal shell, shorter legs, and a more distinct top and bottom.

size 2 inches to 2 feet long, ½ pound to 2 pounds each.

my notes The cuttlefish you'll most likely find have been caught off Spain or Portugal and shipped frozen. They can often be purchased with the ink sac intact; the ink is a crucial ingredient in dishes like cuttlefish and squid risotto.

finnan haddie (smoked haddock)

water Haddock is fished from the same waters as Atlantic cod.

appearance Pearly white flesh.

size Haddock can grow up to 20 pounds, but you'll buy smoked haddock in significantly smaller quantities.

my notes From its name, it's pretty easy to guess that smoked haddock, known as "finnan haddie," was first made in Scotland. Today, it's also produced in New England. I like cooking it in milk, which moderates the smoky and fishy qualities.

flounder

water Atlantic and Pacific Coasts.

appearance Firm, small, white flake.

size Because of the wide variety (see My Notes), it's difficult to generalize. Halibut, for example, can grow up to 700 pounds, while fluke can be as small as 2 pounds.

my notes "Flounder" is a name given to a wide variety of flat fish that includes everything from fluke (below) to halibut (page 8) to sand dab.

fluke (summer flounder)

water Atlantic Coast of the United States.

appearance Orange or brown skin, which changes to match the ocean floor, giving way to a firm, small, white flake.

size 2 to 5 pounds

my notes Fluke is a great receiver of flavor. Try the recipe on page 36 and see how well it takes on the saké reduction's taste.

frog's legs

water Florida lakes and swamps.

appearance Plump and light pink.

size 2 to 8 ounces per pair.

my notes I prefer firm, medium-size frog's legs. Just cook them until they're warmed through to preserve their sweet flavor and delicate texture. Do not buy frozen frog's legs; buy fresh ones in the spring and summer.

grouper

water Atlantic Ocean off the Florida coast and, to a lesser extent, the Pacific waters off Southern California.

appearance Unattractive red- or black-skinned fin fish with a protruding lower jaw.

size Grouper can grow up to 1,200 pounds, but your fish source will have them somewhere between 2 and 20.

my notes Both black and red grouper are found on both coasts of the United States. I prefer the black, which has a fluffier, lighter meat. I love the firm, sweet flesh of this fish; it's leaner than a lot of other white-fleshed fish.

hake (blue hake, sow hake, russet hake, white hake)

water North Atlantic.

appearance Slender-bodied, white-fleshed fin fish.

size Can weigh up to 30 pounds, but usually 3 to 4 pounds.

my notes This lean, delicate flesh—a member of the codfish family—is my favorite, for its large, soft flake and sublime flavor.

halibut (atlantic halibut)

water When most chefs talk about halibut, they're talking about Atlantic halibut, which has the most desirable firm flesh and delicate flavor. That said, there are West Coast halibut, namely Pacific (fished during an insanely short season of just a few days and frozen) and California (which is really a flounder).

appearance Snowy white-fleshed fin fish with a large flake.

size Usually caught at about 10 pounds, this fish can grow up to about 750 pounds.

my notes Do not purchase frozen halibut.

lobster, american

water Cold waters of the Atlantic Coast and Pacific Coast off California. Warm-water species from Florida.

appearance Orange-black shell. You can determine the sex by looking at the underside of the tail and following the legs to where the tail joins the head. There are two small hind legs there—male hind legs are stiff and hard; female's legs are flimsy and soft.

size Generally 1 to 2 pounds in the market, but they grow significantly larger.

my notes One of the most luxurious shellfish there is. If you can get them, the blue lobsters from Brittany are the best on the planet. It's interesting to note that the Canadian lobster is the same species as the one we call Atlantic or Maine lobster here, but it doesn't taste as good owing to its waters and diet.

lobster, spiny (california spiny lobster, lobster tail)

water California spiny lobster is found along the Southern California coast. Western Mexico Florida spiny lobster (aka Caribbean lobster) is caught off the east coast of Florida, all the way down to the Carribbean.

appearance No claws, long antennae.

size The ones you see in a fish store generally are 1 to 2 pounds.

my notes: My favorite lobster, with a texture and flavor all its own.

mackerel

water North Atlantic and Pacific.

appearance Pacific mackerel are fin fish with long, green bodies, dark stripes, and pale flesh; Atlantic mackerel are greenish blue with slate-blue lines along the back.

size ½ pound to 7 pounds.

my notes I love eating this relatively fatty fish in raw (sashimi) dishes. Generally, that which is sold as mackerel here is the Atlantic mackerel, sometimes also called the Boston mackerel. Spanish mackerel, which are generally found in the Mediterranean, are also fished along the East Coast of the United States. These are less oily and much larger than Atlantic mackerel.

mahi mahi (dolphinfish, dorado)

water These fish flourish in the warm waters off Florida and the Pacific Coast of the United States, including Hawaii.

appearance Grayish, large-flaked flesh that lightens when cooked.

size 5 to 10 pounds, with the capacity to grow to 50 pounds.

my notes I enjoy the mild, sweet flavor of this fish after it's been cooked and chilled.

monkfish

water The Atlantic Coast, from North Carolina northward.

appearance Large bulbous head with sharp teeth and firm, white flesh. The head is usually cut off and the fish is sold in portions called "tails" or "loins."

size Grows up to 50 pounds, but 1 to 10 pounds is normal.

my notes The ugliest fish in the sea, monkfish has the sweet flavor and firm texture reminiscent of lobster tail meat.

mussels

water Atlantic Ocean from North Carolina northward; Pacific Ocean from Alaska to California.

appearance Castanet-like shell surrounding pale orange meat.

size ½ inch to 3 inches in length. Medium size are best.

my notes Blue mussels are cultivated in the United States, but you're just as likely to find larger, green-lipped Prince Edward Island mussels from New Zealand in your market. Whatever their origin, most mussels cultivated today are "rope" mussels, bred on ropes hung from rafts in the ocean to avoid sand and grit.

octopus

water Several species are available up and down the Atlantic and Pacific Coasts.

appearance A bulbous head with 8 tentacles around it.

size 1 to 4 pounds.

my notes Because it's so naturally tough, octopus is best if braised and grilled. I often cool it and serve it cold in salads. I especially like baby octopus because they're more tender; you may have to seek them out in Greek, Spanish, or Italian markets.

oysters

water All coasts of the United States.

appearance Hard, tightly closed shell encasing slimy meat.

size Up to 6 inches in diameter.

my notes There are almost countless oysters in the United States, but they are all the same species. The different varieties are named for the waters from which they come (e.g., Wellfleet, Bluepoint). There are two important exceptions to this: Maine Milan oysters and the famed Kumamoto, the latter of which is cultivated on the West Coast of the United States.

pike, walleye (yellow pike, pike perch)

water Lake fish.

appearance Long body covered by silver skin with brown or yellow areas and white flesh beneath.

size Most are 1 to 2 pounds, but they can grow larger.

my notes For my money, this is the best-tasting lake fish.

pompano

water Caught off coasts of Florida, North and South Carolina, and in the Gulf of Mexico.

appearance Light silver-skinned fin fish with white flesh.

size ¾ pound to 2 pounds.

my notes The smaller the better with this fish because it has a strong flavor that's more pronounced in larger specimens. Great for grilling.

rockfish (rosefish, blackfish, wolffish)

water Except for Atlantic Ocean perch, the only commercially important rockfish are caught along the Pacific Coast as far south as Baja California and as far north as the Bering Sea.

appearance Rockfish are among the most colorful and beautiful of all fish. They have long spiny dorsal fins, usually bright colors, big eyes, and a generally jagged appearance.

size Varies according to species.

my notes These fish are perfect for fish soup and stock. They're also deep-fried a lot in Asian cooking.

salmon, atlantic

water Most sold in the United States is farmed. Somewhat confusingly, some Atlantic salmon is farmed in the Pacific Ocean.

appearance Atlantic salmon has moist flesh and a beautiful, rich pink color.

size 10 to 15 pounds.

my notes Atlantic salmon has a fairly high fat content, which accounts for its melting texture and rich flavor.

salmon, copper river king (chinook salmon)

water The Copper River flows through the state of Alaska. Almost 300 miles in length, this wild rushing river empties into Prince William Sound at the town of Cordova. The Copper River King salmon is fished only from mid-May to mid-June.

appearance A muscular-looking fin fish with silver skin.

size Up to 50 pounds, with an average weight of 20 pounds.

my notes Fighting against the strong, cold current of the Copper River makes these salmon strong, with a high level of stored oils and fats. These qualities make the salmon among the richest, tastiest fish in the world.

The white Alaskan salmon is a King salmon that, for some unknown reason, eats a carotene-free, or krill-free, diet, so its flesh stays white, but it tastes very similar to other salmon.

salmon, copper river sockeye (red salmon)

water The Copper River (see Copper River King Salmon).

appearance Copper River Sockeye are prized for their intense red color and high oil content.

size 3 to 8 pounds.

my notes I love grilling this fish; its firm, moist flesh responds very well to the high heat.

sardines

water Most U.S. sardines are caught off the coast of Maine. Pacific sardines (from off the California coast) are now almost extinct.

appearance Small, herring-like bodies.

size Approximately 5 ounces.

my notes I love these small, delicate fish grilled.

scallops, sea

water Deep Atlantic waters from Canada to North Carolina.

appearance Ivory to pinkish white.

size 10 to 20 pieces per pound.

my notes There are three sources for sea scallops: The best are diver-harvested (or diver) sea scallops, which are gathered by divers who go on one-day or half-day fishing trips just off-shore, bringing in the freshest scallops and ensuring that their shells do not trap mud, which you end up paying for because it contributes to the weight of the scallop. The second best are dry-packed scallops (sold in supermarkets as "dry" scallops), gathered by larger boats that spend about one week in the water. They're not as fresh as diver-harvested, but are generally of very high quality. By far, the least meritorious scallops are those packed in a milky solution (sold as "chemically preserved"), which is an unpleasant-tasting chemical preservative that turns them a pure white rather than their natural off-white or cream color.

scallops, bay

water Protected bays, harbors, and salt ponds from North Carolina to Canada. The best come from Nantucket and Cape Cod, though many also come from Southern California.

appearance Tiny, firm, white, and shaped like a thimble.

size 50 to 100 per pound.

my notes Little known fact: Nantucket and Cape Cod scallops are actually sweeter than Taylor Bay scallops. The best are almost like candy. They are only in season from October through April.

scallops, taylor bay

water Fairhaven, Massachusetts. (Taylor is the name of the company, not the bay.)

appearance Tiny, firm, white, and shaped like a thimble.

size 70 to 100 per pound.

my notes Taylor Bay scallops are cultivated to be spectacularly sweet. If you cook them, be sure to do so quickly; they can overcook before you know it.

sea urchin

water Atlantic and Pacific Coasts.

appearance Small, spiny orbs. The Pacific urchin has larger, orange roe. The East Coast urchin is smaller and sweeter with a less intensely orange roe.

size Up to 10 inches in diameter.

my notes I especially like the iodine flavor of sea urchin on its own, with a squeeze of lemon or gently warmed in cream.

shrimp and prawns

water The most commonly available shrimp in the United States are Gulf white and Gulf pink. Both are caught off the Atlantic Coasts of the Carolinas and Florida, and in the Gulf of Mexico.

appearance The classic shrimp shape and pink or gray-white to blue in color.

size Shrimp are size-categorized by how many come to a pound. The common designations are 7 or less; 10 or less; 10/15 (meaning 10 to 15); 16/20; 21/25; 26/30; 31/35; 35/40; 41/50, and so on. It's important to note that the lower the first number, the larger the individual shrimp.

It's also useful to remember that although shrimp are commonly sold as small, large, jumbo, and so on, these designations are not officially defined by the industry. However, a good guideline is: small, 56/65; medium, 41/50; jumbo, 21/25; colossal, 10/15 or larger.

my notes Technically, prawns are just another name for shrimp. As the names suggest, the white are white and the pink are pink (or orange) when raw.

shrimp, rock

water Cold waters off the Florida coast.

appearance Small and curled, almost in a nugget shape.

size About the size of a marble.

my notes These shrimp actually do have heads, but they're usually sold pre-peeled with the heads cut off.

skate

water Both the Atlantic and Pacific Coasts of the United States.

appearance Flat, like a ray, with a long tail. Because of its shape, the meat from this fish is referred to as "wings" (actually enlarged pectoral fins) rather than fillets. The wings can be up to 2 inches thick at their center and taper off toward the edges.

size Skate wings, the only edible portion, average about 1 pound.

my notes Be sure to serve this fish as soon as you finish cooking it, and leave it a bit under-cooked and moist. Its high gelatin content causes it to become unpleasantly sticky when it chills. For this reason, butter is the best cooking medium as it almost serves to baste the fish.

snails

water American snails are farm-raised in California.

appearance Grayish-brown shell and meat.

size 20 to 30 pieces of harvested meat per pound. Each snail in its shell is approximately 1 inch in diameter.

my notes Escargot are *petit-gris* snails, which were originally from France but are now farmed in the United States. These escargot are recognizable by their brown-gray shells. You can also buy canned snails at gourmet stores and via mail order.

snapper, red

water From Newfoundland to North Carolina; Gulf of Mexico; Pacific Ocean, including around Hawaii.

appearance Pink in color and a bit rounder than most other fin fish.

size Grow up to 50 pounds, but average market fish is 2½ pounds.

my notes Large, flaky pieces and pleasingly oily texture.

snapper, yellowtail

water Gulf of Mexico and Northern and Southern Florida.

appearance Pink meat that turns white when cooked.

size Up to 4 pounds.

my notes Deliciously, mildly sweet.

squid (calamari)

water Atlantic and Pacific waters, both shallow and deep, off the United States coast.

appearance A cephalopod with 8 arms, 2 fins, and a siphon used for propulsion. It has firm flesh and off-white meat.

size Anywhere from 1 to 80 feet long.

my notes Even if the fish has been cleaned by your fishmonger, rinse it well to get any lingering grit out. The ink sac is the source of a black liquid used in pastas, risottos, and other Mediterranean dishes.

swordfish

water All along the Atlantic Coast and off the Pacific Coast near California.

appearance A long-bodied fish with a swordlike extension of its mouth.

size Up to 1,000 pounds, but more commonly found at 250 pounds.

my notes A great grilling fish.

note: Pink swordfish is a swordfish that (like the King salmon) eats a carotene-free, or krill-free, diet. Its flesh can be white or as pink as a "regular" salmon. It's most commonly found in the North Atlantic and is also known as the pumpkin swordfish.

trout, rainbow and brown

water Lakes and streams, but some make it out to sea water. They are also the most commonly farmed trout.

appearance White flesh that turns a bit pink at the lateral line.

size 12 to 16 ounces.

my notes Steelhead trout are actually rainbow trout that make it out to sea; they can reach sizes of up to 12 pounds and have a pleasingly strong flavor. Smoked trout is delicious, its oily character softened by smoking. If you come across any other trout, especially Steelhead from the northern Pacific Coast, by all means try them to learn the difference between the species.

tuna, bluefin

water Atlantic and Pacific Coasts of the United States.

appearance Blue-black skin giving way to silver on the underside; dark red flesh.

size Up to 1,400 pounds.

my notes Easily the best tuna for sushi and other raw preparations.

tuna, yellowfin

water Yellowfin tuna swim in warm waters worldwide. Here, most are fished in the Pacific, but also along the Atlantic Coast in the summer months.

appearance Yellow bellies and fins; dark pink/medium red flesh.

size Up to 500 pounds.

my notes   This is one of the most abundant tunas. If you see a sign in the market that just says "tuna," it's probably Yellowfin.

note: ahi tuna   Ahi is actually the Hawaiian name for two popular tunas: Yellowfin and Bigeye. Bigeye is plumper, with a higher fat content.

note: toro   Toro is a cut from the belly of Bluefin tuna that has a high fat content. In Japanese markets, *chutoro* signifies a moderately high content; *otoro* is very fatty. This is a prized sushi cut that's very pale and very expensive.

whitebait

water   Bays and inlets.

appearance   Tiny little fish, just like the name says.

size   Almost pin-sized.

my notes   Scientifically speaking, there is no such thing as whitebait. They are any fish small as minnows, silvery in color, and practically transparent, found in waters worldwide. These include silversides and sand lances. They are almost always fried.

BUYING AND STORING FISH AND SHELLFISH

Let me start out by saying something that might surprise you: buying and storing great fish is easy. It's easy because you don't have a lot of decisions to make. If you follow a few simple guidelines, you'll be able to buy excellent-quality fish and make sure it stays in good condition right up until the time you cook it.

The best advice I can give you for buying fresh fish is to find a fishmonger, market, or online source you trust. If you have such a source, you're practically all set because you can get what you need and know that they'll only sell you the best. It's especially important to find a good source because fin fish are not "regulated" in the United States; the USDA simply does not inspect them the way it does beef and poultry.

As for signs of a good fish market, the rule of thumb is to "follow your nose." Steer clear of markets or fish departments that have a fishy or ammonia scent in the air. Markets should smell fresh and clean. They should also be immaculately well kept, and the fish should be perfectly cut and attractively presented. Why am I so concerned with appearances? For this simple reason: If they don't take pride in what you see in the front of the store, just imagine what goes on in the back!

If you catch your own fish or shellfish, then you have probably developed a good eye and nose for freshness. Nevertheless, I strongly suggest that you contact the local department of fish and game to be sure the waters in which you're fishing are free of contaminants like pesticides and pollutants like sewage and PBCs.

AFTER PURCHASING FISH

Once you purchase fish, you should keep it as cold as possible at all times. If you don't live very close to your source, keep it on ice, or pack it in amongst your frozen food. (I've never understood why the seafood department isn't the last department in the supermarket. It should be after the frozen food and before the checkout counter.) At home, keep fish in the coldest part of your refrigerator. If you don't keep your refrigerator very cold (40°F or lower), store the fish on ice in the fridge, changing the ice as it melts. This is most important with fatty fish like mackerel and salmon, which spoil more quickly.

I urge you to cook fresh fish and shellfish as soon as possible, certainly within one day of when you buy it. I don't recommend freezing fish yourself, although it's sometimes okay to buy it frozen (see page 21). Most seafood is very delicate and its moisture can turn to ice.

Mussels, clams, cockles, and oysters should be kept similarly cold, but with a few important distinctions: do not keep them on ice because they're alive when you buy them and can literally freeze to death. Also, don't keep them in plastic bags or they might suffocate. Store them in a large bowl covered with a wet towel. You can keep mollusks for up to three days, but it's better to cook them as soon as possible.

Crabs should be stored in a brown paper bag ventilated with a few small holes. Lobsters should be held in a wet cloth or newspaper. Both should be cooked on the day you buy them.

SIGNS OF FRESHNESS: FISH

Eyes should retain their full shape. There's a common misconception that they shouldn't be clouded, but this isn't necessarily so. Many fish's eyes film over when they are caught.

Fins are delicate, so check them for the best gauge of whether or not a fish has been carefully handled on its journey to the market.

Flesh You can't touch fish in a store, but firm flesh is a sign of freshness. It should give a little, then rise back up when depressed.

Gills should be bright red with no brown whatsoever. You may need to ask your fish purveyor to show them to you, but don't hesitate to do this. The gills are a great place to further gauge freshness by smelling them; they should smell clean. (Fish might be bled through the gills, which can drain them of their color; this is okay.)

Scales should be more or less all intact, and should glisten, but not be slimy.

Smell All fresh fish, whether whole or filleted, should have a very faint smell of the sea, but otherwise be practically odorless. Whole fish should still be rigid (literally from rigor mortis).

SIGNS OF FRESHNESS: SHELLFISH

CRUSTACEANS (CRAB, LOBSTER, AND SHRIMP)

Crab and Lobster The most important thing about crabs and lobsters is that they should be alive. Buy them from a busy store that sells them as soon as they come in; crabs and lobsters that have been confined to a tank for a long time are lifeless and therefore flavorless. A good test for lobster freshness is that if you pull the tail toward its body and release it, it should snap back quickly. Soft-shell crabs are easier to gauge: they have a siphon that should retract when touched.

Shrimp should smell fresh, be firm to the touch, and have no black spots on the meat, which indicates oxidation.

MOLLUSKS AND CEPHALOPODS (CLAMS, MUSSELS, OYSTERS, SCALLOPS, SQUID, AND OCTOPUS)

Clams, oysters, and mussels are inspected in wholesale units. Look for the USDA sticker indicating they are approved. You need to buy clams, mussels, and oysters alive. Shells should be tightly closed, but if tapping causes an ajar one to close, that's acceptable as well. Avoid broken shells, or discard them if purchasing a bag of mussels. Mussels or clams that feel very heavy for their size, or in relation to others in the batch, are probably filled with mud. Discard them.

Scallops and squid are sold out of the shell. They should be super-fresh in smell. Do not buy scallops stored in a milky preservative; they take on too much of its flavor.

Squid and octopus should be firm, with a nice, shiny skin. Squid should have a light, fresh, oceanic smell.

BUYING FISH FROM THE SUPERMARKET

For a number of reasons, the supermarket is a less than ideal place to purchase fish. For one thing, the market doesn't specialize in fish. Fish is just one of the many things they buy and sell. Because fish is so perishable, it's probably the last thing you want to buy at the supermarket.

But there are other reasons. When you buy fish at the average supermarket, it's usually in fillets or steaks presented on a Styrofoam or cardboard tray that's wrapped in plastic. So you can't really touch it, smell it, or even tell if it's glistening because the plastic and the way the light catches it can throw you off. (Although you can often smell bad fish right through the plastic.) And, obviously, you can't see its eyes or gills.

Look for the following signs if purchasing fish fillets from a supermarket:

○ Flesh should look moist and solid, with no gaps or conspicuous imperfections.

○ If it's not too tautly wrapped, be sure the fish is firm.

○ Make sure darker-fleshed fish like tuna, monkfish, and swordfish do not have rainbow-like streaks.

FROZEN FISH

Freezing is one of the most misunderstood fish topics. Most so-called gourmets think that any fish that has been frozen is bad. But this is far from the truth. In reality, many fishermen who work for large seafood companies do their work so far from shore that they have to freeze the fish before it's even brought in. In other words, a lot of "fresh" fish has been frozen. But it's flash-frozen at temperatures below 20°F, which keeps large deposits of ice from forming and also kills parasites, a benefit if the fish will be served raw or rare.

If you purchase your fish frozen, look for the same signs you would seek in fresh fish, such as a fresh, clean smell and no white or discolored areas. To thaw frozen fish, let it rest in the refrigerator overnight, preferably on a large plate to catch any gathering moisture. Do not thaw it at room temperature, which provides ideal breeding conditions for bacteria.

SMOKED FISH

Smoked fish should be moist, firm, and well refrigerated at all times.

When preparing fish, your utensils and cutting board or work surface should be immaculate, to guard against salmonella contamination.

RAW FISH AND OTHER COLD APPETIZERS

Tomato Bruschetta with Manchego
and Anchovy

Sea Bass Ceviche with
Lemon Verbena Oil

Crab Roll

Peekytoe Crab in Vine-Ripe Tomato
Gelée

Stone Crab with Avocado
and Grapefruit Juice

Slivered Fluke with Saké Reduction

Lobster Roll

Lobster Salad with Roasted Beets and
Soft-Boiled Egg Mayonnaise

Copper River Salmon, Osetra Caviar,
and Cipolline Onions

Marinated Salmon and Cold Citrus
Nage with Sunflower Seeds

Oysters with Daikon Vinaigrette

Taylor Bay Scallops in Green
Apple–Coriander Sauce

Steamed Shrimp with Heirloom
Tomato and Lime-Ginger Sauce

Tuna Tartar with Crispy Shallots

Curry-Scented Tuna with
Sun-Dried Tomato

Sweet Yellowtail Sashimi with Wasabi

When I moved to New York, sushi quickly became one of my favorite kinds of food, even before I became a seafood specialist. It's probably the ultimate example of the power of great raw ingredients: fish so superior and fresh that it can be eaten in its pure, natural state, with just some soy sauce to coax out the flavor, some wasabi to balance it with heat, and pickled ginger to refresh the palate for the next taste.

There's one sashimi recipe in this chapter, Sweet Yellowtail Sashimi with Wasabi (page 56). There are also many recipes featuring raw or partially cooked fish. If you've never been a sushi eater, these recipes are a great way to ease yourself into it. For example, Slivered Fluke with Saké Reduction (page 36) is a sushi-like dish featuring the popular Japanese rice wine.

Raw fish is, of course, something that needs to be handled very carefully, not just for health concerns, but also for flavor. Here are a few important guidelines:

- Keep raw fish as cold as possible, from the moment you buy it. If you live a long way from your market or fishmonger, keep it wrapped in plastic and on ice all the way home. It's also not a bad idea to let it chill for 5 or 10 minutes in the freezer before you begin working with it at room temperature; this will keep it cold and firm, making it easier to manipulate. Ideally, you should prepare and serve raw fish on the same day as you buy it.

- The surfaces on which you prepare and serve raw fish are very important. Cutting boards should be cleaned with antibacterial soap and cooled, and plates should be chilled in the refrigerator. Again, not only will these steps keep the fish at a safe temperature but because the fish is so delicate, it will maintain its flavor as well.

Even with a cold dish, there's room for plenty of contrast. I like situating raw fish in a cool broth, as in Marinated Salmon and Cold Citrus Nage with Sunflower Seeds (page 44), Taylor Bay Scallops in Green Apple–Coriander Sauce (page 48), or Oysters with Daikon Vinaigrette (page 47). I look for different textures, as in Tuna Tartar with Crispy Shallots (page 52) and Copper River Salmon, Osetra Caviar, and Cipolline Onions (page 42). I also find that tomato has a great affinity with raw or cold fish, as in Peekytoe Crab in Vine-Ripe Tomato Gelée (page 32), Curry-Scented Tuna with Sun-Dried Tomato (page 54), and Tomato Bruschetta with Manchego and Anchovy (page 26).

This chapter doesn't just include raw fish; it also features a number of recipes in which shellfish is cooked, cooled, and served cold. I find that this is often the best way to appreciate their texture and flavor, as in a Lobster Roll (page 38) or Crab Roll (page 30). Moreover, in dishes like Steamed Shrimp with Heirloom Tomato and Lime-Ginger Sauce (page 50), Stone Crab with Avocado and Grapefruit Juice (page 34), and Lobster Salad with Roasted Beets and Soft-Boiled Egg Mayonnaise (page 40), having the shellfish cold keeps it from cooking or wilting the other ingredients.

Finally, there's one type of dish that's sort of a hybrid between raw and cooked: ceviche. In Sea Bass Ceviche with Lemon Verbena Oil (page 28), as in all ceviches, the acid in the marinade "cooks" the fish without any heat. If you don't eat raw fish on a regular basis, this is another good way to introduce it to your palate.

TOMATO BRUSCHETTA WITH MANCHEGO AND ANCHOVY

serves (6) This is my version of a bruschetta, the Italian hors d'oeuvre that features grilled bread topped with tomatoes, garlic, and basil. If you can't find Spanish manchego cheese, substitute a light locatelli Romano. For an interesting alternative to pesto mayonnaise, make this with Tapenade (recipe follows) instead.

1	**cup basil leaves,** tightly packed, plus 10 leaves, chopped
3	**garlic cloves**
3	**tablespoons mayonnaise**
¾	**pound round tomatoes or cherry tomatoes of various colors,** halved
⅓	**cup thinly sliced red onion**
1	**tablespoon balsamic vinegar**
3	**ounces aged manchego or dry, aged locatelli Romano,** cut into small dice (about ¾ cup)
3	**tablespoons olive oil**
2	**tablespoons sliced pitted Kalamata olives**
	Fine sea salt and freshly ground black pepper to taste
6	**slices country bread or ciabatta,** cut into 4 pieces each
24	**anchovy fillets,** preferably white anchovies

MAKE THE PESTO MAYONNAISE Put the whole basil and the garlic in a blender and puree until chunky. Add the mayonnaise and puree until incorporated. Set aside, covered, in the refrigerator.

MAKE THE TOMATO TOPPING In a bowl, stir together the tomatoes, onion, vinegar, cheese, olive oil, olives, and chopped basil. Season with salt and pepper. Cover and let marinate for at least 4 hours in the refrigerator.

TO SERVE Grill the bread or toast it in the toaster or oven. Divide among 6 plates. Spread each slice of bread with a generous amount of pesto mayonnaise. Top with some tomato mixture and an anchovy fillet.

Wine Suggestion: Musso, Barbera d'Alba 2000. A light Italian red with cherry and spice tones.

TAPENADE

makes about ① cup   This is my version of the famous Mediterranean olive paste.

1 **cup pitted Niçoise or Kalamata olives,** rinsed and dried
1 **tablespoon capers,** rinsed and dried
4 **salted anchovy fillets,** rinsed and dried
2 **tablespoons olive oil**
2 **cloves garlic**
  Freshly ground black pepper to taste

PUT ALL THE INGREDIENTS in a food processor fitted with the metal blade. Process until smooth. (At home, I make a version for spreading on toast that includes ¼ cup grated Parmigiano-Reggiano cheese and 1 dried chile processed along with the other ingredients.)

MAYONNAISE

makes about ① cup   Mayonnaise-based condiments are always better when you use homemade mayonnaise. Here's a recipe for making your own.

1 **egg yolk**
1 **tablespoon Dijon mustard**
1 **teaspoon red wine vinegar**
¾ **cup canola oil**
  Fine sea salt and cayenne to taste

IN A BOWL, whisk together the egg yolk, mustard, and vinegar. Gradually whisk in the oil in a thin stream; continue whisking until a thick emulsion forms. Season with salt and cayenne.

SEA BASS CEVICHE WITH LEMON VERBENA OIL

serves ⑥ A ceviche is a Peruvian dish in which the fish is "cooked" by the acid of the citrus marinade. Marinating time can vary from a few minutes to several hours. I generally marinate for a few hours, but if you have a fondness for sushi, you can certainly serve the fish after a shorter period. This can be made into a more traditional ceviche by omitting the lemon verbena oil and using the classic grouper in place of the bass. It can also be made with red snapper (page 14) or striped bass (page 2).

For a simpler version of this dish, simply leave out the lemon verbena oil.

⅓ **cup olive oil**

40 **dried lemon verbena leaves** (available bottled in the dried-spice section of supermarkets)

1 **pound sushi-grade sea bass,** skinned and cut into ¾-inch dice

¼ **cup finely diced red onion**

1 **tablespoon chopped cilantro leaves**

1 **jalapeño pepper,** diced

3 **tablespoons extra-virgin olive oil**

3 **tablespoons freshly squeezed lime juice**

2 **mint leaves,** chopped

½ **cup finely diced vine-ripened tomato**

½ **avocado,** peeled, pitted, and cut into small dice

Fine sea salt and freshly ground black pepper to taste

MAKE THE LEMON VERBENA OIL Warm the olive oil in a small pot set over medium-high heat. Remove the pot from the heat and add the lemon verbena, pushing the leaves into the oil with a wooden spoon to make sure they're submerged. Cover and set aside to infuse and cool. When cool, strain through a fine-mesh strainer set over a bowl. Discard the leaves and set the oil aside.

MAKE THE CEVICHE Put all the remaining ingredients except the salt and pepper in a bowl and stir together gently but thoroughly. Season with salt and pepper. Cover and let marinate in the refrigerator for 3 hours.

TO SERVE Divide the ceviche among 6 chilled martini glasses or small bowls set in larger bowls filled with crushed ice. Drizzle some lemon verbena oil over the top and serve at once.

Wine Suggestion: Pazo de Señorans, Albariño 2001; Rías Biaxas. A bright, citrusy white from Galacia, Spain. This would also be delicious with a light-style beer like Corona.

CRAB ROLL

serves ⑥ to ⑧ as an hors d'oeuvre This is not intended as a plated appetizer, but rather as a passed hors d'oeuvre. For this recipe, it's essential to get very fresh crabmeat and handle it gingerly to keep the pieces firm and large; wearing latex gloves is a good way to further protect its texture.

¾ **pound jumbo lump crabmeat,** cartilage fragments picked out and discarded
Grated zest of 2 limes, plus 3 tablespoons lime juice
3 **tablespoons mayonnaise**
2 **tablespoons chopped cilantro leaves**
Fine sea salt and freshly ground black pepper to taste
6 **sheets Asian rice paper,** 8½-inch diameter (available in the international section of many supermarkets)
24 **large mint leaves**
½ **large seedless cucumber,** cut into matchstick pieces
3 **jalapeño peppers,** seeded and cut into matchstick pieces
¾ **teaspoon red curry paste or hot sauce**
½ **cup olive oil**
2 **tablespoons rice vinegar**

DRESS THE CRABMEAT Put the crabmeat in a bowl. Add the lime zest, mayonnaise, and cilantro. Season with salt and pepper and stir gently so as not to damage the delicate meat.

PREPARE THE ROLLS Fill a wide, shallow bowl with cold water. Lower 1 rice paper sheet into the water and leave there for 2 minutes. Remove very carefully and lay on a clean, dry towel to drain. Lay 4 mint leaves from one end of the paper to another. Top with about one-sixth of the cucumber. Spoon about one-sixth of the crab over the cucumber. Top with one-sixth of the jalapeño. Season the contents of the roll with salt and pepper. Roll the paper up as tightly as possible without tearing it. Roll in plastic wrap and twist the ends repeatedly until they begin to curl up and the roll is firmly sealed. Repeat with the remaining rice papers and filling. Chill the rolls in the refrigerator for at least 4 hours, but no more than 12 hours.

MAKE THE SAUCE In a bowl, whisk together the curry paste, lime juice, olive oil, and vinegar.

TO SERVE With the plastic coating still in place, cut each roll into 6 pieces, then remove the plastic. Arrange the segments on a chilled platter or two, and pour the sauce into a small bowl or two. Place the bowl(s) in the center of the platter(s).

Wine Suggestion: Schiopetto, Tocai Friulano 2001; Friuli. A white from Italy with aromas of pear, citrus, herbs, and wildflowers.

PEEKYTOE CRAB IN VINE-RIPE TOMATO GELÉE

serves ⑥ This dish combines two delicious components, a delicate crab salad and a tomato gelée, subtly uniting them with the sun-dried tomato in the salad. Don't be intimidated by the gelée; the word just means "jelly," and it's actually very easy to prepare. It also makes for a beautiful and sophisticated presentation. In fact, the trickiest thing about a gelée is the easiest one to control: the seasoning. Because it's made with nothing but tomatoes and unflavored gelatin, you must carefully taste and adjust its flavor with salt, pepper, and sugar until a pleasing balance is reached.

If you can't find Peekytoe crab, substitute jumbo lump crabmeat, but don't use any tomatoes other than vine-ripened; they have the best flavor and texture for this recipe.

10 **very ripe vine-ripened tomatoes,** coarsely chopped
    Fine sea salt, freshly ground white pepper, and granulated sugar to taste
¼   **teaspoon powdered unflavored gelatin**
1   **pound crabmeat,** preferably Peekytoe, cartilage fragments picked out and discarded
1   **tablespoon minced red onion**
3   **basil leaves,** minced
3   **tablespoons coarsely chopped sun-dried tomatoes packed in olive oil**
¼   **cup olive oil**
1   **tablespoon sherry vinegar**
1   **teaspoon cracked coriander seeds**
1   **avocado,** peeled, pitted, and diced

MAKE THE TOMATO GELÉE Put the chopped tomatoes in a pot. Season lightly with salt, white pepper, and a pinch of sugar. Set the pot over high heat and cook, stirring occasionally, until the tomatoes give off their liquid and the liquid begins to boil. Strain the tomatoes through a fine-mesh strainer lined with cheesecloth, set over a bowl, and let the liquid drain into the bowl. Do not squeeze the tomatoes or press down or the liquid will turn cloudy.

Pour the liquid into a small pot and set over high heat. Bring it to a boil, and cook over high heat until reduced by two-thirds. Meanwhile, put the gelatin in a cup with 1 tablespoon cold water and let soften and swell for 5 minutes. Stir in the gelatin until dissolved. You should have about ¾ cup of liquid. Season to taste with salt and white pepper. Transfer the tomato liquid to a shallow vessel, such as a baking dish. Cover with plastic wrap, and refrigerate for at least 6 hours.

MAKE THE CRAB SALAD When ready to proceed, put the crabmeat in a bowl with the onion, basil, sun-dried tomatoes, olive oil, vinegar, coriander seed, and avocado. Season with salt and white pepper. Toss gently.

TO SERVE Remove the gelée from the refrigerator. Divide the crabmeat mixture among 6 chilled shallow bowls, spreading the meat over the bottom of each bowl to cover. Run a tablespoon under hot tap water and shake it dry. Skim a very thin section of gelée from the vessel and lay over a portion of the crabmeat on 1 plate. Repeat until the entire portion is covered by a thin layer of gelee. Repeat with the remaining gelée and crabmeat, rewarming the spoon as necessary. Serve at once.

Wine Suggestion: Lucien Crochet, Sancerre 2001; Loire Valley. A refreshing and bright French white with aromas of citrus, stones, and a slight grassiness.

STONE CRAB WITH AVOCADO AND GRAPEFRUIT JUICE

serves (6) Based on a French cocktail sauce, the dressing here is best appreciated when tasted in tandem with the emulsified grapefruit juice vinaigrette. Add the oil to the juice gradually so the vinaigrette emulsifies. If stone crab is not in season, use jumbo lump crabmeat instead of the claw. For a simple dip for stone crabs and other boiled seafood, try my Horseradish Mayonnaise (recipe follows).

 3 **tablespoons mayonnaise,** preferably homemade (page 27)
 1 **tablespoon ketchup**
 1½ **teaspoons Cognac**
   Pinch cayenne
   Fine sea salt and freshly ground white pepper to taste
 1¼ **pounds picked stone crabmeat,** plus 6 cracked stone crab claws
 ¾ **cup diced avocado**
 ¾ **cup diced grapefruit segments,** seeds removed, drained on paper towels
 1 **cup freshly squeezed grapefruit juice**
 ⅓ **cup extra-virgin olive oil**
 1 **cup baby mustard greens or other small greens**

MAKE THE DRESSING AND DRESS THE CRABMEAT In a small bowl, stir together the mayonnaise, ketchup, Cognac, and cayenne. Season with salt and white pepper; then fold in the crabmeat, avocado, and grapefruit.

MAKE THE SAUCE Pour the grapefruit juice into a mixing bowl. Add the oil to the juice a few drops at a time, blending it with an immersion blender to form an emulsified vinaigrette. If you don't have an immersion blender, do this in the bowl of a small conventional blender. Season with salt and white pepper.

TO SERVE Use a 2½-inch ring mold or tuna fish can with the bottom cut out to mound a portion of the dressed crabmeat in the center of each of 6 chilled plates. Spoon some sauce around the perimeter of the mound on each plate. Place a claw on top of each serving and top with mustard greens.

Wine Suggestion: Vavasour, Sauvignon Blanc 2002; Marlborough. A New Zealand Sauvignon Blanc with grapefruit and passionfruit notes.

HORSERADISH MAYONNAISE

makes about (1¼) **cups** Here's an easy dipping sauce for shellfish.

1 cup Mayonnaise (page 27)
2 to 3 tablespoons prepared white horseradish
¼ cup heavy cream, whipped
Fine sea salt and freshly ground black pepper to taste

IN A BOWL, whisk together the mayonnaise and 2 tablespoons of the horseradish, or more to taste. Fold in the cream and season with salt and pepper.

SLIVERED FLUKE WITH SAKÉ REDUCTION

serves ⑥ Gently flavored fluke is a perfect background for a reduced sauce of Asian flavors like soy, sesame, yuzu, and saké. If you can't get fluke, substitute red snapper. This dish is delicious with grilled toast and/or homemade Pickled Ginger (recipe follows), a traditional sushi garnish.

¼	cup saké
2	tablespoons reduced-sodium (lite) soy sauce
2	tablespoons chopped fresh ginger
1½	teaspoons sesame oil
10	leaves basil
¼	cup olive oil
2	teaspoons yuzu, Meyer lemon juice, or regular lemon juice
	Grated zest of 2 lemons
1¼	pounds skinless fluke fillet
	Fine sea salt and freshly ground black pepper to taste
¼	cup diced fennel
12	paper-thin slices jalapeño pepper
2	tablespoons Crispy Shallots (page 53)
1	cup alfalfa sprouts

MAKE THE SAKÉ REDUCTION In a medium saucepan, combine the saké, soy sauce, ginger, and 2 tablespoons water. Set over high heat and reduce to 4 to 5 teaspoons of a syrupy liquid, approximately 8 minutes. Remove from the heat, add the sesame oil and basil, and let infuse until cool. Strain through a fine-mesh strainer set over a bowl and stir in the olive oil and yuzu.

DRY THE LEMON ZEST Preheat the oven to 200°F. Spread the lemon zest out on a cookie sheet and dry in the oven until completely free of moisture, approximately 3 minutes. Remove and set aside.

TO SERVE Cut the fluke crosswise into ⅛-inch slices and season with salt and pepper. Divide the slices among 6 chilled plates, overlapping them in the center of each plate. Drizzle with the sauce and sprinkle with the lemon zest. Top each serving with some diced fennel, 2 slices of jalapeño, some crispy shallots, and some alfalfa sprouts.

Wine Suggestion: Chiyomisubi, Tokebetsu Junmai. An aromatic spicy saké with apple and pear notes, or any Junmai-level saké.

PICKLED GINGER

makes about ½ cup, enough for 6 people This is how to make the ginger that's served alongside sushi. It's a great way to cleanse your palate between bites.

> 1 **large piece fresh ginger,** peeled and sliced paper-thin (about ½ cup sliced)
> ½ **cup sugar**
> 1 **cup rice vinegar**

COOK THE GINGER in boiling salted water for 1 minute, then drain it. Pour the sugar and vinegar into a pot and bring to a boil over high heat. Add the ginger and return to a boil. Remove the pot from the heat and let cool.

YUZU is a Japanese citrus fruit that makes a nuanced impact; its flavor—preceded by an alluring perfume—is more like that of a lemon's zest than its highly acidic juice, and it's less sweet than a lemon, as well. Yuzu juice is a popular dressing for sushi and sushi-related dishes. If you can't find yuzu or its juice in bottles, substitute the juice of Meyer lemons in recipes that call for it.

LOBSTER ROLL

serves ⑥ to ⑧ as an hors d'oeuvre Because they balance the lobster with a variety of vegetables, lobster rolls are a very economical way to enjoy the most elegant of crustaceans, as you can see from this recipe, in which three lobsters offer enough meat to serve six to eight people. Whenever using lobster meat in a recipe, do not use the meat that comes from the very tip of the claw. It tends to be watery and mushy.

2 **portobello mushrooms,** stems removed
   Fine sea salt and freshly ground black pepper to taste
¼ **cup olive oil**
2 **tablespoons sesame oil**
1 **large carrot,** cut into matchstick pieces
1 **large jalapeño pepper,** halved lengthwise, seeds from one half discarded, chopped
2 **tablespoons chopped fresh ginger**
2 **garlic cloves,** chopped
2 **tablespoons chopped cilantro leaves**
3 **lobsters,** 1¼ pounds each, boiled, meat removed and cut into 1-inch pieces
   (see page 274; approximately 20 ounces meat)
6 **sheets Asian rice paper,** 8½-inch diameter (available in the international section of
   many supermarkets)
24 **large mint leaves**
1 **avocado,** peeled, pitted, and thinly sliced lengthwise
   About ¼ cup reduced-sodium (lite) soy sauce
   About 1 tablespoon wasabi paste

ROAST THE PORTOBELLO MUSHROOMS Season the mushrooms with salt and pepper. Warm 2 tablespoons of the olive oil in a sauté pan set over medium-high heat. Add the mushrooms, stem side down, and cook until tender, approximately 4 minutes. Turn over and cook until tender on the other side, approximately 4 more minutes. Transfer to a cutting board and let cool. When cool enough to handle, cut into ½-inch-thick slices.

COOK THE OTHER VEGETABLES Heat the sesame oil in the same pan set over high heat. Add the carrot, jalapeño, ginger, and garlic. Season with salt and pepper and sauté quickly until the vegetables are softened but still holding their shape, approximately 2 minutes. Remove the pan from the heat, turn the vegetables out into a bowl, add the cilantro, and set aside to cool.

COOK THE LOBSTER Warm the remaining 2 tablespoons of olive oil in the same sauté pan set over high heat. Add the lobster, season with salt and pepper, and cook until the lobster turns bright orange, approximately 1 minute. Transfer to another bowl.

MAKE THE ROLLS Fill a wide, shallow bowl with cold water. Lower 1 rice paper sheet into the water and leave there for 2 minutes. Remove very carefully and lay on a clean, dry towel to drain. Lay 4 mint leaves from one end to the other. Top with about one-sixth of the carrot and mushrooms. Spoon about one-sixth of the lobster over the mint. Top with one-sixth of the avocado. Season the contents of the roll with salt and pepper. Roll the paper up as tightly as possible without tearing it. Roll in plastic wrap and twist the ends repeatedly until they begin to curl up and the roll is firmly sealed. Repeat with the remaining rice papers and filling. Chill the rolls in the refrigerator for at least 4 hours, but no more than 12 hours.

MAKE THE SAUCE In a bowl, whisk together the soy sauce and wasabi. Taste and, if desired, add more soy sauce or wasabi.

TO SERVE With the plastic coating still in place, cut each roll into 6 pieces, then remove the plastic. Arrange the segments on a chilled or cool platter or two and pour the sauce into a small bowl, or two if using two platters. Place the bowl(s) in the center of the platter(s).

Wine Suggestion: Trevor Jones, "Virgin" Chardonnay 2002; Barossa. A clean, crisp un-oaked Chardonnay from Australia, with bright tropical and citrus notes.

LOBSTER SALAD WITH ROASTED BEETS AND SOFT-BOILED EGG MAYONNAISE

serves ⑥ Lobster and mayonnaise are a perfect, luxurious combination, balanced here by sweet, roasted beets and a variety of fresh herbs in the sauce. The lobster itself is flavored with a poaching liquid of vegetables, peppercorns, thyme, and bay. Plan to make this dish a bit ahead of time because each component features an ingredient that has to be cooked, then cooled.

- 6 ounces yellow wax beans and green beans
- 18 yellow and red baby beets, ideally 9 of each
- ¼ cup olive oil
- Fine sea salt and freshly ground black pepper to taste
- 3 live lobsters, 1½ pounds each
- Soft-Boiled Egg Mayonnaise (recipe follows)
- 1 tablespoon chopped fresh dill
- 1 tablespoon chopped tarragon leaves
- 1 tablespoon chopped chives
- 1 tablespoon chopped mint leaves
- 1 tablespoon freshly squeezed lemon juice
- 1½ teaspoons red wine vinegar
- ½ garlic clove, chopped

BLANCH THE BEANS Bring a pot of salted water to a boil. Fill a large bowl halfway with ice water. Add the beans to the boiling water and blanch for 2 minutes. Drain and transfer to the ice water to cool them and stop the cooking. Drain and set aside.

ROAST THE BEETS Preheat the oven to 300°F. Rub the beets with 2 tablespoons of the olive oil and season with salt and pepper. Wrap the red beets together loosely in aluminum foil, and the yellow beets together in another tinfoil package. Place both packages on the center rack of the oven and roast until tender throughout, 1 hour to 90 minutes. (The beets are done when a sharp, thin-bladed knife can pierce easily to the center of 1 beet.)

COOK THE LOBSTERS Poach the lobsters in court bouillon, cut tail meat in half lengthwise, and reserve claw and knuckle meat separately (see page 274).

MAKE THE SAUCE Put the mayonnaise in a bowl and stir in the dill, tarragon, chives, mint, and lemon juice. Season with salt and pepper. Set aside.

SLICE AND DRESS THE BEETS When the beets are done cooking, remove and set aside to cool. When they are cool enough to handle, remove their skins with a paring knife (they should come right off), cut in half, and put them in a large bowl. Add the remaining 2 tablespoons olive oil, the vinegar, and garlic. Toss very gently to combine.

TO SERVE Spoon some mayonnaise over the center of each of six chilled plates. Arrange 6 beet halves and some wax beans over the mayonnaise on each plate. Top with the meat of half a lobster tail and some claw and knuckle meat.

Wine Suggestion: Veuve Clicquot, Yellow Label, NV; Champagne. A sparkling wine with slight hints of toast and biscuits with crisp apple fruit.

SOFT-BOILED EGG MAYONNAISE

makes about ① cup If you're concerned about eating raw egg in mayonnaise, try this recipe, which uses a partially cooked egg instead. The texture is smoother, as well.

1 egg, soft-boiled and peeled (see page 275)
1 tablespoon Dijon mustard
1 tablespoon red wine vinegar
¾ cup grapeseed oil
Fine sea salt and freshly ground black pepper to taste

PUT THE EGG, mustard, and vinegar in the bowl of a food processor fitted with the metal blade. With the motor running, slowly add the oil in a thin stream to make an emulsified sauce. Season with salt and pepper.

COPPER RIVER SALMON, OSETRA CAVIAR, AND CIPOLLINE ONIONS

serves (6) Salmon and cream sauce are a classic combination that recalls Nordic cuisine. Rounded out with cippoline onions, cucumbers, and caviar, the pair makes the foundation of a memorable carpaccio-like dish here. If Copper River salmon is out of season, use Scottish or Atlantic salmon. In my restaurants, I make this only with luxurious Osetra caviar because I simply adore its silky salinity, but at home you should feel free to substitute American caviar. If you like to eat salmon and caviar with toast points, serve this with toasted rye bread with the crust removed.

18 ounces salmon fillet, preferably Copper River
Fine sea salt and freshly ground white pepper to taste
3 tablespoons heavy cream
2 tablespoons crème fraîche
3 tablespoons freshly squeezed lemon juice
¼ cup chopped cippoline or pearl onions
4 ounces Osetra caviar
1 cup diced (¼-inch) peeled cucumber
¼ pound microgreens or other small greens
2 tablespoons extra-virgin olive oil

SLICE AND PRESS THE SALMON Using a very sharp knife, slice the salmon horizontally as thin as possible, just as you would smoked fish. Put one-sixth of the slices in the center of a large, chilled dinner plate in a circular pattern. Cover with a sheet of plastic wrap and lightly tap with a small pot, the bottom of a ramekin, or any flat, heavy object, until the pieces are flattened out and cover the surface of the dinner plate. Repeat with the remaining salmon on 5 additional chilled plates. Remove the plastic wrap, season the salmon with salt and pepper, and set aside while you make the sauce.

MAKE THE SAUCE In a bowl, whisk together the cream, crème fraîche, and lemon juice. Stir in the onions and season with salt and pepper.

TO SERVE Spoon some sauce over each portion of salmon and use the spoon to spread it out and lightly cover the fish. Scatter some caviar and cucumber all over each portion. In a small bowl, toss the greens with the olive oil and season with salt and pepper. Scatter some of this salad over each portion and serve at once.

Wine Suggestion: Billecart-Salmon, Brut Rosé, NV; Champagne. A fresh rosé Champagne with hints of berries.

CIPOLLINE ONIONS are small, flat white onions. Their name comes from *cipolla,* the Italian word for "onion." If you can't find any, it's generally okay to substitute pearl onions or chopped, large sweet onions, like Vidalia.

MARINATED SALMON AND COLD CITRUS NAGE WITH SUNFLOWER SEEDS

serves ⑥ Technically, a *nage* is an aromatic court bouillon used to cook fish or shellfish, then served with the fish itself. Here I'm using it to describe an intensely flavored cold sauce. The cured fish (gravlax) can be made with any salmon, including Atlantic. Just be sure to ask your fishmonger to give you a fillet cut from the head end of the fish, where it's thickest. Also, be sure to plan ahead; the fish has to marinate for at least 18 hours.

Grilled bread and a Watercress and Cucumber Salad (recipe follows) are perfect accompaniments to this dish.

⅔ cup **kosher salt,** plus more for seasoning

1½ cups **packed light brown sugar**

¼ cup **chopped cilantro leaves**

2 tablespoons **chopped fresh dill**

Grated zest of 1 orange

¼ cup **Cognac**

2 pounds **salmon fillet,** cut from the top (see headnote) or center cut

2 tablespoons **sunflower seeds**

1 tablespoon **honey**

1 teaspoon **fennel seeds**

2 tablespoons **olive oil**

¼ cup **freshly squeezed lemon juice**

2 teaspoons **grated lemon zest**

1 teaspoon **minced mint leaves**

2 tablespoons **mustard oil** (available from Middle Eastern shops; also see Mail-Order Sources)

Fine sea salt and freshly ground black pepper to taste

MARINATE THE SALMON In a bowl, stir together the salt, brown sugar, 1 tablespoon of the cilantro, the dill, orange zest, and Cognac. Put the salmon on a cookie sheet and rub all over with the marinade. Cover with plastic wrap and let marinate in the refrigerator for 18 to 24 hours, depending on the thickness of the fish.

ROAST THE SUNFLOWER SEEDS Preheat the oven to 200°F. Put the sunflower seeds on a baking sheet in a single layer and roast in the oven until lightly toasted, approximately 5 minutes. Remove from the oven and let cool. (The seeds can be prepared at the same time as the salmon, covered, and held at room temperature until ready to proceed.)

CLEAN AND SLICE THE SALMON Scrape off the excess marinade and spices and wipe the salmon with a clean towel. (The salmon can be prepared up to this point up to 1 week in advance, wrapped snugly with plastic wrap, and stored in the refrigerator.) Slice the salmon crosswise into 18 equal portions.

MAKE THE NAGE In a bowl, stir together the honey, fennel seeds, olive oil, lemon juice, lemon zest, remaining cilantro, mint, and mustard oil. Season with salt and pepper and stir again.

TO SERVE Lay 3 salmon slices across the center of each of 6 chilled shallow bowls. Spoon the nage around the salmon. Garnish with sunflower seeds.

Wine Suggestion: Cantina Terlano, Quarz 2000; Alto Adige. A steely Sauvignon Blanc from Italy with nuances of grapefruit and black currant.

WATERCRESS AND CUCUMBER SALAD

serves ⑥ as a side dish This simple, clean, and refreshing salad is a perfect accompaniment to assertively seasoned dishes.

> ¼ cup crème fraîche
> 1 tablespoon chopped fresh dill
> 1 tablespoon freshly squeezed lemon juice
> 1 large bunch **watercress,** tough stems removed, cleaned
> 1 large **seedless cucumber,** peeled and thinly sliced crosswise
> Fine sea salt and freshly ground black pepper to taste

IN A BOWL, stir together the crème fraîche, dill, and lemon juice. Add the watercress and cucumber and season with salt and pepper. Toss and serve at once.

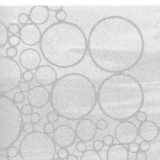

CRÈME FRAÎCHE is a cultured cream that's reached the point when it begins to thicken. Because cream must be pasteurized in the United States, domestic producers of crème fraîche often add buttermilk or sour cream to heavy cream to produce the desired effect.

TOMATO BRUSCHETTA WITH MANCHEGO AND ANCHOVY   page 26

MARINATED SALMON AND COLD CITRUS NAGE WITH SUNFLOWER SEED, PLATED WITH CUCUMBER SALAD   page 44

SPICY SHRIMP NOODLES   page 88 >>

SPICE-CRUSTED SCALLOPS WITH CURRY-LEMON RELISH   page 84

<< TAYLOR BAY SCALLOPS IN GREEN APPLE-CORIANDER SAUCE   page 48

NEW ENGLAND CLAM CHOWDER page 106

OYSTERS WITH DAIKON VINAIGRETTE

serves (6) Whenever I can get Kumamoto oysters, I use them because their buttery flavor is unique. This is one of my my favorite preparations for raw Kumamoto oysters, though it will be a winner with any oyster variety. Top each oyster with sea urchin, if you have it, for an extra luxurious touch.

2 tablespoons finely grated daikon radish

2 tablespoons saké

2 tablespoons rice vinegar

2 tablespoons reduced-sodium (lite) soy sauce

3 dozen oysters, preferably Kumamoto, shucked (see page 276)

1 small lime, halved

1 tablespoon chopped chives

MAKE THE DAIKON VINAGRETTE In a bowl, whisk together the daikon, saké, vinegar, and soy sauce.

TO SERVE Arrange the oysters on their half-shells on a chilled platter or on crushed ice. Place a scant amount of daikon and sauce on each oyster. Squeeze a drop of lime juice onto each oyster. Top with chives. Serve at once.

Wine Suggestion: Brocard, Chablis 2002; Yonne. A clean, minerally French white with lemony acidity.

TAYLOR BAY SCALLOPS IN GREEN APPLE–CORIANDER SAUCE

serves (6) Taylor Bay scallops are delicate, sweet little scallops that are very receptive to all kinds of flavor. Here, they're dressed in a simple sauce of honey, mustard oil, Tabasco, and lime juice. The key to this dish is keeping it as fresh as possible by topping the scallops with the sauce *at the very last second* to prevent the acid of the lime juice from "cooking" them as they would in a ceviche.

For a sensational presentation, make a bed of crushed ice on the surface of a serving platter. Arrange 30 serving shells (available from specialty stores and gourmet Web sites) on the ice and put 3 scallops in each shell.

For an extra flourish, serve Bricelet (recipe follows) alongside; they're quick-to-prepare little crackers that make a big impression.

3 teaspoons honey
2 tablespoons mustard oil (available from Middle Eastern shops; also see Mail-Order Sources)
2 tablespoons olive oil
1 teaspoon chopped cilantro leaves
1 teaspoon cracked coriander seeds
4 drops Tabasco Green Pepper sauce
¼ cup freshly squeezed lime juice
¼ cup diced Granny Smith apple
Fine sea salt and freshly ground black pepper to taste
90 Taylor Bay scallops, cleaned and shucked (about 1 pound shucked)
Cayenne to taste

MAKE THE GREEN APPLE–CORIANDER SAUCE In a bowl, whisk together the honey, mustard oil, olive oil, cilantro, coriander, Tabasco, and lime juice. Stir in the apple. Season with salt and black pepper.

TO SERVE Put 15 scallops on each of 6 chilled salad plates. Spoon some sauce over each cluster of scallops and top with a scant pinch of cayenne. Serve at once.

Wine Suggestion: Navarro, Gewürztraminer 2001; Anderson Valley. A dry California white with aromas of lychee and citrus, with a spicy finish.

BRICELET

serves ⑥ as an accompaniment These tiny biscuits are delicious alongside salads and soups. Choose from the optional seasonings to tailor the flavor to the dish they'll accompany.

> 1 cup all-purpose flour
> 2 cups heavy cream
>   Salt and freshly ground black pepper to taste
>   Fleur de sel
>   Pinch crushed red pepper flakes
>   **Cracked coriander seeds,** cumin seeds, fennel seeds, black peppercorns,
>   or chopped Spiced Preserved Lemon (page 253; optional)

MAKE THE DOUGH In a small bowl, stir together the flour and cream until smooth. Season with salt and pepper. Cover and refrigerate for 6 hours.

FORM AND BAKE THE BISCUITS Preheat the oven to 375°F. Divide the dough into tablespoon-sized portions and spread them out on a cookie sheet. Top each bricelet with 2 or 3 grains of fleur de sel and red pepper flakes. If desired, also top with cracked coriander seeds, cumin seeds, fennel seeds, black peppercorns, and/or chopped Spiced Preserved Lemon, or other toppings. Bake until the edges are golden brown, 5 to 6 minutes.

STEAMED SHRIMP WITH HEIRLOOM TOMATO AND LIME-GINGER SAUCE

serves (6) Make this dish in the late summer, when farmers' markets sell a beautiful variety of heirloom tomatoes. You can personalize the recipe by adding mint, lemongrass, and/or basil to the simmering water used to steam the shrimp.

6	ounces **green beans,** preferably French green beans (*haricots verts*)
1¼	pounds **assorted heirloom or beefsteak tomatoes,** cut into wedges
⅓	cup **thin slices red onion**
¼	cup **olive oil**
1	tablespoon **freshly squeezed lemon juice**
1	tablespoon **chopped cilantro leaves**
	Fine sea salt and freshly ground white pepper to taste
1	cup **Soft-Boiled Egg Mayonnaise (page 41)**
1	teaspoon **curry powder**
¼	cup **ginger juice**
	Grated zest and juice of 1 lime
24	**medium shrimp (about 1¼ pounds),** peeled, deveined, and halved lengthwise
2	bunches **baby arugula,** stems removed, well rinsed in several changes of cold water, and spun dry

BLANCH THE BEANS Fill a large bowl halfway with ice water and set aside. Bring a pot of lightly salted water to a boil. Add the beans to the boiling water and blanch for 2 minutes, then drain them and plunge them into the ice water to stop the cooking and preserve their color. Drain and set aside.

MAKE THE TOMATO SALAD In a bowl, toss together the tomatoes, red onion, and beans. Add 2 tablespoons of the olive oil, the lemon juice, and cilantro. Season with salt and pepper. Set aside at room temperature.

MAKE THE LIME-GINGER SAUCE Put the mayonnaise in a bowl. Whisk in the curry, ginger juice, and lime juice. Season with salt and pepper. Cover and refrigerate.

STEAM THE SHRIMP Bring a pot of salted water to a simmer. Put the shrimp in a steamer basket and set over the simmering water. Steam until firm and pink, 5 to 6 minutes. Use tongs to transfer the shrimp to a bowl. Add the remaining 2 tablespoons olive oil and the lime zest; toss to coat the shrimp. Season with salt and pepper.

TO SERVE Put some tomato salad in the center of each of 6 chilled plates. Place 8 shrimp halves on top of the tomatoes on each plate. Place the arugula in the bowl with the remaining olive oil and lime juice and toss briefly. Pile some arugula on top of the shrimp. Spoon a tablespoon or so of sauce around the perimeter of each plate. Serve at once.

Wine Suggestion: Hofstatter, "Kolbenhof" Gewürztraminer 2001; Alto Adige. An exotic Italian white with aromas of ginger, lychee, and lime sorbet.

GINGER JUICE is now available in small bottles from specialty-food producers. If you can't find it, it's easy (and far less expensive) to make your own: Peel a large knob of ginger and grate about ½ cup. Wrap the grated ginger in cheesecloth, hold over a bowl, and twirl the ends of the cheesecloth over and over, as though wringing a towel, until the desired amount of juice accumulates in the bowl.

TUNA TARTAR WITH CRISPY SHALLOTS

serves (6) This recipe is based on contrasts: cold, clean-flavored tuna dressed with a slightly spicy sauce and topped with hot, crunchy shallots that taste like tiny onion rings. For a more formal presentation, use a ring mold or tuna fish can with the bottom cut out to shape the tartar into a perfect circle in the center of each plate. Bluefin is my tuna of choice here because it's especially delicious cold (it's also the preferred tuna of most sushi chefs), but any sushi-grade tuna will work well.

Serve this with a simple green salad for a light meal.

2	tablespoons thinly sliced scallions, white part only
1½	tablespoons minced fresh ginger
1½	tablespoons chopped fresh dill
1½	tablespoons chopped chives
¼	cup extra-virgin olive oil
2	tablespoons sherry vinegar
1	tablespoon Worcestershire sauce
1	tablespoon freshly squeezed lime juice
	Fine sea salt and freshly ground black pepper to taste
18	ounces tuna, preferably Bluefin, cut into ¼-inch dice and kept in the refrigerator
	Crispy Shallots (recipe follows)
3	ciabatta rolls, halved and grilled or toasted

MAKE THE SAUCE Put the scallions, ginger, dill, chives, olive oil, sherry vinegar, Worcestershire sauce, and lime juice in a bowl. Stir together and season with salt and pepper.

TO SERVE Divide the tuna among 6 chilled salad plates. Drizzle some sauce over each serving and top with some crispy shallots. Place a grilled ciabatta half alongside the tuna on each plate.

Wine Suggestion: Strub, "Niersteiner-Bruckchen" Riesling-Kabinett 2001; Rheinhessen. A clean, fresh German white with aromas of honey and lime.

CRISPY SHALLOTS

makes about ¼ cup, enough to garnish 6 dishes   These little onion crisps, my version of onion rings, are a fun garnish for salads, soups, and raw fish dishes.

3   tablespoons coarsely chopped shallots
2   tablespoons Wondra flour
    Vegetable oil, for frying
    Fine sea salt to taste

Toss the shallots in the flour. Pour oil into a small saucepan to a depth of about 1 inch. Warm over medium-high heat for 3 minutes. Add the shallots to the hot oil and fry until golden brown, 30 to 60 seconds. Remove with a slotted spoon and set on a paper towel–lined plate to drain. Season with a pinch of salt.

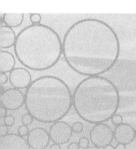

WONDRA FLOUR is a granular mixture of wheat and barley flour. I generally prefer it to powdery all-purpose flour for frying fish and shellfish because it becomes crispier when fried.

CURRY-SCENTED TUNA WITH SUN-DRIED TOMATO

serves (6) The tuna in this dish is seared on the outside but raw in the center, which accomplishes two important goals: fusing the curry to the fish and creating a compelling temperature contrast. The salad adds all sorts of complementary flavors to the plate, from cooling avocado to peppery radish to sweet apple and piquant mustard oil.

Bigeye tuna is my first choice here because it is so unctuous, but you can use Bluefin or Yellowfin as long as it is sushi grade. When you purchase the tuna, ask your fishmonger to cut as close to the bone as possible; you want a bright, ruby red portion with no white striations.

2 **tablespoons diced daikon radish** (if not available, skip Step 1 and increase the amounts of fennel and cucumber by 1 tablespoon each)

2 **tablespoons curry powder**

1 **tablespoon fine sea salt,** plus more to taste

2 **tablespoons cracked black peppercorns**

6 **bricks sushi-grade tuna,** preferably Bigeye, 3 ounces each (ask your fishmonger to cut them 2 by 2 by 3 inches)

2 **tablespoons extra-virgin olive oil,** plus more if necessary

2 **tablespoons finely diced cucumber**

2 **tablespoons finely diced fennel**

2 **tablespoons finely diced peeled Granny Smith apple,** tossed with 1 tablespoon freshly squeezed lime juice

2 **tablespoons finely diced avocado,** tossed with 1 tablespoon freshly squeezed lime juice

2 **tablespoons finely diced tomato**

3 **tablespoons mustard oil** (available from Middle Eastern shops; also see Mail-Order Sources)

Freshly ground black pepper to taste

½ **cup sun-dried tomatoes packed in olive oil,** drained and pureed in a blender

1 **bunch watercress,** preferably baby

BLANCH THE DAIKON RADISH Bring a pot of salted water to a boil. Fill a large bowl halfway with ice water. Add the daikon radish to the boiling water and blanch for 2 minutes. Drain and transfer to the ice water to cool it and stop the cooking. Drain and set aside.

COAT AND SEAR THE TUNA Spread the curry powder, 1 tablespoon salt, and cracked black pepper over the surface of a plate. Dredge each piece of tuna in the spice mixture to coat, pressing down to make sure the spices adhere to the fish. Warm 2 tablespoons of the olive oil in a large sauté pan set over high heat. Put 3 tuna pieces in the pan without crowding and sear on each side until nicely caramelized, approximately 20 seconds per side. Remove to a cutting board and repeat with the remaining tuna rectangles, adding more oil if necessary.

SLICE THE TUNA Cut each tuna rectangle crosswise into 4 or 5 pieces.

MAKE THE SALAD Put the daikon, cucumber, fennel, apple, avocado, tomato, and 2 tablespoons of the mustard oil in a bowl. Toss and season with salt and pepper.

TO SERVE Overlap the slices of each tuna portion in the center of a chilled salad plate. Spoon the vegetables over the center of the tuna in a thin path running lengthwise from end to end. Spoon the sun-dried tomato puree over the vegetables. Top with watercress and drizzle some mustard oil around the edge of the plate. Serve at once.

Wine Suggestion: Marcel Deiss, Burg 1999; Alsace. A rich Alsatian white featuring Gewürztraminer, Riesling, and Pinot Gris grapes, with complex, exotic, tropical aromas.

SWEET YELLOWTAIL SASHIMI WITH WASABI

serves ⑥ If you're a sashimi lover, this recipe will show you a way to create a sushi-like experience at home, building it out with a complex sauce. This dish would also be delicious with Yellowfin tuna.

1½ teaspoons wasabi powder

4 teaspoons cold water

2 tablespoons white mirin

3 tablespoons reduced-sodium (lite) soy sauce

1 tablespoon mustard oil (available from Middle Eastern shops; also see Mail-Order Sources)

1 tablespoon rice wine vinegar

¼ teaspoon honey

Freshly ground white pepper to taste

1 pound skinless yellowtail snapper fillet (hake or red snapper can be substituted)

Fine sea salt to taste

2 jalapeño peppers, sliced paper-thin crosswise

1 teaspoon chile paste

1 cup cilantro leaves

Olive oil

1 lime, halved (optional)

MAKE THE WASABI SAUCE In a bowl, stir together the wasabi powder and the cold water. Whisk in the mirin, soy sauce, mustard oil, vinegar, and honey. Season with pepper. Cover and refrigerate while you prepare the fish.

SLICE AND CHILL THE FISH Slice the snapper into 60 thin slices, about ⅛ inch thick. Arrange the fish slices in a flower pattern in the center of 6 cool plates. Cover the plates with plastic wrap and refrigerate for up to 4 hours.

TO SERVE Lightly season the fish with salt and pepper. Top each slice with a slice of jalapeño and dot each pepper slice with a dab of chile paste. Top with cilantro leaves. Drizzle each serving with approximately 1½ tablespoons of the sauce. Drizzle some olive oil around the perimeter of the plate and add a squeeze of lime juice, if desired. Serve immediately.

Wine Suggestion: Selbach-Oster, Riesling-Kabinett 2002; Mosel-Saar-Ruwer. A slightly off-dry Mosel Riesling with peach and slate notes.

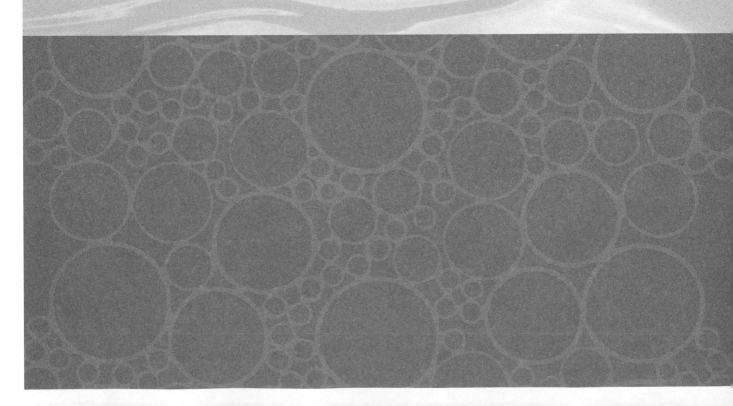

HOT APPETIZERS

Provençal Matchsticks

Bacalao Fritters

Fried Calamari with Half-Cooked
Tomato Broth

Hot and Salty Calamari

Crab Shepherd's Pie

Crispy Soft-Shell Crab with a Curried
Orange Dressing

Crab Cake Remoulade

Frog's Legs with Preserved Lemon
and Garlic

Grilled Baby Octopus and
Cumin–White Bean Salad

Bay Scallop, Blue Cheese, and Fig Salad

Breaded Sea Scallops with
Soy Brown Butter

Spice-Crusted Scallops with Curry-
Lemon Relish

Shrimp "Viet Nem"

Spicy Shrimp Noodles

Poached Skate with Spicy Lime-Yogurt
Vinaigrette

Blackened Tuna Toro with Yuzu
Vinaigrette

Fried Whitebait with Lime-Chile Dip

At restaurants, I sometimes order nothing but appetizers, filling the table with small dishes that my friends and I can taste. It's a less formal way to experience more flavors, most of them more intense than the ones you encounter in a main course. When I make hot appetizers at home, I also like to have some fun, setting a creative, festive mood for the meal.

One of my favorite types of hot appetizers is crispy fish dipped in a cool sauce—a combination that never fails to please a crowd. This is the dynamic at work in Crab Cake Remoulade (page 72), Fried Whitebait with Lime-Chile Dip (page 95), Poached Skate with Spicy Lime-Yogurt Vinaigrette (page 90), and Bacalao Fritters (page 62).

Then there are times when I look at hot appetizers as smaller versions of main courses, with a few components on one plate. This is how I approach Grilled Baby Octopus and Cumin–White Bean Salad (page 77), Breaded Sea Scallops with Soy Brown Butter (page 82), Spice-Crusted Scallops with Curry-Lemon Relish (page 84), Frog's Legs with Preserved Lemon and Garlic (page 75), and Crispy Soft-Shell Crab with a Curried Orange Dressing (page 70).

I also like to play with conventions in hot appetizers, presenting a twist on a classic. My Fried Calamari with Half-Cooked Tomato Broth (page 64) and Hot and Salty Calamari (page 66) are take-offs on Italian-American fried calamari, and Spicy Shrimp Noodles (page 88) is my answer to *pad thai*. Crab Shepherd's Pie (page 68) is my version of a dish that usually features ground beef or lamb. I do a seared version of sushi in Blackened Tuna Toro with Yuzu Vinaigrette (page 93) and a seafood version of a classic fall salad in Bay Scallop, Blue Cheese, and Fig Salad (page 80).

I also love creating appetizers that freely combine ingredients from more than one exotic culture, such as Shrimp "Viet Nem" (page 86), which isn't based on any dish in particular but, rather, takes its inspiration from the cuisine of the Far East in general.

PROVENÇAL MATCHSTICKS

serves (6) These slender little filled breadsticks are great on their own as an hors d'oeuvre or with a pesto mayonnaise (see Step 1, page 26) for dipping. Start a dinner party with them and your guests will be very impressed. They're also a witty, colorful accompaniment to Pesto Minestrone with Rock Shrimp (page 120) or Curry-Scented Tuna with Sun-Dried Tomato (page 54).

  2 **sheets puff pastry dough,** 8 by 12 inches each (from a 17¼-ounce package)
50 pitted Niçoise olives
12 **salt-packed anchovy fillets,** rinsed and patted dry
  4 **basil leaves,** cut lengthwise into 3 strips each
10 **sun-dried tomatoes,** cut lengthwise into thirds
  2 **egg yolks mixed with 2 tablespoons water**
½ **cup grated Parmigiano-Reggiano cheese**
    Pinch cayenne

BEGIN THE MATCHSTICKS Place one sheet of puff pastry on a shallow cookie sheet with the longer side running from left to right in front of you. Starting about ½ inch from the left side, arrange a column of olives from the top of the sheet to the bottom. About ½ inch to the right of the olive column, arrange a column of anchovies, topping it with pieces of basil. About ½ inch to the right of the anchovy column, arrange a column of tomato slices. Repeat twice, making a total of 9 columns, ending about ½ inch from the right side of the pastry sheet.

ADD THE OTHER PASTRY SHEET Roll out the other pastry sheet on a clean, dry work surface. Brush it with egg wash and invert on top of the first pastry sheet. Gently press the sheets together. Use your fingers to press down between the columns of ingredients, forming ridges. Brush the top of the pastry with egg wash and scatter the grated Parmigiano-Reggiano over the top. Season with cayenne. Wrap with plastic wrap and freeze for at least 3 hours or as long as 2 weeks.

BAKE THE PASTRY Preheat the oven to 375°F. Remove the puff pastry from the freezer and unwrap it. Without thawing, slice it lengthwise into ¼-inch-wide strips with a serrated knife. Arrange on a cookie sheet and bake until lightly golden and they begin to puff up, 12 to 14 minutes.

TO SERVE Serve the matchsticks from a basket as an hors d'oeuvre.

Wine Suggestion: Cava, Avinyo, NV; Penedes. A simple sparkling wine from Spain, with notes of citrus.

BACALAO FRITTERS

serves ⑥ *Bacalao* is the Spanish name for salt cod, which you can read about on page 4. If you don't want to make the sauce, serve these fritters simply with a squeeze of lemon juice and a few drops of Tabasco. To spice up the sauce, add crushed red pepper flakes. These fritters—known as *acra* in the Caribbean—would also be delicious made with crab or shrimp, or dipped in Tartar Sauce (recipe follows). These also make an ideal passed hors d'oeuvre.

Note that the salt cod requires 24 hours of soaking.

9	ounces salt cod
⅓	cup extra-virgin olive oil
7	garlic cloves, chopped
2	teaspoons thyme leaves
1½	pounds vine-ripened tomatoes, seeded and coarsely chopped (about 2½ cups)
	Pinch sugar
5	large basil leaves, chopped
1	dried chile, chopped
¼	cup finely diced onion
1	tablespoon chopped parsley
1	cup self-rising flour
½	cup milk
1	egg
⅓	cup water
	Freshly ground black pepper to taste
	Vegetable oil, for frying

SOAK THE SALT COD Put the salt cod in a bowl, cover with cold water, cover, and soak in the refrigerator for 24 hours, changing the water 3 times. Drain and flake fairly fine into a large bowl and refrigerate until ready to proceed.

MAKE THE SAUCE Preheat the oven to 400°F. Heat the olive oil in a flameproof casserole set over medium-high heat. Add 5 of the chopped garlic cloves and the thyme, and stir. Add the tomatoes and sugar, and cook, covered, for 2 minutes. Remove the cover, transfer the casserole to the oven, and bake until the tomatoes break down and appear dry, approximately 1 hour. Remove the casserole from the oven, transfer the sauce to a bowl, and let it cool. Stir in the basil and set aside. (This sauce is served at room temperature.)

PREPARE THE FRITTERS Add the chile, onion, parsley, and remaining 2 chopped garlic cloves to the bowl with the salt cod. In another bowl, whisk together the flour, milk, egg, and ⅓ cup water. Season with pepper. Add the salt cod to this mixture and gently toss to coat the fish.

FRY THE FRITTERS Pour the vegetable oil into a wide, deep pot to a depth of 4 inches. Heat the oil over high heat to a temperature of 375°F. Use a teaspoon to scoop up the cod and form it into small balls, about ¾ inch in diameter. Lower the fritters into the oil and fry in batches without crowding until golden brown, approximately 2 minutes. As the fritters are done, transfer them to a paper towel–lined plate to drain.

TO SERVE Put the hot fritters in a basket lined with a clean towel or linen napkin and pass the sauce on the side for dipping.

Wine Suggestion: Hildago, "La Gitana" Manzanilla; Jerez. A dry-style sherry with aromas of almonds and a slight saltiness.

TARTAR SAUCE

makes about 1½ cups In place of the tomato sauce in the main recipe here, you can use this sauce for the fritters or for other fried fish and shellfish sandwiches.

- 1 cup Soft-Boiled Egg Mayonnaise (page 41)
- 3 tablespoons chopped chives
- 2 tablespoons chopped spring onion
- 1 tablespoon freshly squeezed lemon juice

PUT THE MAYONNAISE in a bowl and stir in the chives, onion, and lemon juice.

FRIED CALAMARI WITH HALF-COOKED TOMATO BROTH

serves (6) This is my take on fried calamari, which is usually served with an Italian marinara sauce for dipping. My version features a lighter flour coating instead of the usual cornmeal, a tomato broth, and a salad piqued with the addition of mustard oil.

When making this dish, use your largest pot to keep the calamari from crowding. To add extra flavor, top the tomato salad with a spoonful of mayonnaise enlivened with chopped fresh herbs or pesto mayonnaise (see Step 1, page 26) before adding the calamari.

¾ **cup green beans,** preferably French *haricots verts*, sliced crosswise into ¼-inch segments
¼ **cup plus 1 tablespoon extra-virgin olive oil**
½ **medium onion,** cut into small dice
6 **vine-ripened tomatoes,** chopped, plus ¼ cup diced seeded tomato
1 **sprig thyme**
1 **tablespoon sugar**
½ **teaspoon Tabasco sauce**
2 **tablespoons sherry vinegar**
   Fine sea salt and freshly ground black pepper to taste
2 **tablespoons finely diced red onion**
2 **tablespoons mustard oil (available from Middle Eastern shops; also see**
      Mail-Order Sources)
3 **bunches watercress,** tough stems removed
2 **pounds calamari (squid),** cleaned and cut into 1-inch rings
1 **cup Wondra flour (see page 53)**
   Vegetable oil, for frying

BLANCH THE BEANS Bring a pot of salted water to a boil. Fill a large bowl halfway with ice water. Add the bean segments to the boiling water and blanch for 2 minutes. Drain and transfer to the ice water to stop the cooking. Drain and set aside.

MAKE THE TOMATO BROTH Heat ¼ cup of the olive oil in a medium saucepan set over medium-high heat. Add the onion and sauté until translucent, approximately 4 minutes. Add the chopped tomatoes, thyme, and sugar. Stir, cover, and cook just until the tomatoes begin to break apart, 3 to 5 minutes. Remove from the heat and transfer the tomatoes with their juices to a food processor. Puree until as smooth as possible, then strain through a fine-mesh strainer set over a bowl. Discard the solids. Add the Tabasco and sherry vinegar to the tomato broth and season with salt and pepper. Let cool, cover, and refrigerate for at least 3 hours.

MAKE THE VEGETABLES Put the diced tomato, red onion, and green beans in a bowl. Season with salt and pepper and drizzle with the mustard oil. Set aside.

DRESS THE WATERCRESS Put the watercress in a small bowl. Pour the remaining 1 tablespoon olive oil over it and season with salt and pepper. Toss and set aside.

FRY THE CALAMARI Toss the calamari in the flour in a strainer and shake to remove any excess. Pour the vegetable oil into a pot to a depth of 4 inches and heat to a temperature of 375°F. Add the calamari to the pot in batches and fry until golden brown, 2 to 4 minutes. Remove with a slotted spoon and drain on a paper towel–lined plate. Season with salt as soon as it comes out of the oil.

TO SERVE Mound some vegetables in the center of each of 6 shallow bowls. Top with some calamari, then some watercress. Ladle some tomato broth around the vegetables.

Wine Suggestion: Vincent Raimbault, Vouvray 2000; Loire Valley. A white with melon and pear fruit that has a nice acidity and a touch of earthiness.

HOT AND SALTY CALAMARI

serves (6) In hopes of showing how many things are possible with fish and shellfish, here's another variation on fried calamari using a coriander batter and an Asian-accented dipping sauce. If you can find cuttlefish, make this with them instead.

3 **large calamari (squid) or cuttlefish,** cleaned and cut into 2-inch triangles
     by your fishmonger
¼ **cup reduced-sodium (lite) soy sauce**
½ **teaspoon Vietnamese fish sauce** (*nuoc mam*)
2 **teaspoons rice wine vinegar**
1 **tablespoon freshly squeezed lime juice**
1 **tablespoon light mirin**
2 **dried chiles,** finely chopped
¼ **teaspoon fine sea salt**
½ **bunch cilantro,** chopped
1 **egg white**
1 **cup Wondra flour (see page 53)**
    Canola oil, for frying

CUT THE CALAMARI With the tip of a very sharp, thin-bladed knife, score the flesh on one side in a cross-hatch pattern without cutting through the meat.

MAKE THE SAUCE In a bowl, stir together the soy sauce, fish sauce, vinegar, lime juice, and mirin.

MAKE THE CHILE SALT In a small, shallow bowl, stir together the chiles and sea salt.

DREDGE THE CALAMARI In another bowl, whisk together the cilantro and egg white. Roll the calamari pieces in the egg white mixture, then dredge them in the flour.

FRY THE CALAMARI Pour the canola oil into a pot to a depth of 3 inches and heat to 375°F. Lower the calamari into the pot in batches without crowding and fry until golden brown and crispy, 2 to 3 minutes. Use a slotted spoon to transfer the pieces to a paper towel–lined plate and season them immediately with the chile salt. Repeat with the remaining pieces and chile salt.

TO SERVE   Present the calamari in a linen towel- or napkin-lined basket with the sauce alongside for dipping.

Wine Suggestion: Calera, Viognier 2000; Mt Harlan. A rich California white with aromas of nectarine, nougat, and ginger.

NUOC MAM is Vietnamese fermented fish sauce, used in cooking and as a condiment for the majority of dishes cooked there. The best of the sauces are made from anchovies, which are also a powerful flavor enhancer in Mediterranean cooking. The sauce ferments for about 6 months, producing an intense salty flavor and fish odor that somehow disappears in whatever dish it is used.

CRAB SHEPHERD'S PIE

serves (6) This dish is fashioned in the style of a *parmentier,* a family of recipes named for Antoine Parmentier, the Frenchman credited with first discovering that potatoes were edible and delicious. Many dishes featuring potato are named *parmentier* in his honor. If you own a "cream whipper" for piping potatoes, using it here will ensure that the puree topping each serving will be very light and fluffy. If you don't have one, use a pastry bag and substitute the mashed potato recipe on page 242.

Serve this with a Mâche Salad with Lemon-Parmesan Dressing (recipe follows).

    2 cups Blue Crab Bisque (page 100)
    1 tablespoon Cognac
    3 medium Yukon Gold potatoes
  1⅓ cups heavy cream
     Fine sea salt and freshly ground black pepper to taste
  18 ounces jumbo lump crabmeat, picked of any shell fragments
  1½ tablespoons chopped tarragon leaves
  ¼ cup plus 2 tablespoons dry bread crumbs
    1 tablespoon Old Bay Seasoning

PREPARE THE SAUCE In a medium saucepan, simmer the crab soup over medium-high heat until it is reduced by half, 20 to 30 minutes. Strain, then stir in the Cognac.

MAKE THE POTATO PUREE Put the potatoes in a pot, cover them with cold water, and season with salt. Bring the water to a boil over high heat and cook until the potatoes are done, 15 to 20 minutes from when the water boils. Drain the potatoes and, when they are cool enough to handle, peel them and run through a food mill into a bowl. Stir in the cream. If the mixture appears grainy, press it through a fine-mesh strainer. Season the puree with salt and pepper. While still warm, transfer the puree to a canister loaded with 2 gas charges. Test the consistency by piping a small amount of puree onto a plate.

TO SERVE Preheat the broiler. Rewarm the sauce in a heavy-bottomed pot set over medium heat. Add the crabmeat and tarragon to the sauce, and stir gently to warm through. Divide the crabmeat and sauce among 6 ovenproof ramekins. Pipe a dome of potato puree over the top of each. Sprinkle with bread crumbs to cover. Put the cups on a baking sheet and broil until browned on top, 3 to 5 minutes. Sprinkle with a dusting of Old Bay Seasoning and serve piping hot.

Wine Suggestion: Merry Edwards, Sauvignon Blanc 2001; Russian River Valley. An American white with a little richness from some oak aging and natural, mouthwatering flavors of citrus.

MÂCHE SALAD WITH LEMON-PARMESAN DRESSING

serves (6) **as a side dish** The dressing is the star here. It can be used to dress tender mâche, as suggested, or watercress as an alternative.

- 3 tablespoons freshly squeezed lemon juice
- 2 tablespoons extra-virgin olive oil
- ¼ teaspoon minced garlic
- 3 tablespoons freshly grated Parmigiano-Reggiano cheese
   Fine sea salt and freshly ground black pepper to taste
- 4 to 6 cups mâche or watercress, tough stems discarded, rinsed and spun dry

IN A BOWL, whisk together the lemon juice, olive oil, garlic, and cheese. Season with salt and pepper. Add the mâche and toss.

OLD BAY SEASONING is so commonly used that it's strange to think that it's actually a proprietary name owned by McCormick & Company. In 1990, the corporation purchased the formula from Gustav Brunn, a German immigrant who developed the spice mixture in 1939, when he set up camp in the crab capital of the United States, Baltimore, Maryland. Old Bay Seasoning is made with celery salt, paprika, clove, and other spices. In addition to crab cakes, it's delicious on fish, as well as on French fries and chicken.

CRISPY SOFT-SHELL CRAB WITH A CURRIED ORANGE DRESSING

serves ⑥ This is a wonderful, original way to enjoy soft-shell crabs when they come into season each May. These crabs would also be delicious with the grapefruit emulsion and vegetables that accompany the stone crabs on page 34, the Soy Brown Butter and vegetables served with the breaded sea scallops on page 82, or Tomato-Coriander Vinaigrette (recipe follows). You can also make this treatment into the basis for a sandwich: Put the crabs on ciabatta spread with chili mayonnaise or Tartar Sauce (page 63). Top with arugula, sliced tomato, and onion.

As with all soft-shell crab recipes, take care when cooking the crustaceans; they can actually "explode" when heated. To avoid this, poke tiny holes in their legs with a sewing needle or straight pin.

  2 cups freshly squeezed orange juice
1/4 cup peanut oil
  1 tablespoon cracked juniper berries
  1 tablespoon sherry vinegar
1/2 teaspoon curry powder
  2 tablespoons chopped cilantro leaves
12 small, or 6 large, soft-shell crabs, cleaned
    Fine sea salt and freshly ground black pepper to taste
1/2 cup Wondra flour (see page 53)
1/3 cup clarified butter (see page 275) or canola oil
  1 tablespoon hot paprika
    Wilted Pea Leaves (page 131) or spinach
1/4 cup chopped roasted peanuts

MAKE THE SAUCE Pour the orange juice into a pot and bring to a boil over high heat. Let it boil until reduced to 1/2 cup, approximately 8 minutes. Remove the pot from the heat and let it cool. Pour the peanut oil into a small saucepan and warm it over medium heat. Add the juniper berries, remove the pot from the heat, and let the juniper berries infuse the oil as it cools, then strain the oil. Add the juniper oil, vinegar, curry powder, and cilantro to the pot with the orange juice and stir. Set aside at room temperature.

COOK THE CRABS Season the crabs with salt and pepper and dredge them in the flour. Shake off any excess. Divide the butter between 2 wide, deep sauté pans and melt it over medium-high heat. Add half the crabs to each pan and cook until golden brown, 3 to 4 minutes on each side. Remove them to a paper towel–lined plate to drain. Dust them with hot paprika.

TO SERVE Mound some pea leaves in the center of each of 6 dinner plates. Divide the crabs evenly among 6 dinner plates, leaning them against the pea leaves. Spoon some sauce and sprinkle some chopped peanuts around the crab(s) on each plate.

Wine Suggestion: Troubadour, Belgium. An aromatic beer from Belgium, with notes of flowers, oranges, lemon, and spices.

TOMATO-CORIANDER VINAIGRETTE

makes enough to dress (6) servings This versatile sauce can top many white-fleshed fish. It is flavored with both coriander seeds, which have a mild citrus flavor, and the more pungent fresh coriander leaves, more commonly called cilantro.

- 8 **medium tomatoes,** peeled, seeded, and coarsely chopped
- 1 **tablespoon tomato paste**
- 3 **tablespoons extra-virgin olive oil**
  Pinch sugar
- ¾ **cup chopped shallots**
- 2 **tablespoons aged sherry vinegar**
- 1 **tablespoon cracked toasted coriander seeds**
- 1 **tablespoon chopped cilantro leaves**
  Fine sea salt and freshly ground black pepper to taste

PUT THE TOMATOES, tomato paste, olive oil, and sugar in a pot and cook for 5 minutes. Transfer to a food processor and process until smooth. Let cool, then add the shallots, vinegar, coriander, and cilantro, and season with salt and pepper. Cover and refrigerate for at least 1 hour. Serve very cold.

CRAB CAKE REMOULADE

serves ⑥ French and American traditions meet in this dish with superb results. Crab cakes are a Maryland institution because some of the country's best crab comes from the nearby Chesapeake Bay. Remoulade is a cold mayonnaise-based French sauce, zesty with gherkins and capers. Traditionally served with fried fish, cold salads, and other dishes, here the remoulade is the perfect cool accompaniment to the hot, crispy crab cakes. Because the sauce is founded on mayonnaise, it will be much better if you make the mayonnaise yourself.

This crab cake recipe comes from one of my former sous chefs, Matt Evers, who is—appropriately enough—a Maryland native.

1 **pound jumbo lump crabmeat,** picked over to remove any bits of cartilage
1 **tablespoon chopped shallot**
½ **teaspoon minced garlic**
1 **tablespoon chopped cilantro leaves**
1 **tablespoon chopped parsley leaves**
1 **tablespoon chopped tarragon leaves**
¼ **cup finely diced fennel**
¼ **cup finely diced celery**
5 **tablespoons Mayonnaise (page 27)**
⅓ **cup dry bread crumbs**
   Pinch cayenne
   About 1 teaspoon Old Bay Seasoning (see page 69)
   Fine sea salt and freshly ground black pepper to taste
1 **cup all-purpose flour**
2 **eggs, beaten**
1 **cup panko or regular dry bread crumbs**
   Vegetable oil, for frying
   Remoulade Sauce (recipe follows)
2 **cups baby greens or mesclun greens**

MAKE THE CRAB CAKES In a bowl, gently stir together the crabmeat, shallot, garlic, cilantro, parsley, tarragon, fennel, celery, mayonnaise, dry bread crumbs, cayenne, and Old Bay Seasoning. Taste and season with salt, pepper, and more Old Bay Seasoning, if desired. Shape the mixture into 6 cakes and set them aside on a plate. (The cakes can be made up to this point, lightly covered with plastic wrap, and held in the refrigerator for up to 8 hours.)

DREDGE THE CRAB CAKES Spread the flour out on a plate, pour the eggs into a shallow bowl, and spread the panko on another plate. Dredge the crab cakes in the flour. Dip in the egg wash, letting any excess wash run off, and then coat with the panko.

FRY THE CRAB CAKES Pour vegetable oil into a deep-sided pan to a depth of ¼ inch and heat it over medium-high heat. Add the crabcakes and cook until golden brown and crisp on the bottom, approximately 4 minutes. Lower the heat, carefully turn the crab cakes over, and cook until golden brown and crisp on the other side, another, 3 minutes or so. Transfer to a paper towel–lined plate to drain.

TO SERVE Put 1 crab cake in the center of each of 6 plates. Spoon some Remoulade Sauce around the perimeter of each plate and top with baby greens.

Wine Suggestion: Ronco del Gnemiz, Pinot Grigio 2001; Friuli. A lean, racy white from Italy, with slightly fruity overtones.

PANKO, also known as Japanese bread crumbs, are made from bleached wheat flour, dextrose, partially hydrogenated soybean oil, palm oil, yeast, and salt. They are perfect for frying because the "crumbs" are much more resilient than they look; when cooked in hot oil, the exterior browns while the interior retains its dry texture. The flakes are also larger, crispier, and lighter than regular bread crumbs.

REMOULADE SAUCE makes about ② cups

½ cup plus 2 tablespoons mayonnaise, preferably homemade (page 27)
1 tablespoon Dijon mustard
1 tablespoon capers, rinsed, drained, and minced
¼ cup minced peeled celery root
1 tablespoon minced gherkins
1 tablespoon finely chopped parsley leaves
1½ teaspoons finely chopped tarragon leaves
1½ tablespoons freshly squeezed lemon juice
Fine sea salt and freshly ground black pepper to taste

IN A BOWL, stir together the mayonnaise, mustard, capers, celery root, gherkins, parsley, tarragon, and lemon juice. Season with salt and pepper and set aside. Cover and refrigerate for up to 1 hour before serving.

FROG'S LEGS WITH PRESERVED LEMON AND GARLIC

serves (6) Frog's legs, one of the great French delicacies, can still be difficult to find in the United States, but they are worth the effort, even if means mail-ordering them (see page 277). Not only are they tender and full of flavor but also they are very easy to cook. The legs are sold skinned and cleaned, so they require no preparation whatsoever. Though they are available frozen, it's better to purchase them fresh—and essential to do so for this dish.

You might serve these with a Raw Porcini and Arugula Salad (recipe follows) dressed with olive oil and lemon.

36 **medium pairs frog's legs,** separated into 72 individual legs
   Fine sea salt and freshly ground black pepper to taste
 1 **cup Wondra flour (see page 53)**
 3 **tablespoons vegetable oil**
 3 **tablespoons unsalted butter**
 2 **garlic cloves,** minced
 3 **tablespoons chopped parsley**
   Juice of 2 lemons
 2 **tablespoons chopped Spiced Preserved Lemon peel (page 253),** rinsed and drained
   (chopped Meyer lemon peel can be substituted)

DREDGE THE LEGS Season the frog's legs and dredge them in flour, shaking off the excess flour.

SAUTÉ THE LEGS Heat half of the oil in a wide and deep nonstick sauté pan set over high heat. Add half of the legs in a single layer and sauté them until golden brown outside and firm and opaque to their centers, about 1 minute per side. Do not overcook or they will dry out. Add half of the butter and half of the garlic and toss to coat the legs. Add half of the parsley and half of the lemon juice, and toss to coat the legs again. Stir for 20 seconds, then add half of the preserved lemon. Toss and transfer the legs and sauce to a platter. Cover with foil to keep them warm. Repeat these steps with the remaining ingredients.

TO SERVE Present the platter family style, from the center of the table.

Wine Suggestion: Paul Blanck, Pinot Blanc 2001; Alsace. An Alsatian white with aromas of apples and minerals with tangy acidity.

RAW PORCINI AND ARUGULA SALAD

serves (6) **as a side dish** This Italian-style salad would also be delicious alongside many pasta dishes.

3 **medium porcini,** stems removed, cleaned and dried, thinly sliced
   Lemon-Parmesan Dressing (page 69), whisked with 2 chopped garlic cloves
3 **bunches arugula,** large stems removed
   Fine sea salt and freshly ground black pepper to taste

PUT THE PORCINI and dressing in a large bowl and gently toss. Add the arugula, season with salt and pepper, toss again, and serve.

GRILLED BABY OCTOPUS AND CUMIN–WHITE BEAN SALAD

serves (6) Grilling octopus is a multistep process: the octopus must be precooked before it's grilled. But it's worth the effort because the flavor is sensational. This recipe is intended for baby octopus because they are more tender and presentable. If you can't get baby octopus, use larger ones and cut them into 2-inch pieces after grilling.

This is also delicious with Aïoli (page 165) or Lime-Ginger Sauce (page 50) on the side.

> 4 **pounds baby octopus,** cleaned
> 3 **cups dry white wine**
> 1 **teaspoon black peppercorns**
> 1 **sprig thyme**
> 1 **tablespoon coarse sea salt**
> 1 **head garlic,** halved
> 1 **medium carrot,** cut into small dice
> ½ **medium onion,** cut into small dice
> 1 **celery stalk,** cut into small dice
> ¼ **cup plus 2 tablespoons olive oil**
> 2 **tablespoons balsamic vinegar**
> **Fine sea salt and freshly ground black pepper to taste**
> 2 **bunches arugula,** tough stems removed
> **Cumin–White Bean Salad (recipe follows)**

COOK THE OCTOPUS Put the octopus in a large pot. Pour in the wine and about 8 cups of water. Add the peppercorns, thyme, sea salt, garlic, carrot, onion, and celery. Bring the liquid to a boil over high heat, then lower the heat and let simmer until the octopus is tender, 1 to 1½ hours, depending on size. Periodically skim any impurities that rise to the surface. (While the octopus is cooking, you can make the Cumin–White Bean Salad.)

FINISH THE OCTOPUS Remove the octopus from the cooking liquid. Strain the liquid and return it to the pot over high heat. Cook until reduced to 3 tablespoons. Remove the pot from the heat and let the liquid cool.

MAKE THE VINAIGRETTE Put the cooled cooking liquid in a bowl. Add ¼ cup of the olive oil and the balsamic vinegar. Whisk together, taste, and adjust the seasoning, if necessary.

GRILL THE OCTOPUS Prepare an indoor or outdoor grill for grilling. Grill the octopus until charred on both sides, approximately 6 minutes total.

TO SERVE Put the arugula in a bowl and toss with the remaining 2 tablespoons olive oil. Spoon some bean salad in the center of each of 6 plates. Top with the octopus and arugula. Drizzle some vinaigrette around the plate.

Wine Suggestion: Marisa Cuomo, Furore 2001; Costa de Amalfi. A coastal Italian white reminiscent of the sea.

CUMIN–WHITE BEAN SALAD

serves ⑥ as a side dish This salad is wonderful on top of grilled bread and accompanied by a simple salad.

½ **pound dried cannellini beans,** soaked overnight in cold water
Coarse sea salt
2 **tablespoons chopped red onion**
3 **tablespoons diced seeded tomato**
⅓ **cup diced jicama**
⅓ **cup diced seedless cucumber**
1 **jalapeño pepper,** minced
1 **teaspoon ground cumin**
3 **tablespoons rice vinegar**
Grated zest of 1 lime
2 **tablespoons freshly squeezed lime juice**
¼ **cup olive oil**
1 **tablespoon chopped cilantro leaves**
1½ **teaspoons chopped mint leaves**
Fine sea salt and freshly ground black pepper to taste

DRAIN THE BEANS and add them to a pot with about 5 cups of cold water and a pinch of sea salt. Bring the water to a boil over high heat, then lower the heat and let simmer, covered, until the beans are tender, approximately 1½ hours. Let the beans cool, then toss them with the red onion, tomato, jicama, cucumber, jalapeño, cumin, rice vinegar, lime zest, lime juice, olive oil, cilantro, and mint. Season with salt and pepper.

BAY SCALLOP, BLUE CHEESE, AND FIG SALAD

serves ⑥ This is my adaptation of a typical fall salad of blue cheese, figs, and walnuts, adding small bay scallops to the mix. If you like, you can replace bay scallops with 3 or 4 dry sea scallops per person. For an even more flavorful dish, strain the burgundy-colored fig marinade, reduce it to a syrup over high heat, and drizzle it around the scallops and salad on the finished dish.

(Note that the figs must soak for 24 hours.)

½	cup port wine
½	cup balsamic vinegar
2	tablespoons sugar
1½	teaspoons ground cinnamon
6	fresh Black Mission figs
20	walnut halves, coarsely chopped
6	ounces bacon, cut into ¼-inch dice (about 1½ cups)
1	Belgian endive, tough core discarded, cut into thin julienne strips
2	bunches watercress, thick stems discarded
2	heads frisée lettuce, yellow part only
½	apple, cut into thin julienne strips
5	ounces Fourme d'Ambert or other mild blue cheese, crumbled
	Mustard Vinaigrette (recipe follows)
	About ¼ cup olive oil
	Fine sea salt and freshly ground black pepper to taste
1¼	pounds medium bay scallops (about 54 scallops)

MARINATE THE FIGS Put the port, vinegar, sugar, and cinnamon in a nonreactive saucepan and bring to a boil over high heat. Make a small X incision on the top of each fig. Remove the pan from the heat and add the figs. Let cool, then cover and marinate for 24 hours in the refrigerator.

TOAST THE WALNUTS Warm the walnuts in a dry sauté pan over medium heat, shaking occasionally, until lightly toasted and fragrant, approximately 5 minutes.

SAUTÉ THE BACON Crisp the bacon in a sauté pan over medium heat; drain on paper towels.

MAKE THE BACON-FRISÉE SALAD In a large bowl, toss together the endive, watercress, toasted walnuts, frisée, bacon, apple, and blue cheese. Toss with most of the vinaigrette, then taste and add more vinaigrette until it is as thickly dressed as you like.

SAUTÉ THE SCALLOPS Heat 2 tablespoons of the olive oil in a deep, wide sauté pan over high heat. Season the scallops with salt and pepper, add them to the pan in batches and sauté them quickly, shaking the pan to ensure even cooking, until golden brown, approximately 1 minute per batch, adding more oil between batches if necessary.

TO SERVE Divide the scallops evenly among 6 plates. Quarter the figs and arrange 4 pieces on each plate. Top with some salad.

Wine Suggestion: Leacocks 10-year-old, Bual Madeira, or another Bual-style Madeira, with aromas of dried fruits, fig, and smoke.

MUSTARD VINAIGRETTE makes about ① cup

  2 tablespoons Dijon mustard
  1 tablespoon red wine vinegar
  ¼ cup canola oil
      Fine sea salt and freshly ground black pepper to taste

IN A SMALL BOWL, whisk together the mustard and vinegar. Slowly add the canola oil in a thin stream, whisking until the dressing is thick and emulsified. Season with salt and pepper.

FOURME D'AMBERT is one of my favorite blue cheeses, much creamier and less assertive than, say, Roquefort. It comes from the Auvergne region of France, which I'm also very fond of. If you're wondering how a blue cheese can be served on the same plate as bay scallops, you'll understand when you taste this gentle giant. If you can't find it, opt for a mild American blue like Point Reyes.

JULIENNE refers to long, thin slices of vegetables or other ingredients that resemble long matchsticks.

BREADED SEA SCALLOPS WITH SOY BROWN BUTTER

serves (6) Scallops are very rich and are able to stand up to a lot of big flavors. Here, I pair them with soy sauce, brown butter, and herbs. This is a beautiful dish with tiny cubes of breading rather than crumbs, creating a pronounced texture. The key to cooking it properly is to use very fresh, very dry scallops so that the bread stays crisp.

If you expand the recipe to allow 4 or 5 scallops per person and serve it with parsnip puree or celery root puree, this could be a main course.

1 **pound medium sea scallops,** preferably diver-harvested (about 18 scallops)
Fine sea salt and freshly ground black pepper to taste
½ **cup all-purpose flour**
2 **eggs,** lightly beaten
5 **slices white bread,** crusts removed, cut into ⅛-inch dice
¼ **cup olive oil**
¼ **cup plus 2 tablespoons heavy cream**
½ **cup (1 stick) unsalted butter**
½ **tablespoon chopped garlic**
1 **tablespoon chopped shallot**
3 **tablespoons reduced-sodium (lite) soy sauce**
2 **tablespoons freshly squeezed lime juice**
1 **tablespoon chopped tarragon leaves**
2 **teaspoons chopped cilantro leaves**
1 **teaspoon chopped parsley leaves**
1 **teaspoon chopped chives**

BREAD THE SCALLOPS Season the scallops with salt and pepper. One by one, dip the scallops in the flour, then the egg, then the bread cubes, to coat 1 flat side of each one. Press firmly on the bread to make sure it adheres to the scallops. (The scallops can be made to this point, covered with plastic wrap, and refrigerated for up to 6 hours.)

PREHEAT THE OVEN to 350°F.

SAUTÉ THE SCALLOPS Heat the olive oil in a wide sauté pan over high heat. Add the scallops, breaded side down a few at a time, and cook, turning once, until golden brown on the outside and opaque in the center (cut one open), approximately 2 minutes per side. Remove to a baking sheet, crust side up, and set aside. Repeat with the remaining scallops, adding more oil between batches if necessary.

MAKE THE SOY–BROWN BUTTER SAUCE Put the cream and butter in a sauté pan set over high heat and cook until melted and browned. Add the garlic and shallot, then the soy sauce, lime juice, tarragon, cilantro, parsley, and chives.

TO SERVE Reheat the scallops in the oven. Mound some vegetable puree, if using, in the center of each of 6 plates. Arrange 3 scallops on each serving and spoon some sauce around the puree.

Wine Suggestion: Au Bon Climat, Talley Vineyard Chardonnay 2001; Santa Barbara. A rich California white with ripe pear and apple fruit with a slight bit of butteriness.

SPICE-CRUSTED SCALLOPS WITH CURRY-LEMON RELISH

serves (6) To make this recipe, try to find scallops that are fresh out of the shell; they have to be dry to keep the spice mixture from becoming too wet. The relish is a new take on chutney, a spiced sweet-and-sour fruit puree that's usually served alongside curry dishes; here, the curry is part of the chutney.

2 teaspoons coriander seeds
4 teaspoons cumin seeds
4 teaspoons fennel seeds
1 cup water
⅔ cup granulated sugar
4 lemons, peeled, seeded, and separated into segments
5 tablespoons olive oil
1 cup chopped shallots (about 5 shallots)
1 teaspoon curry powder
⅔ cup dry white wine
1 tablespoon rice wine vinegar
2 tablespoons chopped cilantro leaves
Fine sea salt and freshly ground black pepper to taste
2 fennel bulbs, shaved and kept in ice water
2 tablespoons extra-virgin olive oil
2 tablespoons freshly squeezed lemon juice
2 teaspoons mace
2 tablespoons plus 2 teaspoons confectioners' sugar
5 teaspoons ground star anise
2 teaspoons ground cardamom
1 pound medium dry sea scallops (about 18 scallops)

TOAST THE SPICES Preheat the oven to 200°F. Put the coriander, cumin, and fennel seeds on a baking sheet and toast until fragrant, approximately 5 minutes. Remove the baking sheet from the oven and set the spices aside to cool.

MAKE THE CURRY-LEMON RELISH In a small saucepan, combine the water with the granulated sugar. Bring to a boil over high heat, stirring, until the sugar dissolves. Cut each lemon segment crosswise into 3 pieces. Put the lemon segments in a bowl. Pour the boiling syrup over the lemon segments; let cool. Heat 2 tablespoons of the olive oil in a pot set over medium-high heat. Add the shallots and curry, and cook, stirring, until the shallots are softened but not browned, approximately 3 minutes. Add the wine and cook until almost dry, approximately 4 minutes. Add the vinegar, cilantro, and cooled lemon pieces. Season with salt and pepper.

MAKE THE FENNEL SALAD Toss the fennel with the extra-virgin olive oil and lemon juice, and season with salt and pepper. Set aside at room temperature.

MAKE THE SPICE MIX In a blender, grind as fine as possible the toasted seeds, mace, confectioners' sugar, star anise, cardamom, and 2 teaspoons of fine sea salt. Strain the mixture through a fine-mesh strainer.

COOK THE SCALLOPS Heat the remaining 3 tablespoons olive oil in a wide, deep sauté pan set over high heat. Dip the lower half of each scallop in the spice mix. Add the scallops to the pan, coated side down, and cook, turning once, until golden brown, approximately 3 minutes per side.

TO SERVE Mound some relish in the center of each of 6 plates. Arrange 3 scallops around each mound of relish. Top the scallops with some fennel salad.

Wine Suggestion: Weingut Bründlmayer, "Langenloiser" Grüner Veltliner 2002; Kamptal-Donauland. A spicy, peachy wine with bright, citrus acidity, from Austria's indigenous white varietal.

SHRIMP "VIET NEM"

serves (6) This is my own version of the Vietnamese dish called *nem,* an appetizer traditionally made with pork and vermicelli rice noodles. Part of the fun of eating a dish like this in Vietnamese restaurants is wrapping the spring rolls with Bibb lettuce and mint, which adds fresh flavor and plenty of crunch. If you like, do this at home, as well.

To prepare these in advance, fry them until three-quarters done as soon as you've made them (this will keep the dough from cracking). Then refry them when you are ready to serve.

These rolls also make a wonderful passed hors d'oeuvre; double the recipe, if desired, to serve more people.

1   **tablespoon honey**
2   **tablespoons white mirin**
3   **tablespoons rice vinegar**
2   **teaspoons reduced-sodium (lite) soy sauce**
¼   **teaspoon crushed red pepper flakes**
½   **teaspoon grated fresh ginger**
1   **teaspoon peeled and grated carrot**
1   **pound medium shrimp,** peeled, deveined, and halved lengthwise
1¼   **teaspoons Chinese chile paste**
1   **tablespoon chopped cilantro leaves**
1   **scallion,** green part only, chopped
Fine sea salt and freshly ground black pepper to taste
6   **rice paper sheets,** 8½ inches in diameter
Vegetable oil, for frying
Large Bibb lettuce leaves and fresh mint, for serving (optional)

MAKE THE SAUCE In a bowl, stir together the honey, mirin, vinegar, soy sauce, red pepper flakes, ginger, and carrot. Set aside.

MARINATE THE SHRIMP Put the shrimp in a bowl. Add the chile paste, cilantro, and scallion. Season with salt and pepper. Cover and refrigerate for 1 hour.

MAKE THE ROLLS Fill a wide, shallow bowl with cold water. Lower a rice paper sheet into the water and leave there until softened, approximately 2 minutes. Remove very carefully and lay on a clean, dry towel to drain. Once dry, remove it from the towel and set it before you.

Remove one-sixth of the shrimp from the marinade and lay in a cigar shape 1 inch from the side nearest you. Roll the wrapper around the filling for one turn. Fold the sides over to seal the ends, then continue rolling. When finished, press the edges to seal the roll. Repeat with the remaining shrimp filling and rice papers.

FRY THE ROLLS Pour the oil into a wide, deep pot and heat it over high heat to a temperature of 375°F. Carefully lower the rolls into the hot oil and fry until golden brown and crisp, approximately 8 minutes. Remove the rolls, drain briefly on paper towels, and cut each one crosswise into 5 pieces using a serrated knife.

TO SERVE Arrange the pieces on a platter and use the sauce for dipping. Serve with lettuce and mint leaves, if desired.

Wine Suggestion: Bott-Geyl, Gewürztraminer 1999; Alsace. A spicy and aromatic white from Alsace, with exotic aromas of quince and lychee.

SPICY SHRIMP NOODLES

serves (6) If you love Thai food, then you've probably eaten *pad thai* (the name means "Thai fry"), a wok-cooked noodle dish that features pork, eggs, tofu, and dried shrimp. A lot of American restaurants make the dish with chicken and cooked shrimp. This recipe is a clean and simple variation on *pad thai*. It's not fried; rather, the noodles are cooked and tossed with traditional spices and sauces, then the poached shrimp are simply laid on top.

To make the shrimp more flavorful, poach them in a court bouillon (see page 274) rather than in plain water.

Fine sea salt to taste
6 ounces white *pad thai* noodles
1 tablespoon brown sugar or palm sugar
1 tablespoon Vietnamese fish sauce (*nuoc mam*; see page 67) or
    nam pla (Thai fish sauce)
1 tablespoon freshly squeezed lime juice
1 tablespoon chopped garlic
1 tablespoon chopped fresh ginger
1 tablespoon Chinese chile paste
2 tablespoons chopped Thai basil or cilantro leaves
1 tablespoon chopped mint leaves
2 tablespoons chopped scallion, green part only
1 tablespoon reduced-sodium (lite) soy sauce
1 tablespoon sesame oil
1 cup bean sprouts
⅓ cup chopped roasted peanuts
24 medium shrimp, peeled, deveined, and split lengthwise

COOK THE NOODLES Bring a pot of lightly salted water to a boil. Add the noodles and cook according to the package directions. Drain and set aside.

MAKE THE SAUCE In a large bowl, toss together the brown sugar, fish sauce, lime juice, garlic, ginger, chile paste, cilantro, mint, scallion, soy sauce, and sesame oil.

DRESS THE NOODLES Add the pasta to the bowl with the sauce. Add the bean sprouts and peanuts. Toss, cover, and let marinate in the refrigerator for 1 hour.

TO SERVE Bring a pot of salted water to a simmer. Put the shrimp in a steamer basket and set over the simmering water. Steam until the shrimp are firm and pink, 5 to 6 minutes. Add half the shrimp to the bowl with the pasta and sauce, toss, and transfer to a large serving bowl. Arrange the remaining shrimp decoratively on top. Serve at once.

Wine Suggestion: Domaine Weinbach, Cuvée Theo 2001; Alsace. An Alsatian Riesling with aromas of peaches, limes, and spice.

POACHED SKATE WITH SPICY LIME-YOGURT VINAIGRETTE

serves ⑥ This dish dresses poached skate with a sauce of curry, garlic, apricot, and cilantro. The gentle flavor of the fish lets each flavor really shine. Skate is as delicate as it is delicious, which means that it has a tendency to fall apart when poached. But that isn't a problem with this recipe; if the fish breaks into pieces, simply arrange equal amounts decoratively on each plate. Be sure to purchase fresh feta preserved in a briny liquid, and allow at least 2 hours to marinate before preparing the skate.

This can easily become a main course if you pair it with boiled fingerling potatoes. It's also delicious with Fried Green Tomatoes (page 238).

¼ **teaspoon cumin seeds**

7 **ounces feta cheese,** cut into ⅛-inch-thick slices

1 **teaspoon harissa**

1 **teaspoon extra-virgin olive oil**

½ **teaspoon fennel seeds**

3 **cups dry white wine**

8 **cups water**

1 **teaspoon black peppercorns**

1 **sprig thyme**

½ **cup finely diced onion**

1 **tablespoon coarse sea salt**

1 **head garlic,** halved crosswise

1 **medium carrot,** peeled and cut into small dice

1 **celery stalk,** cut into small dice

6 **skate wings,** 4 ounces each

Fine sea salt and freshly ground black pepper to taste

1 **large seedless cucumber,** cut into very thin julienne strips

3 **slices white bread,** crusts removed, toasted and cut into croutons

Lime-Yogurt Vinaigrette (recipe follows)

TOAST THE CUMIN SEEDS Toast the cumin seeds in a sauté pan over medium heat, shaking, until fragrant, approximately 1 minute.

MARINATE THE CHEESE Put the cheese in a plastic or glass container. In a small bowl, stir together the harissa, olive oil, toasted cumin seeds, and fennel seeds. Drizzle this mixture over the cheese, cover, and let marinate in the refrigerator for at least 2 hours or overnight.

POACH THE SKATE Pour the wine and water into a large pot. Add the peppercorns, thyme, onion, coarse sea salt, garlic, carrot, and celery. Bring the liquid to a boil over high heat. Season the skate with salt and pepper, and add it to the pot. When the water returns to a boil, lower the heat and let simmer until the skate is just opaque at the center, 3 to 4 minutes, depending on the thickness of the fish. Remove very carefully using a spatula or two and let drain on a paper towel–lined plate.

TO SERVE In a bowl, gently toss the feta cheese with a few drops of marinade, the cucumber, and the croutons. Divide the skate among 6 plates. Top with some of the cheese mixture. Spoon the vinaigrette around the fish.

Wine Suggestion: Hadjimichalis, Laas 2000; Attica. An exotic, refreshing Greek white, with notes of mango.

HARISSA is an extremely hot and spicy North African condiment made from red chiles and olive oil that is most closely associated with Moroccan cuisine. Because of its intensity, don't use any more than the recipe calls for. It is also delicious as an accompaniment to couscous, soups, and dried meats.

LIME-YOGURT VINAIGRETTE

makes about (1¼) **cups**   For a change of pace, serve this alongside poached and grilled fish and shellfish.

1	**sweet white onion,** quartered
4	**garlic cloves**
¼	**cup apricot jam**
¼	**cup plus 1 tablespoon freshly squeezed lime juice**
1	**tablespoon curry powder**
½	**teaspoon harissa**
¼	**cup olive oil**
1½	**teaspoons plain yogurt**
2	**tablespoons water**
	Fine sea salt and freshly ground black pepper to taste
1	**tablespoon chopped cilantro leaves**

PUT THE ONION, garlic, jam, lime juice, curry powder, harissa, olive oil, yogurt, and water in a blender. Puree until smooth. Season to taste with salt and pepper, and fold in the cilantro. Refrigerate until ready to serve.

BLACKENED TUNA TORO WITH YUZU VINAIGRETTE

serves (6) This recipe is sublime when made with authentic toro, the fatty underbelly of a tuna, which is one of the most desirable sushi cuts, prized for its silky texture. The high fat content allows the flavor of the fish to register, even with such spices as curry powder and coriander. It also helps the fish stand up to a high-heat searing without overcooking the entire toro, much like foie gras.

Even the best sushi restaurants sometimes don't have toro. If you can't find it, use sushi-grade tuna. If you have a sharp knife, slice the tuna after blackening it for a more striking presentation.

- ¼ cup plus 3 tablespoons water
- ¼ cup sugar
- ⅓ cup white wine vinegar
- 1 tablespoon whole-grain mustard
- 6 tablespoons yuzu (see page 37) or Meyer lemon juice
- ¼ cup plus 1 tablespoon olive oil
  Fine sea salt and freshly ground black pepper to taste
- 1 teaspoon ground cumin
- 1 teaspoon ground coriander
- 1 teaspoon chopped thyme leaves
- 1 teaspoon curry powder
- ¾ teaspoon cayenne
- 6 pieces sushi-grade tuna, preferably toro, each about 4 ounces and 1 inch thick
- 2 lemons, preferably Meyer lemons, separated into segments
- 2 bunches baby watercress, tough stems discarded, rinsed and spun dry
- ¼ cup Crispy Shallots (page 53)
- ½ seedless cucumber, peeled and finely diced
- 2 tablespoons mustard oil (available from Middle Eastern shops; also see Mail-Order Sources)

MAKE THE SAUCE Put 2 tablespoons of water in a deep pot with the sugar. Cook over high heat, stirring constantly, until reduced to a syrup. Add the vinegar, boil until reduced by two-thirds, then remove from the heat and let the mixture cool. Stir in the mustard, yuzu juice, 2 tablespoons of the olive oil, and remaining ¼ cup plus 1 tablespoon of water, and season with salt and pepper.

SEASON THE TUNA In a bowl, stir together the cumin, coriander, thyme, curry, and cayenne. Roll the tuna pieces in the spices to coat all over.

SEAR THE TUNA Heat the remaining 3 tablespoons olive oil in a large nonstick skillet over medium-high heat. Add the tuna pieces and cook, turning, until seared on both sides, less than 1 minute per side. You want the tuna raw in the middle, so as soon as each side is darkened, turn the fish.

TO SERVE Spoon some sauce around the perimeter of each of 6 salad plates. Arrange some lemon segments and watercress in the middle of each plate. Place 1 piece of tuna on top of the watercress on each place. Garnish with Crispy Shallots and diced cucumber. Drizzle each serving with mustard oil.

Wine Suggestion: Chateau Ste. Michelle/Dr. Loosen, Riesling "Eroica" 2001; Columbia Valley. An American Riesling from Washington, with aromas of white peach and fresh apricot.

FRIED WHITEBAIT WITH LIME-CHILE DIP

serves ⑥ to ⑧ as an appetizer Whitebait are almost always fried until crisp and served with a dipping sauce. I like to experiment with different flavors because the tiny fish get along with almost anything—in this case, an Asian-style sauce. These also make a fine passed hors d'oeuvre.

This recipe is most successful when made with the smallest whitebait possible, which will be the crunchiest when fried. It would also be delicious with Remoulade Sauce (page 74) or Lime-Ginger Sauce (Step 3, page 50).

6 tablespoons **mayonnaise,** preferably homemade
2 teaspoons **Chinese chile paste**
Grated zest of 1 lime
1½ tablespoons **freshly squeezed lime juice**
Fine sea salt and freshly ground black pepper to taste
1 cup **Wondra flour (see page 53)**
1 pound **fresh whitebait,** rinsed and dried
Vegetable oil, for frying

MAKE THE LIME-CHILE SAUCE In a small bowl, whisk together the mayonnaise, chile paste, lime zest, and lime juice. Season with salt and pepper. Cover and refrigerate until serving time.

DREDGE AND FRY THE WHITEBAIT Spread the flour out on a plate. Dredge the whitebait in the flour. Pour the oil into a large saucepan or deep fryer to a depth of 5 inches. Heat the oil to a temperature of 375°F. Carefully lower the fish into the oil, a few at a time, and fry until golden brown, just a few seconds. Remove with a slotted spoon and transfer to a paper towel–lined plate to drain. Immediately season with salt.

TO SERVE Serve the whitebait at once from a linen basket, presenting the dipping sauce alongside.

Wine Suggestion: Weingut Dr. V. Bassermann-Jordan, Riesling-Spätlese 2001; Rheinpfalz. A German Riesling with notes of spice and nectarine.

SOUPS AND CHOWDERS

Gazpacho with Dungeness Crab

Blue Crab Bisque

Chilled Asparagus Soup with American Caviar

Manhattan Clam Chowder

New England Clam Chowder

Cream of Cauliflower with Salt Cod

Mediterranean Fish Soup with Rouille

Corn and Haddock Chowder

Mushroom Velouté with Truffle Sabayon

Mussel Soup with Red Curry and Coconut

Butternut Squash Soup with Nutmeg and Bay Scallops

Pesto Minestrone with Rock Shrimp

Chilled Green Pea Soup with Spicy Shrimp

Cream of Lettuce with Smoked Trout

One of the nicest things anyone ever said about my cooking was when *GQ* magazine's food writer Alan Richman called me the "Picasso of Soup." I'm not foolish enough to think that he meant I was anything like Picasso himself. I think he merely was trying to say that I look at soups a little differently from most people.

I grew up eating soups such as vichyssoise, lentil soup, and *pot au feu*. Many of my favorite childhood recipes have been adapted for this book, including Mediterranean Fish Soup with Rouille (page 110), Cream of Lettuce with Smoked Trout (page 125), and Cream of Cauliflower with Salt Cod (page 108).

Here in the United States, I came to love a whole new family of classic hearty American soups like New England Clam Chowder (page 106), Corn and Haddock Chowder (page 113), and Manhattan Clam Chowder (page 104). And it's no wonder I like chowders in particular; many people assert that their name comes from the French word for cauldron, *chaudron*.

I love to make soups interesting and surprising. Two of my favorite ways of doing this are by making sure they have a distinct texture and by adding a garnish. The garnish can be fish or shellfish itself, as in Gazpacho with Dungeness Crab (page 99); or it can be a condiment, as in Pesto Minestrone with Rock Shrimp (page 120), where the pesto stirred into the soup gives it a much more complex flavor than minestrone usually has.

I also love soups because they can be one of the most effective ways to harness the ingredients of a season. Chilled Green Pea Soup with Spicy Shrimp (page 122) and Chilled Asparagus Soup with American Caviar (page 102) capture the essence of spring. They're cool and full of fresh, green flavor. Similarly, Butternut Squash Soup with Nutmeg and Bay Scallops (page 118) is a tribute to fall flavors, with a heartier texture that is welcome in the colder months of the year.

There are a few important considerations when making fish and shellfish soups in particular. First and foremost, you need to cook shellfish just enough, being careful not to overcook them, which will cause them to seize up. With soups featuring fin fish, you need to be careful not to overcook them to the point where they will begin to break apart, unless, of course, that's the effect you seek.

You'll also notice that I occasionally use water instead of stock. Because water lets the flavor of the main ingredient show through, I find it's a better choice than chicken or fish stock for many soups.

Don't be afraid to let fish or shellfish soups sit in the refrigerator for a day or two before serving. They are just as convenient as other soups in this respect, and many of them will actually develop flavor as they "age" in the refrigerator.

Finally, I encourage you to not think of soups as just a first course. Many of them can be a main course. Blue Crab Bisque (page 100) and Mussel Soup with Red Curry and Coconut (page 116) are just two examples of soups that are so full of flavor and texture that they just might satisfy as a meal on their own, with a small salad on the side.

GAZPACHO WITH DUNGENESS CRAB

serves (6) Gazpacho is a cold Spanish soup made of finely chopped tomatoes, onions, and sweet red pepper. I enrich mine with mayonnaise and strain it, so you have the flavor of the vegetables but with a smooth, satiny texture. I like to embellish my gazpacho with Dungeness crab, but you can also make this with jumbo lump crabmeat, grilled sea scallops, or jumbo shrimp.

This is delicious with Provençal Matchsticks (page 61) or grilled bread spread with basil pesto (Steps 2 and 3, pages 120–121).

2 **small red bell peppers,** cut into large dice
2 **medium Vidalia or other sweet onions,** cut into large dice
6 **vine-ripened tomatoes,** cut into large dice
1 **large cucumber,** peeled and cut into large dice
4 **garlic cloves,** chopped
1 **tablespoon sherry vinegar**
¼ **cup extra-virgin olive oil**
Fine sea salt and freshly ground black pepper
2 **tablespoons mayonnaise**
Tabasco sauce
1 **pound crabmeat,** preferably Dungeness
1 **avocado,** diced

MARINATE THE VEGETABLES Put the bell peppers, onions, tomatoes, cucumber, garlic, sherry vinegar, and olive oil in a bowl. Toss, season with salt and pepper to taste, and let marinate, covered, in the refrigerator for at least 4 hours or preferably overnight.

MAKE THE SOUP Transfer the vegetables and their liquid to a blender. Add the mayonnaise and blend until coarsely chopped. Turn the contents of the blender into a medium-mesh strainer set over a bowl. Discard the solids and season the drained liquid to taste with Tabasco, salt, and pepper. The soup should be fairly highly seasoned because the flavors will mellow as it stands. (The gazpacho can be made to this point and refrigerated overnight in an airtight container in the refrigerator.)

TO SERVE Use a ladle to divide the gazpacho among 6 chilled bowls. Scatter some crabmeat and avocado over the top of each serving.

Wine Suggestion: Frederic Lornet, Brut Rosé, NV; Jura. A light, refreshing sparkling rosé from the Jura in France.

BLUE CRAB BISQUE

serves ⑥ You probably know bisque as a creamy vehicle for lobster, or maybe shrimp. I love making bisque with blue crab, whose slightly sweet flavor is the perfect foil for the heavy cream. Traditional recipes include white wine and a rich stock, but I've always found that the Cognac in bisques makes the wine unnecessary, and that using water instead of stock, which is much simpler, lets the flavor of the crab shine through.

This bisque is especially delicious with toasted baguette slices spread with the potato-thickened condiment called Rouille (page 112).

¼ **cup extra-virgin olive oil**

6 **pounds blue crabs,** preferably from Maine, rinsed and chopped with their shells into 5 pieces each, plus ¾ pound lump crabmeat

Pinch cayenne

½ **cup Cognac**

1 **large carrot,** cut into large dice

1 **medium onion,** cut into large dice

1 **celery stalk,** cut into large dice

1 **head garlic,** halved crosswise

2 **tablespoons tomato paste**

4 **vine-ripened tomatoes,** chopped

1 **sprig thyme**

1 **bay leaf**

10 **stems parsley,** with no leaves

1 **tablespoon black peppercorns**

3½ **quarts water**

½ **cup heavy cream**

2 **tablespoons chopped fresh tarragon**

Fine sea salt and freshly ground black pepper

PAN-ROAST THE CRAB Heat 2 tablespoons of the olive oil in a large flameproof casserole set over high heat. Add the cut-up crabs and cayenne, and sauté until all of the moisture has been cooked out and the meat has turned red, 8 to 10 minutes. Leaning away from the casserole, add the Cognac and carefully ignite it with a match, then cook until the flames subside and all the Cognac is evaporated. Use a slotted spoon to transfer the crabs to a bowl.

ROAST THE VEGETABLES Add the remaining 2 tablespoons olive oil to the casserole and let it heat up. When the oil is hot, add the carrot, onion, celery, and garlic. Sauté until the onion is translucent, approximately 4 minutes.

CONTINUE MAKING THE SOUP Return the cooked crabs to the casserole. Add the tomato paste and cook, stirring, to coat the vegetables for 3 to 4 minutes. Add the tomatoes, thyme, bay leaf, parsley, and peppercorns. Continue to cook, stirring occasionally, until the tomatoes break down, approximately 5 minutes.

TURN THE SOUP INTO A BISQUE Add the water, raise the heat to high, and bring to a boil, then lower the heat and let the soup simmer for at least 45 minutes. Strain through a fine-mesh strainer set over a bowl. Discard the solids. Return the strained soup to the casserole and set over medium heat. Bring to a boil, then lower the heat and simmer until reduced by half. (The bisque can be made to this point, cooled, covered, and refrigerated overnight in an airtight container in the refrigerator. Reheat gently before proceeding.)

TO FINISH AND SERVE Pour in the cream and bring the bisque to a simmer. Stir in the lump crabmeat and the tarragon. Season the soup with salt and pepper. Ladle the soup into 6 warm bowls.

Wine Suggestion: Cristom, Pinot Gris 2001; Willamette, Oregon. A white with aromas of melon, pear, and slight mineral nuances.

CHILLED ASPARAGUS SOUP WITH AMERICAN CAVIAR

serves ⑥ Like the pea soup on page 122, this dish is perfect for the spring, when asparagus is in season and is sweet. The fresh green flavor of the asparagus provides a perfect backdrop for salty caviar cream. You can also make this without caviar, replacing it with a salty substitute, like chopped anchovy fillets or wasabi-flavored fish eggs.

2	pounds medium-thick asparagus (2 to 3 bunches)
	Fine sea salt and freshly ground black pepper to taste
2	ounces bacon, diced (about ½ cup)
8	small shallots, chopped
3	garlic cloves, chopped
1	sprig thyme
5	cups water
¼	cup heavy cream
2	tablespoons American caviar

CUT UP AND BLANCH THE ASPARAGUS TIPS Trim the asparagus to remove the tough, woody ends. Cut off the tips and reserve 18 of them for a garnish. Cut the stalks into ½-inch pieces and combine with the remaining tips. Bring a pot of salted water to a boil. Fill a bowl halfway with ice water. Add the 18 asparagus tips to the water and blanch them. Remove them with a slotted spoon and shock them in the ice water to stop the cooking and preserve their color. Drain and set aside.

COOK THE SOUP Put the bacon in a pot set over medium heat and cook until it renders enough fat to coat the bottom of the pot, 4 to 5 minutes. Add the shallots, garlic, and thyme, and sauté until the shallots are translucent, approximately 3 minutes. Add the remaining asparagus and tips and the water. Raise the heat to high and bring to a boil. Continue to boil for approximately 8 minutes, or until the asparagus are tender but still vibrantly green.

PUREE THE SOUP While the soup is cooking, fill a large bowl halfway with ice water. Remove and discard the thyme sprig. Pour the contents of the pot into a blender or food processor, and puree until smooth and creamy. (For smoother texture, pour the soup through a fine-mesh strainer set over a bowl.) Set the bowl in the ice water to cool the soup and stir occasionally to cool. (While not essential, if you have time to chill the soup on ice in the refrigerator for 2 hours, that would be optimal. If the soup appears very thick after cooling, stir in a few drops of cold water.)

MAKE THE CAVIAR CREAM Whip the cream to soft peaks. Put the caviar in a small bowl and gently fold in the cream. (This cream can be made up to 2 hours in advance; keep covered and refrigerated.)

TO SERVE Ladle some soup into each of 6 chilled bowls. Spoon 3 teaspoon-size dots of caviar cream on the surface of each serving and garnish each serving with 3 of the asparagus tips, halved lengthwise.

Wine Suggestion: Selene (Carneros), "Hyde Vineyard" Sauvignon Blanc 2001; Napa Valley. A medium-bodied white from California, with hints of herbs, citrus, and minerals.

WASABI-FLAVORED FISH EGGS are flying fish roe flavored and colored with wasabi. They are available from Japanese markets and by mail order (see page 277).

MANHATTAN CLAM CHOWDER

serves ⑥ Manhattan clam chowder—the tomatoey, not the creamy kind—doesn't seem like something that was created in a big city. Nobody really knows where it originated, but its Mediterranean character suggests Italian or Portuguese roots. I take the chowder in a rustic direction and serve it with slices of grilled country bread. I also strongly recommend that you make this a day ahead to give the clams time to soak up the flavor of the soup.

1½ **cups water**

½ **cup dry white wine**

10 **pounds cherrystone clams,** scrubbed

5 **ounces bacon,** finely diced (about 1¼ cups)

3 **tablespoons extra-virgin olive oil**

3 **garlic cloves,** chopped

1 **large onion,** cut into ½-inch dice

¼ **bulb fennel,** cut into ½-inch dice

1 **celery stalk,** cut into ½-inch dice

1 **green bell pepper,** cut into ½-inch dice

1 **medium carrot,** cut into ½-inch dice

2 **bay leaves**

1½ **teaspoons dried oregano**

2 **dried chiles**

1 **tablespoon tomato paste**

¾ **pound Yukon Gold potatoes,** cut into ½-inch dice (about 1 cup)

1 **cup bottled clam juice**

6 **vine-ripened tomatoes,** cut into ½-inch dice

Fine sea salt and freshly ground black pepper to taste

2 **tablespoons chopped parsley**

COOK THE CLAMS Pour the water into a large heavy-bottomed pot and add the wine. Bring to a boil over high heat. Add the clams, cover, and cook until they pop open, approximately 5 minutes. Discard any clams that have not opened and transfer the others to a bowl. Strain the liquid through a fine-mesh strainer set over a bowl. When cool enough to handle, remove the clams from their shells and cut them into ¼-inch pieces.

MAKE THE CHOWDER In a large pot, cook the bacon with the olive oil over medium heat until golden brown, approximately 5 minutes. Add the garlic, onion, fennel, celery, bell pepper, carrot, bay leaves, oregano, and chiles. Cook, stirring occasionally, for 10 minutes or until the onion is translucent but not browned. Add the tomato paste and cook for 2 minutes, stirring to coat the other ingredients. Add the potatoes, reserved clam cooking liquid, and bottled clam juice. Bring to a boil, then lower the heat and simmer until the potatoes are almost tender but still firm in the center, 7 to 8 minutes. Add the diced tomatoes and cook until the potatoes are cooked through, 2 to 3 minutes longer. Stir in the clams. Do not cook any longer at this point or the clams will toughen. Taste and adjust seasoning with salt and pepper. (The soup can be cooled and stored in the refrigerator overnight at this point and will deepen in flavor if you choose to do this.)

TO SERVE If the soup has been refrigerated, reheat it very slowly and gently. Use tongs or a slotted spoon to fish out and discard the bay leaves and chiles. Divide the soup among 6 individual bowls and serve garnished with the parsley.

Beer Suggestion: Brooklyn Brewery, Pennant Ale; Brooklyn, New York. A medium-bodied, slighty hoppy beer with mild maltiness, from New York City.

NEW ENGLAND CLAM CHOWDER

serves (6) This rich, creamy chowder is one of my favorite soups, and I'll often make a meal of it. If you're able to plan ahead, the soup is better after a day in the refrigerator to give the bacon's smoky flavor some time to permeate the cream. If you do make the chowder ahead, don't add the chopped clams to the soup until you're reheating it so that they remain tender; store the two components separately in tightly covered containers.

1½ cups water

½ cup dry white wine

8 pounds cherrystone clams, scrubbed and rinsed

3 tablespoons unsalted butter

5 ounces bacon, diced (about 1¼ cups)

1 large onion, cut into ¼-inch dice

3 garlic cloves, chopped

2 celery stalks, cut into ¼-inch dice

3 sprigs thyme, chopped

2 bay leaves

1½ pounds Yukon Gold potatoes, peeled and cut into ¼-inch dice (about 2 cups)

2 cups heavy cream

2 tablespoons chopped parsley

Fine sea salt and freshly ground black pepper to taste

Oyster crackers or saltines

COOK THE CLAMS Pour the water and wine into a large pot. Bring to a boil over high heat. Add the clams, cover, and cook until they open, approximately 5 minutes. Remove the clams to a bowl, discarding any that have not opened. Strain the liquid through a fine-mesh strainer and reserve. Set aside. When the clams are cool enough to handle, remove them from their shells and cut them into ¼-inch pieces.

COOK THE CHOWDER In a pot, melt the butter with the bacon over medium-high heat and cook until the bacon is crisp, 4 to 5 minutes. Add the onion, garlic, celery, thyme, and bay leaves. Sauté until the onion is translucent, approximately 4 minutes. Add the potatoes, reserved clam juice, and the cream. Simmer until the potatoes are tender, 8 to 10 minutes. Fish out and discard the bay leaves. (The soup can be made to this point, cooled, covered, and refrigerated overnight in an airtight container in the refrigerator. Refrigerate the clams in a separate container.)

TO SERVE   Reheat the soup and let the clams come to room temperature before proceeding. Return the clams to the chowder. Stir in the parsley and season with salt and pepper. Ladle the soup into 6 warm bowls and serve with crackers alongside.

Beer Suggestion: A medium-bodied India pale ale, such as Harpoon, IPA; Boston, Massachusetts.

CREAM OF CAULIFLOWER WITH SALT COD

serves ⑥ Cauliflower is a versatile basis for soup because its neutral palate gets along well with so many other flavors. Here, it's augmented with nutty brown butter and flaked salt cod. If you love smoky flavor, substitute 2 cups of the cod's poaching liquid for 2 cups of the milk in the soup. Serve this with slices of country bread.

This recipe requires some advance planning: The salt cod must be soaked for at least 24 hours before using.

    6   tablespoons (¾ stick) unsalted butter
    1   large head cauliflower (about 2¼ pounds)
    1   teaspoon black peppercorns
    2   medium onions, 1 chopped and 1 cut into small dice
    2   sprigs thyme
    5   garlic cloves, crushed
    7   cups whole milk
  1¼   pounds salt cod, soaked in water to cover for 24 hours in refrigerator,
            changing water 3 times, and drained
    2   tablespoons olive oil
    1   teaspoon curry powder
    1   bay leaf
    4   cups store-bought low-sodium chicken broth
    1   cup heavy cream
    2   tablespoons minced chives

BROWN THE BUTTER Put the butter in a small sauté pan and set it over high heat. Cook until the butter melts and turns brown. Remove the pan from the heat and set it aside.

PREPARE THE CAULIFLOWER Cut out the stem and hard core and divide the cauliflower into large florets. Further separate enough of the cauliflower to make 30 very small florets for garnish.

POACH THE COD Put the black peppercorns, chopped onion, 1 thyme sprig, 3 garlic cloves, and 3 cups of the milk in a large saucepan. Add the salt cod. Cover and bring to a simmer over medium heat. Stop cooking 10 minutes from when you first put the pot over the heat. Carefully transfer the cod to a plate.

MAKE THE SOUP   Heat the olive oil in a large pot set over medium-high heat. Add the diced onion and 2 remaining garlic cloves, the curry powder, bay leaf, and remaining thyme sprig. Sauté until the onion is softened and translucent, 3 to 4 minutes. Add the cauliflower, the remaining 4 cups of milk, and the chicken broth. Bring to a boil, then reduce the heat and simmer until the cauliflower is very tender, 20 to 30 minutes. Strain the contents of the pot through a strainer set over a bowl. Pick out and discard the thyme and bay leaves. Transfer the solids to a blender and add about one-fourth of the liquid. Puree until smooth and creamy. If the soup seems too thick, add a little more liquid. Return the soup to the pot and set over medium heat. Stir in the brown butter and cream, then strain the soup again.

TO SERVE   Divide the soup among 6 bowls, flake some cod over each serving, and garnish with 5 reserved florets and some of the chives.

Wine Suggestion: Colin-Deleger, Les Charmois 2000; St.-Aubin. A white Burgundy with aromas of white flowers, smoke, and pepper.

MEDITERRANEAN FISH SOUP WITH ROUILLE

serves (6) *Soupe de poisson,* a fish soup made with olive oil, tomatoes, and garlic, is one of the most well-known and most popular Mediterranean classics. It has many of the qualities of a bouillabaise but is much simpler to make. This powerfully flavored soup is always served with baguette croutons and rouille, a rust-colored condiment made from red pepper and garlic, with potato used as a thickening agent.

The intensity of this soup will depend on which fish you choose. If the flavor seems weak when you taste it, continue to reduce the base until the fish flavor registers on your palate.

5½ **pounds assorted fish,** such as rockfish, including head and bones, gills removed,
     cleaned, rinsed, and cut into large dice

    Fine sea salt and freshly ground black pepper

1¼ **cups olive oil**

1 **medium onion,** chopped

1 **leek,** white part only, rinsed and chopped

1 **carrot,** cut into medium dice

1 **celery stalk,** cut into small dice

½ **medium fennel bulb,** chopped

1 **sprig thyme**

1 **bay leaf**

2 **heads garlic,** halved crosswise

2 **tablespoons tomato paste**

1 **can (14½ ounces) whole peeled Italian tomatoes,** drained and crushed by hand

2 **cups dry white wine**

9 **cups water**

1 **star anise**

1 **sprig parsley**

1 **teaspoon saffron threads**

    Rouille (receipe follows)

18 **croutons (see page 275)**

1 **cup shredded Gruyère cheese**

BEGIN THE SOUP Season the fish with salt and pepper. Heat ¼ cup of the olive oil in a sauté pan set over medium-high heat. When the oil is hot, add the fish to the pan in batches and sauté until well browned, 8 to 10 minutes per side. As the fish pieces are done, transfer them to a large stockpot.

SAUTÉ THE VEGETABLES Add another 2 tablespoons of the oil to the pan. When the oil is hot but not smoking, add the onion, leek, carrot, celery, fennel, thyme, and bay leaf. Sauté until the onion is translucent, approximately 4 minutes. Add the garlic and tomato paste, and stir to coat the vegetables with the paste. Add the crushed tomatoes and cook, stirring, until they begin to break apart. Carefully pour the contents of the pan into the pot with the browned fish.

CONTINUE MAKING THE SOUP Set the pot over high heat. Add the white wine and cook, stirring, until it evaporates. Add the water, star anise, parsley, and saffron. Lower the heat and let the soup simmer for 45 to 50 minutes. (While the soup is simmering, make the Rouille.)

FINISH THE SOUP Pass the soup through a food mill with the medium blade set over a bowl, or puree it in a food processor, and transfer it to a large bowl. Taste and adjust the seasoning with salt and pepper. (The soup can be made to this point, cooled, covered, and refrigerated for up to 2 days in an airtight container in the refrigerator. It will actually taste better because the flavors will have time to develop and deepen.)

TO SERVE Divide the soup among 6 bowls and serve, passing the croutons, Rouille, and grated Gruyère alongside.

Wine Suggestion: Sola Rosa, Rosé 2002; California. A fuller bodied rosé, with nuances of raspberries and spice.

BOUILLABAISE can be made from this soup by letting it cool and refrigerating it overnight so the flavors have a chance to deepen. The next day, set the pot over high heat, boil to reduce and thicken it, then lower the heat. Add an assortment of seafood, such as squid and mussels, and 2-inch square boneless pieces of John Dory, grouper, hake, red snapper, rockfish, and/or monkfish. Poach the fish just until cooked through, approximately 4 minutes. Serve with croutons and Rouille, but omit the cheese.

ROUILLE makes about (1½) cups

1 large Idaho potato, scrubbed
½ cup extra-virgin olive oil
Scant pinch saffron threads
1 small dried chile
3 garlic cloves, smashed
Fine sea salt and freshly ground black pepper to taste

PUT THE WHOLE POTATO in a medium saucepan and cover with cold water. Set over high heat and bring the water to a boil. Boil until the potato is tender in the center, 15 to 20 minutes. (A sharp, thin-bladed knife should pierce easily to its center.) Drain and set aside to cool. When the potato is cool enough to handle, peel and cut it into ½-inch dice. Pour ½ cup of the olive oil into a blender. Add the saffron, chile, and garlic, and blend until smooth. With the motor still running, add the potato and ¼ cup warm water, and continue to blend until well incorporated and smooth. Season with salt and pepper. Transfer to a bowl and refrigerate until ready to use, but no longer than 2 days.

CORN AND HADDOCK CHOWDER

serves (6) Made with finnan haddie (smoked haddock), this chowder has an understated smokiness. It isn't pureed or strained, so be sure to cut the vegetables uniformly for an appealing appearance. For a special occasion, replace half of the haddock with poached, diced lobster meat.

2½ **cups heavy cream**
1½ **medium onions,** cut into small dice
4 **garlic cloves,** 2 left whole and 2 chopped
1 **tablespoon black peppercorns**
2½ **cups water**
1 **pound finnan haddie (smoked haddock)**
3 **tablespoons unsalted butter**
5 **ounces bacon,** finely diced (about 1¼ cups)
2 **celery stalks,** cut into small dice
3 **sprigs thyme**
2 **bay leaves**
1½ **pounds corn on the cob (about 8),** shucked and kernels scraped off
Pinch cayenne
2 **fresh sage leaves, chopped**

POACH THE FINNAN HADDIE Put the cream, one-third of the onion, 2 whole garlic cloves, and the peppercorns in a large saucepan and add the water. Add the finnan haddie, cover, and bring to a simmer over medium heat. Stop cooking 10 minutes from when you first put the pot over the heat. Let cool, then remove the fish from the liquid. Strain the liquid and set aside the finnan haddie and poaching liquid separately. Pick out and discard the garlic and peppercorns.

MAKE THE SOUP In a pot, cook the butter with the bacon over medium-high until the bacon is crisp, about 8 minutes. Add the remaining onion, chopped garlic, celery, thyme, and bay leaves. Cook until the onion is translucent, about 4 minutes. Add the corn and cook for 3 minutes. Add the reserved poaching liquid and cook until the corn is softened, 15 to 20 minutes. Season with cayenne and add the sage. Flake the poached finnan haddie into the pot.

TO SERVE Divide the soup among 6 bowls.

Wine Suggestion: Domaine Laroche, Vaillons 2000; Chablis. A crisp white with slight hints of smoke and toast and streaks of apply acidity.

MUSHROOM VELOUTÉ WITH TRUFFLE SABAYON

serves ⑥   Aside from side dishes and desserts, this is the only recipe in the book that doesn't feature fish or shellfish. But this velvety mushroom soup is as much a signature dish for me as any other.

A velouté is a creamy soup made by adding stock to a mixture of butter and flour known as a roux. I make mine without flour or stock, instead adding water to a mushroom base and finishing the soup with cream. The soup is garnished with my take on sabayon, a foam made with egg yolks and sugar. Here, too, I've made an adjustment, leaving out the sugar and flavoring the sabayon with truffle oil.

This is a great dish for entertaining because it's very simple to prepare but looks and tastes spectacular. You can also make this incredibly richer by spreading some Truffle Butter (see sidebar) over slices of toasted brioche as an accompaniment.

    2 tablespoons unsalted butter
    4 small shallots, thinly sliced
    2 garlic cloves, chopped
    1 bay leaf
    1 sprig thyme
   12 ounces button mushrooms, cleaned and chopped
   1½ cups plus 2 tablespoons water
    1 cup plus 2 tablespoons heavy cream
       Fine sea salt and freshly ground black pepper to taste
    2 egg yolks
    ½ teaspoon white truffle oil
    6 slices black truffle (optional)

MAKE THE VELOUTÉ Put the butter in a large, heavy-bottomed pot set over medium heat. When the butter has melted, add the shallots, garlic, bay leaf, and thyme, and sauté until the shallots are translucent, approximately 3 minutes. Add the mushrooms, lower the heat, and sauté for 3 minutes. Add 1½ cups of the water, raise the heat to high, bring the water to a boil, and boil until the mushrooms are tender, approximately 5 minutes. Pour the mixture into a blender or the bowl of a food processor fitted with the metal blade and blend until smooth. Pour the velouté back into the pot, stir in the cream, and season with salt and pepper. Cover and set aside. The velouté can be made to this point, cooled, covered, and refrigerated overnight in an airtight container in the refrigerator. Let come to room temperature before proceeding.

MAKE THE SABAYON Put the egg yolks and the remaining 2 tablespoons water in a stainless-steel bowl set over a double boiler, and beat with a whisk until the yolk has a foamy but stable consistency. Remove the bowl from the boiler, stir in the truffle oil, and season with salt and pepper.

TO SERVE Gently reheat the velouté if necessary and divide it among 6 warm soup bowls. Spoon a generous tablespoon of sabayon into the center of each serving and place 1 slice of black truffle, if using, atop the sabayon. Serve at once.

TRUFFLE BUTTER

makes about ⅓ cup This is delicious spread on grilled toast or stirred into mushroom pastas and risotto.

- 3 **tablespoons unsalted butter,** softened at room temperature
- 2 **tablespoons finely chopped black truffle**
- ¼ **teaspoon black truffle oil**
  Fine sea salt and freshly ground black pepper to taste

PUT THE BUTTER, truffle, and oil in a bowl and season with salt and pepper. Incorporate the ingredients with a rubber spatula.

Wine Suggestion: De Suremain, Mercurey, Premier cru les Sazenay 1998; Côtes Challonnais. A simple red from Burgundy with aromas of earth, mushrooms, and bright red berries.

MUSSEL SOUP WITH RED CURRY AND COCONUT

serves ⑥ Mussels are accommodating mollusks, able to take on a world of flavors. As much as I love mussels *marinière* (steamed in white wine with parsley, butter, and shallots), I'm also very fond of taking mussels in an Asian direction. This is a powerfully flavored Thai-style dish, spiked with kaffir lime leaves, curry paste, lime juice, coconut milk, and cilantro. It can also become a main course if you use *all* the mussels and serve it with an accompaniment of Sticky Rice (recipe follows).

1 tablespoon canola oil

1 medium onion, chopped

2 garlic cloves, chopped

1 celery stalk, sliced crosswise into ½-inch pieces

1 cup coarsely chopped lemongrass (see page 153)

4 kaffir lime leaves (see page 153)

2 tablespoons thinly sliced fresh ginger

1 teaspoon Thai red curry paste

½ cup dry white wine

8 pounds mussels, preferably Prince Edward Island, scrubbed and debearded

2½ cups unsweetened coconut milk

1 cup heavy cream

¼ cup chopped cilantro

3 tablespoons freshly squeezed lime juice

1 cup enoki mushrooms or thinly sliced shiitake mushrooms

Fine sea salt and freshly ground black pepper to taste

COOK THE MUSSELS Pour the oil into a large heavy-bottomed pot and warm over medium heat. Add the onion and garlic, and cook until translucent, approximately 4 minutes. Add the celery, lemongrass, kaffir lime leaves, ginger, and curry paste. Cook, stirring, for 1 minute. Pour in the white wine, bring to a boil, and cook until reduced by half. Add the mussels, cover, and cook until they open, 3 to 5 minutes. Turn the contents of the pot into a colander set over a large bowl. Use tongs to remove and discard any mussels that have not opened. Remove 36 mussels in their shells and set them aside. Remove any remaining mussels and reserve for another use.

MAKE THE SOUP Return the vegetables in the colander and the liquid in the bowl to the pot. Add the coconut milk and cream, and bring to a boil over medium heat. Lower the heat and let simmer for 3 minutes. Strain into a bowl and blend with an immersion blender or whisk vigorously. Add the cilantro, lime juice, and mushrooms to the bowl. Season with salt and pepper.

TO SERVE Divide the 36 reserved mussels among 6 bowls. Ladle the soup over the mussels and serve at once.

Wine Suggestion: Domaine Schlumberger, Kitterle Gewürztraminer 1999; Alsace. A spicy, off-dry Alsatian white with aromas of logan, lychee, ginger, and flowers.

STICKY RICE

serves (6) as an accompaniment Serve this with Thai food and other dishes of Asian origin.

- 2 cups sticky rice
- ½ cup coconut milk
- Pinch fine sea salt

RINSE THE RICE in several changes of water until the water is clear, not cloudy, then drain the rice and transfer it to a pot. Pour the coconut milk into a bowl and stir in 1 cup of water, then pour this mixture over the rice. Add a pinch of salt and stir. Place the pot over high heat and bring the liquid to a boil, then reduce the heat to very low, cover the pot, and let it cook until the rice is tender, lifting the pot to stir the rice every few minutes to keep it from scorching.

BOUCHOT MUSSELS If you can find them, tiny Bouchot mussels (from the French word *bouchot*, meaning "small") are a good, delicate alternative to blue mussels, especially for soups.

BUTTERNUT SQUASH SOUP WITH NUTMEG AND BAY SCALLOPS

serves (6) This is a wonderful dish for the fall and winter that finds sweet pureed butternut squash in perfect balance with tiny bay scallops and aromatic nutmeg. Be sure to find the ripest butternut squash possible, with a bright orange flesh that isn't too dry or starchy. This is impossible to confirm from the outside, but optimum squash tend to be relatively heavy for their size. If bay scallops are not available, this soup is also delicious with sea scallops.

8 **ounces bacon,** minced (about 2 cups)
1 **large onion,** chopped
3 **garlic cloves,** chopped
1 **sprig thyme**
1 **bay leaf**
1 **teaspoon cracked black peppercorns**
2½ **pounds butternut squash,** peeled, seeded, and diced
3 **cups canned chicken broth**
2 **cups heavy cream**
  Fine sea salt and freshly ground black pepper
  Pinch grated nutmeg
6 **tablespoons olive oil**
4 **slices country bread,** diced
3 **leaves sage,** very finely chopped
1 **pound bay scallops (about 60)**
2 **tablespoons chopped chives**

MAKE THE SOUP In a large pot, warm the bacon over medium-high heat until enough fat has rendered to coat the bottom of the pot, 4 to 5 minutes. Add the onion, garlic, thyme, bay leaf, and peppercorns, and sauté until the onion is translucent, approximately 4 minutes. Add the squash and sauté until it begins to color, 4 to 5 minutes. Add the chicken broth and cream, raise the heat to high, bring to a boil, then lower the heat and let simmer until the squash begins to fall apart, 20 to 25 minutes. Transfer the soup to the bowl of a food processor fitted with the metal blade and process until smooth and creamy. Strain back into the pot, taste, and adjust seasoning with salt, pepper, and nutmeg; keep covered and warm. (The soup can be made to this point, cooled, covered, and refrigerated for up to 2 days in an airtight container in the refrigerator. Reheat before proceeding.)

MAKE THE CROUTONS Heat 2 tablespoons of the olive oil in a sauté pan set over medium-high heat. Add the diced bread and cook, tossing to coat the bread with the oil. Cook until golden brown on all sides, 3 to 4 minutes. Add the sage and sauté for 1 more minute. Transfer the croutons to paper towels to drain. Season with salt.

SAUTÉ THE SCALLOPS Heat 2 tablespoons of the olive oil in a wide, deep sauté pan. Add half the scallops, season with salt and pepper, and sauté for 1 minute on each side. Set the scallops aside on a plate and repeat with the remaining scallops and remaining 2 tablespoons olive oil.

TO SERVE Divide the soup among 6 bowls. Arrange the scallops and croutons around the surface of the soup. Garnish with chives.

Wine Suggestion: Matanzas Creek, Chardonnay 2001; Sonoma County. A full-bodied California white with hints of toast and spiced apples and balanced acidity.

PESTO MINESTRONE WITH ROCK SHRIMP

serves (6) This is my take on Italian minestrone, or vegetable soup, with pesto stirred in and mushrooms and rock shrimp added. For a more traditional minestrone, add ½ cup dried vermicelli. Don't precook the pasta; just let it cook through in the soup, which will only take a few minutes. (Add it when you add the mushrooms.) Serve this with grilled country bread, drizzled with olive oil and rubbed with a cut garlic clove.

4 **ounces dried cannellini beans,** soaked for 2 hours in cold water
8 **cups cold water**
   Fine sea salt
3 **cups loosely packed basil leaves**
6 **garlic cloves,** 3 left whole and 3 chopped
½ **cup grated Parmigiano-Reggiano cheese**
10 **tablespoons olive oil**
5 **ounces bacon,** diced (about 1¼ cups)
1 **medium onion,** cut into small dice
1 **large carrot,** peeled and diced
1 **sprig thyme**
2 **bay leaves**
1 **large leek, white part only,** well washed and cut into small dice
2 **celery stalks,** cut into small dice
½ **large fennel bulb,** cut into small dice
1¼ **cups diced yellow and green zucchini** (1 or 2 medium zucchini)
3 **(10-ounce) cans clear chicken broth**
3½ **ounces shiitake mushrooms,** thinly sliced (1 cup)
1¼ **pounds rock shrimp,** shelled, or larger shrimp cut into small dice
2 **vine-ripened tomatoes,** seeded and diced
   Freshly ground black pepper to taste

COOK THE BEANS Drain the beans and add them to a pot with 5 cups of the cold water and a pinch of sea salt. Bring the water to a boil over high heat, then lower the heat and let simmer, covered, until the beans are tender, approximately 90 minutes.

BLANCH THE BASIL Bring a pot of salted water to a boil. Fill a large bowl halfway with ice water. Add the basil to the boiling water and blanch for 30 seconds. Drain and transfer to the ice water to cool it and stop the cooking. Drain and set aside.

MAKE THE BASIL PESTO Put the basil, whole garlic, and Parmigiano-Reggiano in a blender. With the motor running, add ¼ cup of the olive oil in a thin steam to form a thick mixture. Scoop into a bowl and set aside.

MAKE THE SOUP Warm 2 tablespoons of the olive oil with the bacon in a very large pot set over medium heat. Cook until the bacon renders enough fat to coat the bottom of the pot, 4 to 5 minutes. Add the onion, chopped garlic, carrot, thyme, and bay leaves, and cook until the onion is translucent, approximately 4 minutes. Turn the contents of the pot into a bowl and set aside. Return the pot to the stove. Add 2 tablespoons of the olive oil, the leek, and celery, and sauté for 4 minutes. Add the fennel and zucchini, and stir. Return the other cooked ingredients to the pot. Add the remaining 3 cups of water and the chicken broth, raise the heat, and bring the liquid to a boil. Lower the heat and let the liquid simmer until the vegetables are tender, 5 to 7 minutes.

COOK THE MUSHROOMS AND SHRIMP While the soup is simmering, heat the remaining 2 tablespoons of oil in a sauté pan. Add the mushrooms and sauté until golden brown, 8 to 10 minutes. Transfer to the pot with the simmering soup. Add the shrimp to the pan and sauté until firm and pink, approximately 2 minutes, then add them to the soup as well. The soup is done when the vegetables are tender and the shrimp is cooked through.

TO SERVE In the final few minutes of cooking, add the diced tomato to the soup and stir in the pesto to taste. Season with salt and pepper. Divide among 6 bowls immediately, while the pesto's green color is still bright.

Wine Suggestion: Jermann, Vinnae 2001; Friuli. An Italian white made from the Tocai Friulano grape, with fresh aromas of pear and melon, with nuances of fresh flowers and spice.

CHILLED GREEN PEA SOUP WITH SPICY SHRIMP

serves ⑥ There's really only one time to eat pea soup, and that's in the late spring and early summer, when peas are in season and a chilled soup makes sense. Fresh peas can be hard to come by, however, so if you can't put your hands on them, make this soup with high-quality frozen peas (*petit pois*). This dish depends on the contrast between hot and cold, so chill the soup in the refrigerator, then pour it into bowls while the shrimp are still hot from the pan.

If you want to make a more luxurious version of this soup, used chopped poached lobster meat (see page 000) in place of shrimp. Or, if you can get them, use sweet-water prawns.

2	tablespoons unsalted butter
2	ounces bacon, cut into very small dice (about ½ cup)
4	medium shallots, chopped
3	garlic cloves
I	sprig thyme
I	bay leaf
3	cups water
I½	pounds fresh green peas or defrosted frozen peas (*petit pois*)
	Fine sea salt and freshly ground black pepper to taste
2	tablespoons olive oil
I	pound medium shrimp or sweet-water prawns (about 18)
	Spiced Oil (recipe follows)
2	tablespoons chopped chives

BROWN THE BUTTER Put the butter in a sauté pan set over medium-high heat and let it melt and brown. Remove the pan from the heat and set aside.

MAKE THE SOUP Put the bacon in a heavy-bottomed pot and brown it over medium heat until it has rendered enough fat to coat the bottom of the pot. Add the shallots, garlic, thyme, and bay leaf, and cook until the shallots are golden brown, approximately 5 minutes. Pour in the water, raise the heat to high, and bring the water to a boil. Add the peas, cook until the water returns to a boil, and continue to boil for I additional minute. Pour the soup into a blender, add the reserved brown butter, and blend until well incorporated, smooth, and creamy.

FINISH THE SOUP Fill a large, wide bowl halfway with ice water. Set a bowl large enough to hold the soup on top of the ice cubes. Pour the blended soup through a fine-mesh strainer into the bowl, pushing down on the solids with a spoon or ladle to extract as much liquid as possible. Discard the solids. Season the soup with salt and pepper, cover it, and keep it on ice in the refrigerator, letting it get very cold. This will also preserve the peas' color. (The soup can be refrigerated like this overnight, if desired.)

COOK THE SHIRMP Heat the olive oil in a wide, deep-sided sauté pan set over high heat. Season the shrimp with salt and pepper, add them to the pan and sauté them until firm and pink, about 2 minutes on each side.

TO SERVE: Divide the soup among 6 chilled or cool bowls and add 3 shrimp to each serving. Drizzle on some Spiced Oil and scatter some chives over each serving and serve at once.

Wine Suggestion: Nigl, Alta Reben, Grüner Veltliner 2001; Kamptal-Donauland. A spicy Austrian white with hints of fresh peas, peaches, and ginger.

SWEET-WATER PRAWNS are freshwater shrimp harvested from Hawaii and the Southern states (and overseas in Brazil, Puerto Rico, and Jamaica). It's essential to purchase them fresh, so they often have to be mail-ordered (see page 277). They are also referred to as blue prawns because they have a blue tint with striking red flares of color on their antennae and claws.

SPICED OIL

makes about ② cups   This oil can also be used as a dressing for a mixed green salad with shrimp or to season calamari before sautéing.

   2 cups olive oil
 1½ teaspoons ground cumin
 1½ teaspoons Tabasco sauce
 1½ teaspoons ground cinnamon
   1 teaspoon curry powder
   1 teaspoon ground ginger
   1 teaspoon paprika
   1 teaspoon ground white pepper

POUR THE OLIVE OIL into a blender. Add the cumin, Tabasco, cinnamon, curry powder, ginger, paprika, and white pepper. Blend for 2 minutes, then pour the mixture into a bowl and set aside. (This oil can be made a day before you plan to use it and kept, covered, in the refrigerator. Let it come to room temperature before proceeding.)

CREAM OF LETTUCE WITH SMOKED TROUT

serves (6) I think of this as a farmer's soup: It uses a lot of lettuce, and trout comes not from the ocean but from inland streams and brooks. Also, though it uses a bit of cream, this is a very healthful soup because of the amount of greens (each person gets an entire head of lettuce).

- 6 large heads Boston lettuce
- 2 cups water or low-sodium canned chicken broth
- 2 tablespoons cornstarch mixed with 1/2 cup water
- 1/2 cup heavy cream
  Pinch grated nutmeg
  Fine sea salt and freshly ground black pepper to taste
- 8 ounces smoked trout, skinned and broken into pieces (smoked eel or Japanese *onagi* can be substituted)
- 6 slices country bread, toasted, rubbed with garlic, and diced
- 2 tablespoons chopped chives

BLANCH AND COOL THE LETTUCE Fill a large bowl halfway with ice water and set aside. Bring a pot of lightly salted water to a boil. While the water is heating, remove the cores from the heads of lettuce. Separate the leaves and rinse them in cold, running water. Blanch them for 30 seconds in the boiling water, then drain them and plunge them into the ice water to stop the cooking and preserve their color. Drain, squeeze out the excess moisture, and set aside.

MAKE THE SOUP Transfer the lettuce leaves to a food processor. Add the water or chicken broth and process until liquefied. Strain through a fine-mesh strainer set over a bowl. Return the liquid to the pot and warm over medium heat. Add the cornstarch and its liquid, cream, and nutmeg, and season with salt and pepper. Bring to a boil.

TO SERVE Divide the soup among 6 bowls. Divide the trout pieces among the bowls and garnish with the bread cubes and chopped chives.

Wine Suggestion: Pascal Jolivet, Pouilly Fumé 2001; Loire Valley. A crisp French white with aromas of smoke and citrus and a zesty acidity.

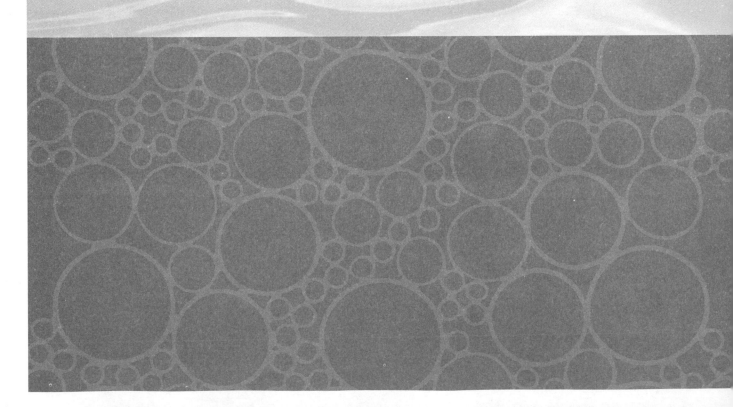

PASTA AND RISOTTO

Lemon-Crab Risotto with Grilled Asparagus

Parma-Style Gnocchi with Calamari

Lobster and Foie Gras Risotto

Penne and Lobster Gratin

Mussel Risotto and Confit Kumquat

Ricotta Tortellini with Grilled Sardines

Bay Scallops with Cippoline Bouillon and Foie Gras Ravioli

Rigatoni with Bay Scallops and Mushrooms

Sea Scallops with Basil-Portobello Ravioli and Parmesan Cream Sauce

Shellfish Bow tie Pasta with Tomatoes and Oregano

Chinatown Shrimp Wontons

Rock Shrimp Risotto with Grilled Pancetta and White Truffle Oil

Parsley Risotto with Snails and Frothy Goat Cheese

Squid Risotto with Garlic Porcini

Of course, I'm proud of my culinary heritage, but I also love the simple flavors and cooking techniques of the Italian kitchen, especially pasta and risotto, with their endless variety of flavors and textures. Maybe it's because my predominantly French ancestry also includes an Italian great-grandmother.

You can find pasta and risotto all over the world. In the past decade or two they have begun to show up in even the most highly rated restaurants. But traditionally, outside of Italy, they have been present only in their most simple form, in bistros and brasseries.

Because I haven't spent much time in Italy, it wasn't until I moved to the United States that I began to appreciate fully the possibilities of pasta and risotto, which have been treated with great creativity by American chefs. It's almost impossible to name an ingredient that somebody hasn't used in a pasta or risotto here. I myself never would have thought of making something as unconventional as Mussel Risotto and Confit Kumquat (page 138) until I came to New York City.

One of the things I appreciate most about pasta is the seemingly infinite number of shapes and sizes that can be made from the same dough. My favorite dried shapes are thick tubes of rigatoni, the chewy bow ties called farfalle, and the quill-shaped penne. I use them all in this chapter, in the Penne and Lobster Gratin (page 136), the Rigatoni with Bay Scallops and Mushrooms (page 146), and the Shellfish Bow Tie Pasta with Tomatoes and Oregano (page 150).

I'm even more fond of fresh pasta, especially when it's used to make filled pasta like ravioli and tortellini. I often turn to these as a way of containing big flavors to be served alongside more delicate fish and shellfish. Examples include Bay Scallops with Cippoline Bouillon and Foie Gras Ravioli (page 143), Sea Scallops with Basil-Portobello Ravioli and Parmesan Cream Sauce (page 148), and Ricotta Tortellini with Grilled Sardines (page 141). This gives diners more control over their experience, letting them decide which flavors they want to include in each and every bite.

Just as I value pasta for its endless possibilities, I love risotto for the way it can absorb so many complementary flavors and textures. Think of how much is going on in the Lobster and Foie Gras Risotto (page 133), the Parsley Risotto with Snails and Frothy Goat Cheese (page 156), or the Lemon-Crab Risotto with Grilled Asparagus (page 130). Each of those dishes has as many flavors as a full meal might contain, but they all get along because the rice itself provides such a sturdy backdrop. In fact, as I think about it, the variety that can be had from pasta and risotto reminds me of all the wildly varied forms potatoes take back in France.

No doubt because pasta and risotto are Italian cooking forms, I find myself using a lot of Italian ingredients when composing them. There's prosciutto and Parmigiano-Reggiano in Parma-Style Gnocchi with Calamari (page 132), pancetta and white truffle oil in Rock Shrimp Risotto with Grilled Pancetta and White Truffle Oil (page 154), and porcini mushrooms in Squid Risotto with Garlic Porcini (page 158).

I have a few strongly held beliefs regarding the cooking of pasta and risotto that I want to share with you. First, when it comes to pasta, the water should be very well salted because the pasta itself is one of the most important ingredients in any pasta dish, and you want its taste, not just its texture, to register on the palate. Second, I differ a bit from Italian chefs in that I don't like my pasta truly *al dente*, which means "to the tooth." To me, pasta cooked *al dente* isn't cooked enough; I find it too chewy, which is probably why I prefer fresh pasta to dried.

As for risotto, I prefer arborio rice, although carnaroli or vialone nano are also perfectly acceptable. These are the best *superfino* varieties, the Italian designation for medium-grain rice that gives off a lot of starch when cooked, which binds the risotto.

There are a number of ways of making risotto. Some prefer it rather dry with the grains *al dente*. I like the individual grains firm in the center, but the overall dish a bit moist, made by stirring the rice nonstop and going just beyond the point where it can absorb any more stock. Also, there is advice out there about making risotto in advance, but I don't believe in it. I think that risotto should always be made at the last moment, just before serving.

You'll also notice a common thread in my risottos: they all feature some type of acidity, such as wine or lemon juice, which lightens them a bit and helps unite the flavors.

If you make your own stocks, or buy your groceries from a market that sells freshly made or frozen stocks, risottos are a time to use them. Because the liquid so permeates the dish, infusing the rice with volume and flavor, better stock will really result in a better risotto.

Finally, I have to mention there's one wildcard in this chapter that has nothing to do with French or Italian cooking. The Chinatown Shrimp Wontons (page 152) are, obviously, based on a dish from Asia, another type of cuisine that I've come to appreciate in my adopted home of New York City.

LEMON-CRAB RISOTTO WITH GRILLED ASPARAGUS

serves (6) Risotto can be rich and heavy, but it can also be surprisingly light, as in this spring risotto with lemon, crabmeat, asparagus, and delicate spring greens. The big pieces of jumbo lump crabmeat make a dramatic impression; Dungeness crabmeat or sautéed shrimp can be substituted to good effect.

1 pound thin asparagus

4 tablespoons unsalted butter

4 garlic cloves, chopped

3 cups pea leaves or baby spinach

Fine sea salt and freshly ground black pepper to taste

3 tablespoons olive oil

1 medium onion, chopped

1 sprig thyme

2 cups arborio rice

1 cup dry white wine

5 cups canned low-sodium chicken broth

1 cup grated Parmigiano-Reggiano cheese

⅔ cup heavy cream

Grated zest of 2 lemons

Juice of 1½ lemons

1 pound jumbo lump crabmeat or Dungeness crabmeat, picked over; or
    1 pound cooked, shelled, and deveined shrimp

BLANCH THE ASPARAGUS Bring a pot of salted water to a boil over high heat. Fill a large bowl halfway with ice water. Add the asparagus to the boiling water and blanch until tender, approximately 2 minutes. Drain, and add them to the ice water to stop the cooking and preserve their color. Drain again.

GRILL THE ASPARAGUS Prepare a hot fire in a barbecue grill or preheat an indoor grill. Grill the asparagus, turning, until lightly charred all over, 4 to 6 minutes, depending on the thickness of the asparagus. Cut off and reserve the tips. Cut the stalks into 2-inch segments; set aside.

SAUTÉ THE PEA SHOOTS Melt 1 tablespoon of the butter with one of the garlic cloves in a sauté pan over medium heat. Add all but a small handful of pea leaves and season with salt and pepper. Cook just until wilted, approximately 30 seconds; remove and set aside.

MAKE THE RISOTTO In a heavy-bottomed saucepan, heat the olive oil over medium heat. Add the remaining 3 garlic cloves, the onion, and the thyme. Cook, stirring, until the onion is translucent, approximately 4 minutes. Add the rice and stir to coat the rice with the oil. Cook for 3 to 4 minutes. Add the white wine and cook, stirring, until evaporated. Add about 1 cup of the broth and cook, stirring constantly, until it is completely absorbed by the rice. Then add another cup of liquid. Continue in this manner until you have used all the broth, which should take approximately 18 minutes. Stir in the grated Parmigiano-Reggiano cheese, remaining 3 tablespoons butter, cream, lemon zest and juice, asparagus stalk pieces, and sautéed pea leaves.

TO SERVE Mound some risotto in each of 6 bowls. Top with crabmeat and garnish with the reserved pea leaves and asparagus tips.

Wine Suggestion: Heidler, "Thal" Grüner Veltliner 2001; Kamptal-Donauland. An Austrian white with herbaceous and citrus aromas.

PEA LEAVES are a delicate, sweet spring green. They are available in some upscale supermarkets and in Asian markets and greengrocers.

PARMA-STYLE GNOCCHI WITH CALAMARI

serves (6) Most Americans probably know calamari, the Italian name for squid, in its breaded and fried form. Before I ever heard the word *calamari*, I was eating its relative, *supion*—a small cuttlefish from the Basque region, which includes the Southwest of France. This recipe matches calamari with sautéed gnocchi and with cheese and prosciutto from Parma, Italy. Notice how slicing and scoring the calamari causes it to curl into attractive little cones.

1½ **pounds calamari (squid),** cleaned by your fishmonger

3 **tablespoons olive oil**

  Parmesan Gnocchi (page 236, Steps 1–2), at room temperature

2 **tablespoons grated Parmigiano-Reggiano cheese**

2 **garlic cloves,** chopped

2 **tablespoons small capers,** rinsed and drained

2 **tablespoons pitted and thinly sliced Niçoise olives**

2 **tablespoons chopped parsley**

  Squeeze of lemon juice

  Fine sea salt and freshly ground black pepper to taste

¼ **pound prosciutto di Parma,** thinly sliced

1 **bunch arugula,** stems removed

PREPARE THE CALAMARI Cut off and set aside the tentacles. Slice the calamari bodies open lengthwise and cut them into triangles. Score the triangles in a cross-hatch pattern on one side with a sharp, thin-bladed knife, being careful not to cut all the way through them.

COOK THE GNOCCHI Heat half of the olive oil in a sauté pan set over medium heat. Add the Parmesan Gnocchi and sauté until golden brown, 2 to 3 minutes per side. Add the Parmigiano-Reggiano cheese and toss so the cheese melts onto the gnocchi, coating them, approximately 30 seconds. Set aside, covered to keep the gnocchi warm.

COOK THE CALAMARI Heat the remaining 1½ tablespoons olive oil in a large sauté pan set over high heat. Add the garlic and calamari. When the calamari are almost cooked, 1 to 2 minutes, add the capers, olives, parsley, and lemon juice. Toss and season with salt and pepper.

TO SERVE Arrange some gnocchi in the center of each plate. Top with calamari, a few slices of prosciutto, and some arugula.

Wine Suggestion: Soave, Inama, Vigneti di Foscarino 2000; Veneto. A crisp Italian white.

LOBSTER AND FOIE GRAS RISOTTO

serves (6) This is a perfect special-occasion dish, for several reasons. First, it's an unusual way to serve lobster and foie gras—ingredients we all associate with celebrations. Second, it's brimming with big flavors, like the cream and Sauternes in the sauce. Finally, let's be honest: this risotto is an orgy of fat and carbohydrates that is best presented at those events when people aren't watching what they eat.

To dress up this dish, perhaps for a special occasion, top each serving with a few curls of Parmigiano-Reggiano cut with a vegetable peeler, and pea shoots or baby greens tossed with olive oil, salt, and pepper. You can also serve Parmesan Crisps (recipe follows) alongside.

4 **lobsters,** 1¼ pounds each, poached in court bouillon (see page 274), cooled,
     bodies reserved, meat removed and cut into 1-inch dice

6 **tablespoons olive oil**

½ **cup chopped carrot**

¼ **cup finely diced celery**

¾ **cup finely diced onion**

⅓ **cup finely diced leek,** green part only

5 **garlic cloves,** 2 halved and 3 chopped

2 **sprigs thyme**

¼ **teaspoon black peppercorns**

1 **bay leaf**

2 **tablespoons Cognac**

1½ **plum tomatoes, chopped**

1½ **teaspoons tomato paste**

½ **cup plus 2 splashes Sauternes wine**

2 **cups heavy cream**

½ **cup loosely packed basil leaves**
     Fine sea salt and freshly ground black pepper to taste

18 **ounces foie gras,** cut into medium dice

2 **cups arborio rice**

1 **cup dry white wine**

3 **cups canned low-sodium chicken broth diluted with 1 cup water**

1 **cup grated Parmigiano-Reggiano cheese**

2 **tablespoons unsalted butter,** at room temperature

2 **tablespoons chopped chives**

CRUSH THE LOBSTER BODIES Put the lobster bodies between two clean kitchen towels. Use a rolling pin or the bottom of a heavy pan to crush the bodies. Set aside.

BEGIN MAKING THE LOBSTER EMULSION Set a large pot over high heat. Add 3 tablespoons of the olive oil and heat until almost smoking. Add the carrot, celery, ¼ cup of the onion, leek, halved garlic, 1 sprig of thyme, the peppercorns, and bay leaf. Cook until the onion is translucent, approximately 4 minutes. Add the lobster bodies. When they begin to turn red, remove the pan from the heat, turn the pan away from you, lean back, add the Cognac, and carefully ignite with a match. Cook until evaporated, approximately 1 minute. Add the tomatoes and tomato paste. Roast until the tomatoes are falling apart, approximately 4 minutes. Add ½ cup of the Sauternes and bring to a boil. Add the cream, bring to a boil, then lower the heat, and cook for 10 minutes. Remove the pot from the heat, add the basil, and cover with plastic wrap. Set aside and let cool.

FINISH MAKING THE LOBSTER EMULSION Once the contents of the pot are cool, strain through a fine-mesh sieve, pressing down on the solids to extract as much flavorful liquid as possible. Season with salt and pepper. Add a splash of Sauternes and blend with a hand blender just until the liquid foams.

SAUTÉ THE FOIE GRAS AND LOBSTER Set a sauté pan over high heat and let it get very hot. Season the foie gras and lobster meat with salt and pepper. Add about a third of the foie gras dice to the pan and cook quickly, just until browned on all sides, approximately 1 minute per side. Remove the foie gras from the pan, collecting it on a plate, and repeat until all of the foie gras has been cooked. Drain off all but 2 tablespoons of the fat from the pan. Add the lobster to the pan and sauté just until warmed through, approximately 1 minute, then add it to the plate with the foie gras.

MAKE THE RISOTTO In a heavy-bottomed pot, heat the remaining 3 tablespoons olive oil over medium-heat. Add the chopped garlic, remaining ½ cup onion, and remaining thyme sprig and cook, stirring, until the onion is translucent, approximately 4 minutes. Add the rice and cook, stirring to coat the rice with the oil, for 3 to 4 minutes. Add the white wine and cook, stirring, until it is evaporated. Add about a cup of broth to the pot and cook, stirring constantly, until the broth is completely absorbed by the rice, then add another cup of liquid. Continue in this manner until you have used all the chicken broth, which should take approximately 18 minutes. Add 1 cup of the lobster emulsion to the pot and stir vigorously until it has been absorbed by the rice.

FINISH THE RISOTTO Stir the Parmigiano-Reggiano into the risotto until it melts and thickens it, then stir in the butter and chives. If the risotto seems too thick at this point, add a bit more stock or water. Stir in a splash of Sauternes wine and season to taste with salt and pepper. Gently fold in the lobster and foie gras.

TO SERVE Divide the risotto among 6 individual plates and serve.

Wine Suggestion: Dorado, Alvarinho 2001; Mihno. A rich Portuguese white with peachy and tropical aromas.

PARMESAN CRISPS

serves ⑥ as a garnish Called *frico* in Italy, these are a fun, crunchy treat to serve along with soups, salads, and risottos.

¾ **cup grated Parmigiano-Reggiano cheese**

PREHEAT THE BROILER. Set a round, 3¼-inch mold on a nonstick cookie sheet and sprinkle 2 teaspoons cheese in an even layer. Repeat all over the pan, forming 20 to 22 circles. Broil in the center of the broiler until lightly golden, 2 to 3 minutes. Carefully remove the rounds from the pan with a spatula, and let cool on a rack. They will be soft out of the oven, but will firm up as they cool. Once cool, test one to see if it's brittle, like a potato chip; if not, return to the pan and bake for a few more minutes.

PENNE AND LOBSTER GRATIN

serves ⑥ This main-course pasta—it's simply too rich to serve as an appetizer—is a real treat for lobster lovers. It uses all parts of cooked lobsters: the bodies flavor a creamy sauce améri-caine—like emulsion that binds the dish, and the chopped meat is tossed into the gratin just before broiling. This pasta was inspired by one served in Nice by the great French chef Jacques Maximin. His version was finished with a shaving of black truffles and, indeed, you can add to the luxurious quality here with a drizzle of truffle oil just before serving.

    If you can't find pennette, use regular penne; obviously, the shape of the pasta won't change the flavor.

   4 **lobsters,** 1¼ pounds each, boiled (see page 274), meat removed and cut into
        1-inch dice (approximately 2 cups)
  ½ cup **olive oil**
  ½ cup **finely diced carrot**
  ½ cup **finely diced celery**
  ¼ cup **finely diced onion**
  ½ cup **finely diced leek greens**
  2 **garlic cloves,** halved
  1 **sprig thyme**
  ¼ teaspoon **black peppercorns**
  1 **bay leaf**
  2 tablespoons **Cognac**
  ¾ cup **chopped plum tomatoes**
1½ teaspoons **tomato paste**
  ½ cup plus a splash **Sauternes wine**
  2 cups **heavy cream**
 10 leaves **basil,** stems reserved, leaves rolled and cut into thin ribbons
    Fine sea salt and freshly ground black pepper to taste
 12 ounces **pennette (small penne) pasta**
  ¾ cup **grated Parmigiano-Reggiano cheese**

CRUSH THE LOBSTER SHELLS AND BEGIN MAKING THE EMULSION Put the lobster shells and other trimmings between 2 clean kitchen towels. Use a rolling pin or the bottom of a heavy pan to crush the bodies. Set aside. Set a large pot over high heat. Pour in 3 tablespoons of the olive oil and heat until almost smoking. Add the carrot, celery, onion, leek, garlic, thyme, peppercorns, and bay leaf. Cook until the onion is translucent. Add the lobster shells. When they begin to turn red, tip the pan away from you, lean back, add the Cognac, and carefully ignite it with a match. Cook until evaporated. Add the tomatoes and tomato paste, and cook until the tomatoes are falling apart, approximately 4 minutes. Add ½ cup of the Sauternes and bring to a boil. Add the cream, bring to a boil, lower the heat, and cook uncovered for 10 minutes. Remove the pot from the heat and add the basil stems. Set aside, covered, to cool.

FINISH MAKING THE LOBSTER EMULSION Once the contents of the pot are cool, strain them through a fine-mesh strainer, pressing down on the solids to extract as much flavorful liquid as possible. Discard the solids and season the liquid with salt and pepper. Add another splash of Sauternes and blend with an immersion blender just until the liquid foams.

SAUTÉ THE LOBSTER Heat 4 tablespoons of the olive oil in a large sauté pan set over medium-high heat. Add the lobster meat and sauté until it turns bright orange, approximately 2 minutes; do not overcook. Season with salt and pepper and set aside.

COOK THE PASTA Bring a pot of salted water with the remaining tablespoon of the oil to a boil over high heat. Add the pasta and cook until *al dente,* about 10 minutes. Drain and transfer to a large bowl.

ASSEMBLE AND BROWN THE GRATIN Preheat the broiler. Add the lobster, emulsion, and basil leaves to the bowl with the hot pasta and toss to ensure all elements are hot. Taste and adjust the seasoning with salt and pepper. Transfer to a large gratin dish and top with the grated cheese. (The gratin can be prepared to this point, covered, and refrigerated for up to 3 hours. Let come to room temperature before proceeding.) Place under the broiler and cook until the pasta on top is crisp and the cheese is golden brown, 5 to 7 minutes.

TO SERVE Present the gratin dish at the table and serve family style.

Wine Suggestion: Domaine Caillot, Meursault 1999; Burgundy. A complex white with smoky, toasty, and mineral notes.

MUSSEL RISOTTO AND CONFIT KUMQUAT

serves (6) Most people know *confit* as an old French culinary term that refers to cooking and preserving something, like duck, in its own fat. But it also refers to fruits and vegetables cooked in a syrup, which I do here to make kumquats extra sweet, almost like candy. If kumquats are not in season, use fresh oranges in their place. In order to provide enough flavorful juice, this recipe makes more mussels than you will need; use the remaining mussels to make a salad.

- 6 **garlic cloves,** chopped
- 1 **cup sliced shallots**
- 2½ **cups dry white wine**
- 10 **parsley stems with no leaves**
- 2 **sprigs thyme**
- 1 **bay leaf**
- 6 **pounds small blue mussels or Prince Edward Island mussels,**
  cleaned and debearded, if necessary
- 1 **cup heavy cream**
- 1½ **tablespoons curry powder**
- 3 **tablespoons olive oil**
- 1 **cup chopped onion**
- 2 **cups arborio rice**
- 3 **tablespoons unsalted butter**
- 1 **cup grated Parmigiano-Reggiano cheese**
  Fine sea salt and freshly ground black pepper to taste
  Confit Kumquat and Baby Spinach Salad (optional; recipe follows)

COOK THE MUSSELS   In a large heavy-bottomed pot, stir together half of the chopped garlic, the shallots, 1½ cups of the wine, the parsley stems, 1 thyme sprig, and the bay leaf. Bring to a boil over high heat. Add the mussels, cover, and cook until the mussels have opened, approximately 5 minutes. Strain the contents of the pot through a strainer set over a large bowl. You should obtain at least 5 cups of liquid; if not, add enough water to yield 5 cups. Discard any mussels that have not opened. Set aside 30 unshelled mussels. Remove half of the remaining mussels from their shells and set aside separately. Discard the shells. Keep the remaining unshelled mussels for another use.

MAKE THE RISOTTO Bring the reserved 5 cups mussel liquid to a boil in a pot set over high heat. Stir in the cream and curry powder, then turn off the heat. In a heavy-bottomed pot, heat the olive oil over medium heat. Add the remaining chopped garlic, onion, and the remaining thyme sprig, and cook, stirring, until the onion is translucent, approximately 4 minutes. Add the rice and stir to coat the rice with the oil. Cook for 3 to 4 minutes. Add the remaining 1 cup wine and cook, stirring, until evaporated. Add about 1 cup of the curried mussel cream to the pot and cook, stirring constantly, until is completely absorbed by the rice, then add another cup of liquid. Continue in this manner until you have used 5 cups, which should take approximately 18 minutes. Stir in the butter and the grated Parmigiano-Reggiano. Season with salt and pepper. Set aside, covered.

TO SERVE Stir the shelled mussels into the risotto. (If the rice seems too firm, add a few more tablespoons of broth and a splash of white wine. It should be a nice, natural sauce.) Mound some risotto in each of 6 bowls. In a pot, warm the mussels in their shells in the remaining bouillon and decoratively arrange 5 of them atop each bowl of risotto. Mound some of the Confit Kumquat and Baby Spinach Salad, if using, atop each serving. Spoon any remaining bouillon around the risotto and serve at once.

Wine Suggestion: Grosset, "Polish Hill" Riesling 2001; Clare Valley. A bright Australian white with orange zest and peachy notes.

CONFIT KUMQUAT AND BABY SPINACH SALAD

- ¼ cup thinly sliced seeded kumquats
- 1¾ cups water
- ⅔ cup sugar
- 1½ cups baby spinach leaves
- 2 tablespoons olive oil

BRING A SMALL POT of water to a boil over high heat; fill a bowl with ice water. Add the sliced kumquats to the boiling water, remove with a slotted spoon, and plunge into the ice water. Repeat twice, then drain the kumquats. Bring the water to a boil with the sugar in a small pot. Add the kumquats, reduce the heat to low, and cook until the syrup has reduced to a glaze and the kumquats are tender. Remove the pot from the heat and let cool. Toss the cooled kumquats with the baby spinach and olive oil.

COLD MUSSEL SALAD

serves ⑥ A great way to use leftover steamed mussels the next day.

¾ cup dry white wine
1 garlic clove, very thinly sliced
Leaves from 2 sprigs thyme
¼ cup finely diced red onion
¼ cup finely diced red bell pepper
1 jalapeño pepper, seeded and minced
¼ cup finely diced celery
1½ tablespoons sherry vinegar
Pinch cayenne
1 teaspoon cracked coriander seeds
2 tablespoons chopped cilantro leaves
2 tablespoons extra-virgin olive oil
Juice of 1 lemon
2 cups cooked mussels in their shells
Fine sea salt and freshly ground black pepper to taste

IN A POT, bring the wine to a boil with the garlic and thyme, then remove the pot from the heat. Add the red onion, bell pepper, jalapeño, and celery. Let cool. Add the vinegar, cayenne, coriander, cilantro, olive oil, lemon juice, and mussels. Season with salt and pepper. Let marinate for at least 4 hours. Serve cold over salad greens or as an hors d'oeuvre.

RICOTTA TORTELLINI WITH GRILLED SARDINES

serves ⑥ This pasta dish is based on a Niçoise, which isn't just a salad; the name also refers to a type of olive and to recipes featuring tomatoes, garlic, capers, anchovies, olives, and French green beans. Here, I add tomatoes, olives, and capers to the pasta sauce, and fresh sardines rather than anchovies are draped over the top.

¾ **cup ricotta cheese**

12 **large basil leaves,** chopped

5 **sun-dried tomatoes,** cut into small dice

1 **garlic clove,** very finely chopped

1 **pound Pasta Dough (page 145)**

1 **egg yolk,** beaten with 2 tablespoons water to make an egg wash

2 **tablespoons capers,** rinsed and drained

40 **Niçoise olives,** pitted and thinly sliced (about 1 cup)

¼ **cup olive oil,** plus more for brushing sardines

2 **tablespoons balsamic vinegar**

1 **plum tomato,** seeded and diced

Fine sea salt and freshly ground black pepper to taste

6 **fresh sardines,** filleted and deboned

2 **bunches arugula,** tough stems removed

Country bread, sliced and toasted

MAKE THE TORTELLINI In a bowl, stir together the ricotta, half the basil, the sun-dried tomatoes, and the garlic. Roll out the Pasta Dough and cut into 2½-inch squares. Put 1 teaspoon of filling in the center of each pasta square. Fold the square diagonally in half, to form a triangle, with the top edges about ⅛ inch inside the bottom edges. Brush the edges lightly with egg wash and press to seal the edges with your fingers. Pick up the triangle, with the pointed side facing upward. Bring together the sides in front and pinch the ends of the triangle together, forcing the filling up by exerting gentle pressure with your finger. Form the 2 pinched ends into a ring and set the tortellini aside on a clean towel as you complete them. Cover and set aside.

MAKE THE VINAIGRETTE Bring a pot of salted water to a boil while you make the vinaigrette. Prepare an indoor or outdoor grill for cooking. In a bowl, stir together the remaining basil with the capers, olives, ¼ cup olive oil, balsamic vinegar, and tomato. Season with salt and pepper.

COOK THE TORTELLINI Add the tortellini to the boiling water and cook until they float to the surface, 1 to 2 minutes. Drain in a colander and set aside to cool.

GRILL THE SARDINES Brush the sardines with olive oil and season them with salt and pepper. Grill the fillets on both sides until lightly charred, 2 to 4 minutes per side.

TO SERVE Toss the room-temperature tortellini and arugula together with the vinaigrette and divide among 6 bowls. Top each serving with 2 sardine fillets and serve with the toasted bread alongside.

Wine Suggestion: Bisson, Marea 2001; Cinqueterre, Liguria. A coastal Italian white from Liguria with aromas of sea salt, herbs, and lemon zest.

GRILLED HAKE "FOUR BY FOUR" SERVED WITH SAGE-POTATO GNOCCHI GRATIN AND BROCCOLI RABE WITH GARLIC   page 187

LEMON CRAB RISOTTO WITH GRILLED ASPARAGUS   page 130

RICOTTA TORTELLINI WITH GRILLED SARDINES   page 141 >>

GRILLED MACKEREL WITH WARM LEEK AND POTATO SALAD, WITH ROASTED RED ONION WITH
HONEY AND BALSAMIC VINEGAR   pages 199, 248

BAY SCALLOPS WITH CIPPOLINE BOUILLON AND FOIE GRAS RAVIOLI

serves ⑥ This is one of my signature dishes: rich foie gras ravioli topped with sautéed bay scallops and an onion bouillon. Cippoline are sweet, flat Italian onions, now found in most upscale supermarkets; pearl onions can be substituted. By using a prepared foie gras terrine you save an incredible amount of time, and because much of the fat is already cooked out of a terrine, it will remain finer than fresh foie gras and give you a more accurate sense of how much will remain in the cooked ravioli.

This recipe calls for a pasta machine. If you do not have one, use store-bought wonton skins instead of making your own ravioli dough. If you own a ravioli mold, by all means use it to make perfectly shaped pasta.

1	tablespoon unsalted butter
3	ounces **bacon,** diced (about ¾ cup)
10	ounces **cippolline onions (see page 43) or pearl onions,** peeled and sliced (about 1½ cups)
1	**garlic clove,** crushed
2	tablespoons sugar
2	tablespoons sherry vinegar
3	cups canned low-sodium chicken broth
1	bay leaf
1	sprig thyme
	Fine sea salt and freshly ground black pepper to taste
	Pasta Dough (recipe follows)
1	**egg yolk,** whisked with 2 tablespoons water to make an egg wash
5	ounces foie gras terrine
1	tablespoon olive oil
⅓ to ½	pound **bay scallops,** preferably Nantucket (about 36)
⅓	cup **walnut halves,** toasted and chopped
3	tablespoons walnut oil
1½	teaspoons truffle oil
2	large black truffles (optional)

MAKE THE BOUILLON In a large pot, heat the butter over medium heat. Add the bacon and cook until the fat is rendered and the bacon is crisp, approximately 5 minutes. Add the onions, garlic, and sugar. Cook, stirring occasionally, until the onions are nicely browned, 6 to 7 minutes. Pour in the sherry vinegar and cook until it evaporates, scraping up any brown bits from the bottom of the pot with a wooden spoon, 30 to 60 seconds. Add the broth, bay leaf, and thyme. Simmer until the liquid is reduced by half, approximately 5 minutes from when it reaches a boil. Pour the contents of the pot through a fine-mesh strainer set over a bowl. Discard the solids and season the bouillon with salt and pepper. Cover and set aside.

ROLL OUT THE RAVIOLI Use a pasta machine to roll the Pasta Dough into 2 paper-thin sheets, about $\frac{1}{16}$ inch thick. (If you favor a more delicate dough, you may roll them even thinner. If you do this, shorten the cooking time accordingly; recipes in this book are tested with $\frac{1}{8}$-inch-thick pasta.) The sheets should have a slight elasticity to them—that is, when pulled, they should give just a bit but snap back into their original shape. Be careful when rolling to ensure that you are creating a uniform thickness across the sheets.

FORM THE RAVIOLI Cut the dough into $1\frac{1}{2}$-inch squares. You should have 36 squares. Cut the foie gras into small cubes (about $\frac{3}{4}$ tablespoon). Brush the edges of half the ravioli squares with egg wash and place a foie gras cube in the center of half of those squares. Cover with the remaining pasta squares and seal the edges by pressing the ravioli squares together.

SAUTÉ THE SCALLOPS AND COOK THE RAVIOLI Bring a pot of salted water to a boil. In a large sauté pan, heat the olive oil over medium-high heat. Season the scallops with salt and pepper, add them to the pan and cook until medium-rare, approximately 1 minute. Meanwhile, add the ravioli to the boiling water and cook until they float to the surface, approximately 2 minutes.

TO SERVE Use a slotted spoon to remove the ravioli from the water, placing 3 ravioli in the center of each of 6 bowls. Top each serving with about 5 bay scallops and some chopped walnuts; ladle about $\frac{1}{4}$ cup onion bouillon over the top of each. Drizzle with walnut oil and truffle oil, and if you have them, scatter some sliced black truffle over the top.

Wine Suggestion: Talley, Arroyo Grande 2000; California. A well-balanced American Chardonnay with tropical fruit notes and bright acidity.

PASTA DOUGH makes about ① pound, enough for 18 ravioli

- ¾ **cup all-purpose flour,** plus more for dusting
- 3 **tablespoons semolina flour**
-    **Pinch fine sea salt**
- 1 **whole egg plus 1 egg white**
- 1 **tablespoon olive oil**

PUT THE FLOURS in a large stainless steel or glass mixing bowl and make a well in the center. In a separate mixing bowl, whisk the whole egg and egg white, then pour it into the well. Pour the olive oil into the well. With a fork, gradually mix the flour and salt into the egg and olive oil mixture. When the flour has just been incorporated, turn the dough out onto a floured work surface. Work the dough, kneading it and flattening it out over and over, until it forms a smooth and elastic ball; this should take about 10 minutes. (If the dough isn't holding together as you knead it, add a few drops of lukewarm water. If the dough is sticky, sprinkle it lightly with flour.) Dust the dough with flour, wrap it in plastic wrap, and refrigerate for at least 30 minutes before rolling out.

RIGATONI WITH BAY SCALLOPS AND MUSHROOMS

serves ⑥ This is a delicious pasta, mushroom, and scallop recipe, but you should feel free to use it as a blueprint for your own variations. You can, for example, add another dimension of flavor and color by incorporating blanched asparagus tips, substituting rock or small Gulf shrimp for the bay scallops, using oyster and/or portobello mushrooms instead of the cremini and shiitakes, and trying different pasta shapes.

- 3 pounds button mushrooms
- 2 cups heavy cream
- Fine sea salt and freshly ground black pepper to taste
- 2 ounces thickly sliced bacon, diced (about ½ cup)
- 12 cremini mushrooms, trimmed, washed, and thinly sliced
- 12 shiitake mushrooms, trimmed, washed, and thinly sliced
- 1 large shallot, chopped
- ¼ cup chopped garlic
- 2 tablespoons olive oil
- 1 cup finely diced country bread
- 2 tablespoons chopped flat-leaf parsley
- 5 tablespoons grated Parmigiano-Reggiano cheese
- 1 pound medium bay scallops (about 60)
- 2 tablespoons unsalted butter
- 10 ounces (3 cups) mezze rigatoni, cooked *al dente* and drained

MAKE THE SAUCE   In batches if necessary, put the button mushrooms in a food processor with about 3 cups of water and puree until smooth. Pour into a pot set over high heat, and bring to a boil. Boil for 5 minutes, then strain through a cheesecloth-lined strainer set over another pot, pressing down on the solids to extract as much liquid as possible. Set the pot over high heat and reduce the mushroom liquid to a glaze, about ¼ cup. Add the cream, bring to a boil, remove from the heat, and season with salt and pepper. (This glaze can be cooled, covered, and refrigerated, for up to 3 days. Let come to room temperature before proceeding.)

SAUTÉ THE MUSHROOMS Sauté the diced bacon in a sauté pan set over medium heat until it is crisp and has rendered enough fat to coat the bottom of the pan, approximately 5 minutes. Add the cremini and shiitake mushrooms, and toss to coat with the fat. Add the shallot and half of the chopped garlic, and season with salt and pepper. Remove the pan from the heat and set aside.

MAKE THE BREADING Heat the olive oil in a sauté pan set over medium-high heat. Add the diced bread and cook, tossing, until golden brown, approximately 2 minutes. Add the remaining garlic and the parsley, and sauté until they stick to the bread cubes. Transfer the breading to a bowl and add the Parmigiano-Reggiano. Season with salt and pepper and set aside.

SAUTÉ THE SCALLOPS You may need to do this in two batches: Season the scallops with salt and pepper. Melt the butter in a wide, deep-sided sauté pan set over medium-high heat. Add the scallops and sauté until golden brown on both sides and opaque in the center, approximately 1 minute.

ASSEMBLE THE DISH Preheat the boiler. In a large pot, bring the mushroom glaze to a boil over high heat. Add the mushrooms and rigatoni, and reheat. Add the scallops and toss. Transfer the contents of the pot to a large, shallow ceramic or cast-iron casserole and add the bread topping. Broil until the dish is cooked through and the topping is browned and crisp, approximately 3 minutes.

TO SERVE Present the dish family-style from the center of the table.

> Wine Suggestion: Matrot-Wittersheim, Meursault 2000; Burgundy. A rich white Burgundy with layers of apply fruit, and earthy, smoky undertones.

SEA SCALLOPS WITH BASIL-PORTOBELLO RAVIOLI AND PARMESAN CREAM SAUCE

serves ⑥ Because they're so big and meaty, diver-harvested sea scallops make an impact even when they share the stage with something as flavorful as basil-portobello ravioli. Most pasta dishes can be a starter or a main course, but this is really meant as the center attraction because it's so satisfying. Note that the scallops should be cooked until warm on the outside but still raw in the center.

5 tablespoons olive oil
2 portobello mushrooms, stems removed
  Fine sea salt and freshly ground black pepper to taste
¾ cup grated Parmigiano-Reggiano cheese plus 2 tablespoons
  Pasta Dough (page 145)
1 egg yolk, whisked with 2 tablespoons of water to make an egg wash
1 cup heavy cream
1½ pounds sea scallops, preferably diver-harvested (about 18 medium scallops)
¼ cup basil pesto (Steps 2 and 3, pages 120–121), plus 1 tablespoon oil drained from the pesto

COOK THE MUSHROOMS Preheat the oven to 325°F. Heat 3 tablespoons of the olive oil in a large ovenproof sauté pan set over medium-high heat. Add the mushroom caps, cut side down, season with salt and pepper, and sauté for 1 minute on each side. Transfer the pan to the oven and roast until the mushrooms are roasted and fragrant, approximately 12 minutes. Remove the pan from the oven, let the mushrooms cool slightly, and cut into ¼-inch dice.

MAKE THE RAVIOLI In a bowl, toss together the diced mushrooms, basil pesto, and 2 tablespoons of the Parmigiano-Reggiano cheese. Roll out the Pasta Dough and cut into 2½-inch squares. Brush the edges of half the pasta squares with egg wash and put teaspoon-size scoops of filling in the center of those squares. Cover with the remaining squares and seal the edges by pressing the ravioli squares together. You will have 18 ravioli.

MAKE THE SAUCE Bring a large pot of salted water to a boil while you make the sauce. Pour the cream into a pot and bring to a boil over high heat. Immediately remove from the heat and whisk in the remaining ¾ cup Parmigiano-Reggiano cheese. Taste and season with salt and pepper, if necessary.

SAUTÉ THE SCALLOPS Heat the remaining 2 tablespoons olive oil in a sauté pan set over high heat. Season the scallops with salt and pepper and add them to the pan. Cook until golden brown on each side and warm in the middle, 2 to 3 minutes per side. Test them by inserting a sharp thin-bladed knife into the center of 1 scallop and making sure it comes out warm.

COOK THE RAVIOLI Add the ravioli to the boiling water and cook them while you sauté the scallops.

TO SERVE Arrange 3 scallops in the center of each of 6 shallow bowls. Use a slotted spoon to remove the ravioli from the water and place 1 square atop each scallop. Emulsify the sauce with a hand blender or whisk, and spoon some sauce and a few drops of pesto oil over each serving.

Wine Suggestion: Belondrade y Lurton, Verdejo 2000; Rueda. A white from Spain, with ripe apple and quince aromas and a touch of oak.

SHELLFISH BOW TIE PASTA WITH TOMATOES AND OREGANO

serves (6) A mix of shrimp, scallops, clams, and mussels make this a festive dish that is actually fairly quick and easy. Most of the shellfish are removed from their shells before serving. Just enough are left intact to offer a striking presentation. You can adjust this dish to suit your own taste, changing the quantities or types of shellfish, leaving out the chile for a less spicy result, or changing the pasta to spaghetti or fresh linguine. I especially enjoy this in the summer, when quickly prepared shellfish dishes are in high demand.

1½ **cups sugar snap peas**

3 **tablespoons olive oil**

3 **ounces bacon,** diced (about ¾ cup)

1 **medium onion,** diced

3 **garlic cloves,** chopped

1 **sprig thyme**

2 **dried chiles**

2 **cups sliced cremini mushrooms (about 6 ounces)**

1 **can (28 ounces) Italian peeled tomatoes,** squeezed by hand and drained

1 **tablespoon chopped oregano leaves or dried oregano**

½ **pound medium shrimp,** peeled and deveined

½ **pound bay scallops**

   Fine sea salt and freshly ground black pepper to taste

1½ **cups dry white wine**

¾ **pound small clams or cockles,** cleaned and scrubbed

½ **pound mussels,** cleaned and scrubbed

   Freshly grated pecorino Romano cheese, for serving

5 **cups farfalle (bow tie) pasta**

BLANCH THE SUGAR-SNAP PEAS Bring a pot of salted water to a boil. Fill a large bowl halfway with ice water. Add the peas to the boiling water and blanch for 2 minutes. Drain and transfer to the ice water to cool and stop the cooking. Drain and set aside.

BEGIN MAKING THE TOMATO SAUCE Heat 1 tablespoon of the olive oil in a pot set over medium heat. Add the bacon and cook until golden brown, approximately 7 minutes. Add the onion, garlic, thyme, and chiles, and cook until the onion is translucent, approximately 4 minutes. Add the mushrooms and cook for 2 minutes. Add the tomatoes and oregano. Cook, stirring, for 3 minutes. Set the tomato sauce aside, covered to keep warm.

MEANWHILE, SAUTÉ THE SHRIMP AND SCALLOPS Heat the remaining 2 tablespoons olive oil in a large sauté pan set over high heat. Season the shrimp and scallops with salt and pepper. Add the shrimp to the pan and sauté until firm and pink, approximately 2 minutes, then transfer to a plate. Add the scallops and sauté until firm and opaque at the center, approximately 1 minute. Transfer them to the plate with the shrimp.

FINISH MAKING THE SAUCE Add the wine to the tomato sauce and bring to a boil. Add the clams or cockles, cover, and cook for 3 minutes. Add the mussels, cover, and steam for 2 to 3 minutes, or until the shells open. Discard any clams or mussels that do not open. Remove about three-fourths of the shellfish from the pot; keep the sauce warm over very low heat. As soon as the removed shellfish are cool enough to handle, shell them. Discard the shells and return the meat to the pot. Add the shrimp and scallops. Fish out and discard the chiles.

COOK THE PASTA In a large pot of boiling salted water, cook the pasta until *al dente,* approximately 8 minutes.

FINISH THE DISH Drain the pasta and add it to the pot with the sauce. Add the sugar snap peas and toss well. Season with salt and pepper.

TO SERVE Transfer the pasta and sauce to a bowl and serve family-style from the center of the table with grated pecorino passed alongside.

Wine Suggestion: Casa Sola, Chianti Classico 1999; Tuscany. A simple Chianti with bright cherry fruit and slight herbaceous aromas.

COCKLES are small mollusks that look like clams but are not from the same family. They are not caught in American waters, but can often be found in fish stores. I highly recommend them for their gentle flavor and the variety they bring to recipes featuring a mix of fish and/or shellfish.

CHINATOWN SHRIMP WONTONS

serves ⑥ I'm very fond of the fish and spices I've discovered in New York City's famed Chinatown and while traveling in Asia. One of my favorite Sunday dinners in New York is Asian food. This dish isn't based on any one wonton I've had; it's more of a composite of many of my favorite Asian flavors, not just Chinese but Thai and Vietnamese as well.

To allow each of your guests to adjust the heat to individual taste, place a bowl of chile paste with a small spoon on the table when you serve this dish. If you don't find the souplike treatment appealing, omit the broth and pan-sear the wontons in hot oil like potstickers, and serve them with soy sauce on the side.

1	**pound medium shrimp,** peeled, deveined, and diced
3	**tablespoons chopped shallot**
1¼	**teaspoons Chinese chile paste**
½	**cup cilantro leaves plus 2 tablespoons chopped cilantro**
	Fine sea salt and freshly ground black pepper to taste
18	**square wonton skins**
1	**cup dry white wine**
1½	**teaspoons Vietnamese fish sauce** (*nuoc mam*)
3	**cups water**
2	**diced kaffir lime leaves**
1	**lemongrass stalk,** cut into pieces
1	**tablespoon chopped fresh ginger**
2	**tablespoons reduced-sodium (lite) soy sauce**
¼	**cup chopped roasted macadamia nuts**
¼	**cup thinly julienned red radishes**
¼	**cup sliced scallions,** green part only
	Sesame oil, for drizzling (optional)

MAKE THE WONTONS   In a bowl, stir together the shrimp, shallot, chile paste, and chopped cilantro. Season to taste with salt and pepper. Lay the wonton skins before you and brush the edges of each with water. Place 1 tablespoon of shrimp filling in the center of each wonton. Fold the dough over to form a dumpling. Seal the edges by pinching them together with your fingers, leaving one corner unsealed. Press out any trapped air, then seal the corner.

MAKE THE BOUILLON In a large pot, combine the wine, fish sauce, and water. Bring to a boil. Add the kaffir lime leaves, lemongrass, and ginger; cover, turn off the heat, and let infuse for 10 to 15 minutes. Remove the cover and strain the bouillon through a fine-mesh strainer set over a bowl. Stir in the soy sauce and set aside.

COOK THE WONTONS Bring a large pot of salted water to a boil. Add the wontons and cook until they rise to the surface, 3 to 4 minutes.

TO SERVE Carefully remove the wontons from the pot with a slotted spoon and place 3 wontons in each of 6 shallow soup bowls. Ladle a generous amount of the bouillon over the wontons in each bowl. Garnish with the nuts, radish, cilantro leaves, and scallions. Drizzle with sesame oil and serve at once.

Wine Suggestion: Sokol Blosser, "Evolution" NV; Willamette Valley. An off-dry white from Oregon, with aromas of ripe peach, honeysuckle, and apricots.

LEMONGRASS
adds a lemony flavor to dishes and has one great advantage over actual lemon peel—it doesn't turn bitter after being cooked for a long time. For dishes in which the lemongrass will actually be eaten, use only the bottom 6 inches of the stalk. To prepare, peel off the tough outer leaves and thinly slice the whitish inner stalk. The outer portion can be used to flavor soups and stews, but be sure to strain it out or remove it before serving because it is too fibrous to ingest. Even if lemongrass will be strained out of a dish, chop it into pieces to release its rich and aromatic oils.

KAFFIR LIME LEAVES,
often paired with lemongrass, are one of the true staples of Thai cooking. They exude a powerful perfume and a flavor that seems to lighten any dish, even soups made with rich coconut milk. Because kaffir lime leaves are harvested by hand, they can be expensive, but they're worth it; see Mail-Order Sources.

ROCK SHRIMP RISOTTO WITH GRILLED PANCETTA AND WHITE TRUFFLE OIL

serves (6) This recipe uses white truffle oil, a relatively economical way of enjoying the flavor of truffles, which are famously expensive but well worth it (they boast one of the most incredible flavors produced by nature). White truffles are more intense and earthy than the more common black truffles. They grow exclusively in Italy's Piedmont region, where truffle "hunters" seek them out every fall with the aid of specially trained hounds.

This risotto would be delicious accompanied by grilled bread spread with basil pesto (Steps 2 and 3, pages 120–121).

5 ounces pancetta (about 1¼ cups), diced, plus 6 paper-thin slices

¼ cup plus 1 tablespoon olive oil

3 garlic cloves, chopped

1 cup chopped onion

1 sprig thyme

2 cups arborio rice

1 cup dry white wine

5 cups canned low-sodium chicken broth

1 cup grated Parmigiano-Reggiano cheese

3 tablespoons unsalted butter

Fine sea salt and freshly ground black pepper to taste

1 teaspoon white truffle oil, plus more to taste

1 pound medium shrimp, preferably rock shrimp (about 18)

3 tablespoons chopped chives

2 medium white truffles (optional)

COOK THE PANCETTA Preheat the broiler. Arrange the pancetta slices on a cookie sheet and broil until crisp. Drain on paper towels and set aside.

MAKE THE RISOTTO In a large heavy-bottomed pot, heat 3 tablespoons of the olive oil with the diced pancetta over medium-heat. Add the garlic, onion, and thyme, and cook, stirring, until the onion is translucent, approximately 4 minutes. Add the rice and stir to coat the rice with the oil. Cook for 3 to 4 minutes. Add the wine and cook, stirring, until evaporated. Add about 1 cup of the broth and cook, stirring constantly, until it is completely absorbed by the rice, then add another cup of liquid. Continue in this manner until you have used all the broth, which should take approximately 18 minutes. Use tongs to remove and discard the thyme sprig. Stir in the grated Parmigiano-Reggiano cheese and the butter. Season to taste with salt, pepper, and truffle oil. Set aside, covered.

SAUTÉ THE SHRIMP   Heat the remaining 2 tablespoons of olive oil in a sauté pan set over high heat. Add the shrimp, season with salt and pepper, and cook until firm and pink, 1 to 2 minutes. Fold the shrimp into the risotto, along with the chives.

TO SERVE   Mound some risotto in the center of each of 6 bowls. Break the pancetta into pieces over each serving. Shave a generous amount of truffle over each bowl and serve at once.

Wine Suggestion: Luca Abrate, "Tabaria" Arneis 2001; Piedmonte. A dry, lemon scented Italian white.

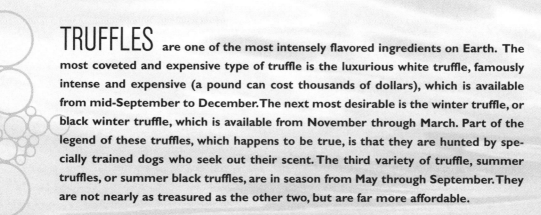

TRUFFLES are one of the most intensely flavored ingredients on Earth. The most coveted and expensive type of truffle is the luxurious white truffle, famously intense and expensive (a pound can cost thousands of dollars), which is available from mid-September to December. The next most desirable is the winter truffle, or black winter truffle, which is available from November through March. Part of the legend of these truffles, which happens to be true, is that they are hunted by specially trained dogs who seek out their scent. The third variety of truffle, summer truffles, or summer black truffles, are in season from May through September. They are not nearly as treasured as the other two, but are far more affordable.

PARSLEY RISOTTO WITH SNAILS AND FROTHY GOAT CHEESE

serves ⑥ You've probably experienced snails only cooked with butter, lots of garlic, and parsley. This recipe presents them with all of those flavors, but does so in a risotto sauced with a goat-cheese emulsion. This is also delicious with boneless frog's legs in place of the snails.

2 cups loosely packed flat-leaf parsley

½ cup olive oil

6 garlic cloves, peeled, 3 left whole and 3 chopped

1 cup plus 2 tablespoons grated Parmigiano-Reggiano cheese
Fine sea salt and freshly ground black pepper to taste

1 cup heavy cream
About 4 ounces aged goat cheese, diced

1 cup chopped onion

1 sprig thyme

2 cups arborio rice

1 cup dry white wine, or more as needed

5 cups canned low-sodium chicken broth, or more as needed

5 tablespoons unsalted butter

2 tablespoons chopped shallot

36 small canned American snails, shelled and rinsed, or canned Burgundy snails

MAKE THE PARSLEY PESTO Bring a small pot of salted water to a boil. Add the parsley and blanch it for 30 seconds. Drain it in a strainer and pass under cold running water to stop the cooking and set the color; drain well. Transfer the parsley to a blender. Add ¼ cup of the olive oil, the 3 whole garlic cloves, and 2 tablespoons of Parmigiano-Reggiano cheese. Process until smooth, transfer the pesto to a small bowl, season with salt and pepper, and set aside.

MAKE THE SAUCE In a saucepot, bring the cream to a boil over medium-high heat, being careful to not let it boil over. Immediately add the goat cheese and blend with an immersion blender. Season with salt and pepper. Remove the pot from the heat and set it aside, covered, to keep the sauce warm.

MAKE THE RISOTTO In a heavy-bottomed pot, heat the remaining ¼ cup olive oil over medium heat. Add the chopped garlic, onion, and thyme, and cook, stirring, until the onion is translucent, approximately 4 minutes. Add the rice and stir to coat the rice with the oil. Cook for 3 to 4 minutes. Add the white wine and cook, stirring, until evaporated. Add about 1 cup of broth to the pot and cook, stirring constantly, until it is completely absorbed by the rice, then add another cup of liquid. Continue in this manner until you have used all the broth, which should take approximately 18 minutes. Cover and keep warm.

SAUTÉ THE SNAILS In a wide, deep sauté pan, heat 2 tablespoons of the butter over medium-high heat. Add the chopped shallot and the snails, and season with salt and pepper. Sauté until cooked through, 3 to 4 minutes.

TO SERVE Stir the remaining 3 tablespoons of the butter, the remaining 1 cup Parmigiano-Reggiano cheese, and the reserved pesto into the risotto. If the risotto seems too firm, add a few more tablespoons of broth and a splash of white wine. Mound some risotto in the center of each of 6 bowls and top with some snails. Emulsify the cheese sauce with an immersion blender and spoon some sauce around the perimeter of the risotto.

Wine Suggestion: Marc Deschamps, "Les Vignes de Berge" Pouilly Fumé 2001; Loire Valley. A traditional French white with citrus and mineral notes.

SQUID RISOTTO WITH GARLIC PORCINI

serves (6) This risotto celebrates fresh, meaty porcini mushrooms. Like the squid, they are perfectly matched with sautéed garlic, which brings out their flavor. If you cannot find fresh porcini, do *not* use dried, but turn to portobello mushrooms instead.

½ **cup olive oil**

5 **ounces bacon,** minced (about 1¼ cups)

2½ **tablespoons chopped garlic (from about 6 cloves)**

1 **cup chopped onion**

1 **sprig thyme**

2 **cups arborio rice**

1 **cup dry white wine,** or more as needed

5 **cups canned low-sodium chicken broth,** or more as needed

1 **cup grated Parmigiano-Reggiano cheese**

3 **tablespoons unsalted butter**

Fine sea salt and freshly ground pepper to taste

3 **fresh medium porcini or portobello mushrooms,** sliced

3 **tablespoons chopped parsley**

1½ **pounds baby squid,** cut into rings

MAKE THE RISOTTO   In a heavy-bottomed pot, heat 3 tablespoons of the olive oil with the diced bacon over medium-heat. Add 2 tablespoons of the chopped garlic, the onion, and thyme, and cook, stirring, until the onion is translucent, approximately 4 minutes. Add the rice and stir to coat the rice with the oil. Cook for 3 to 4 minutes. Add the wine and cook, stirring, until evaporated. Add about a cup of broth and cook, stirring constantly, until it is completely absorbed by the rice, then add another cup of liquid. Continue in this manner until you have used all the broth, which should take approximately 18 minutes. Stir in the grated Parmigiano-Reggiano cheese and the butter. Season to taste with salt and pepper. Set aside, covered.

SAUTÉ THE MUSHROOMS   Heat 3 tablespoons of the olive oil in a sauté pan set over medium-high heat. Add the mushroom slices, season with salt and pepper, and sauté. After a minute or two, add the remaining 1½ teaspoons garlic. Continue to cook until the mushrooms are golden brown, approximately 6 minutes, then toss in the parsley and stir into the risotto. If the risotto seems too firm, add a few more tablespoons of broth and a splash of white wine. Cover and keep warm.

SAUTÉ THE SQUID Heat the remaining 2 tablespoons olive oil in a sauté pan set over high heat. Add the squid, season with salt and pepper, and cook until very lightly golden, 1 to 2 minutes.

TO SERVE Mound some risotto in the center of each of 6 bowls. Top with some cooked squid and serve at once.

Wine Suggestion: Dorigo, Ribolla Gialla 2001; Friuli. A minerally, mouthfilling white from northeastern Italy.

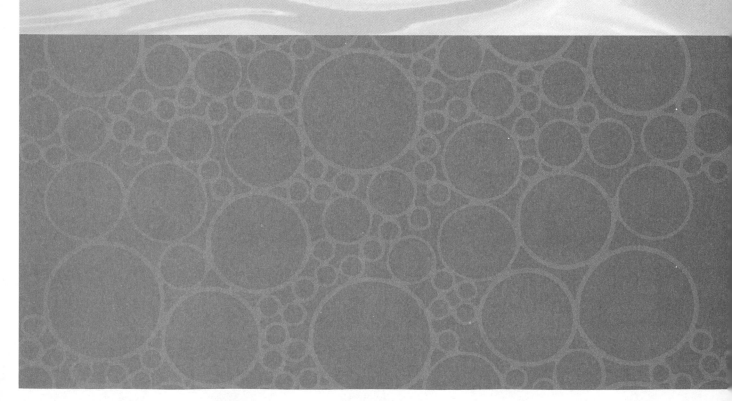

MAIN COURSES

Baked Whole Sea Bass with Meyer Lemon

Broiled Striped Bass with Rosemary-Parmesan Crust

Manila Clams Piperade

Arctic Char and Endive Papillote

Foil-Baked Cod

Poached Cod in Shellfish-Saffron Bouillon

Marinated Black Cod with Acacia Honey

Salt Cod Auvergnate

Crayfish and Chicken Casserole

Lemon-Curry Flounder with Crispy Cauliflower

Roasted Flounder with Cherry Tomatoes and Capers

Grouper with Indian-Style Broth

Grilled Hake "Four by Four"

Bacon-Wrapped Hake with Chilled Artichoke Broth

Mushroom-Crusted Halibut with Truffle Oil Emulsion

Mustard-Crusted Halibut

Lobster in Coconut and Cilantro Broth

Grilled Lobster Tail with Tomato Hollandaise

Poached Lobster with Ice Wine Nage

Roasted Lobster and Aromatic Butter

Grilled Mackerel with Warm Leek and Potato Salad

Grilled Mahi Mahi with Key Lime and Sauternes

Roasted Monkfish with Tomato, Flageolet Beans, and Chorizo

Mouclade

Mussels Steamed in White Wine

Walleye Pike with Bacon-Burgundy Sauce

Grilled Pompano with Vegetable Salsa

Semi-Smoked Salmon with Apple Broth

Salt-Crusted Salmon

Salmon Steak with Ginger-Chile Glaze

Grilled Shrimp Kebabs

Shrimp Omelet

Skate Barbecue with Braised Collard Greens

Red Snapper with Tomato-Ginger Chutney

Spicy Moroccan Swordfish

Prosciutto-Wrapped Rainbow Trout Stuffed with Herb Butter

Tuna Burger

Tuna-Swordfish Skewers

Tuna Panini

Tuna "Surf and Turf" with Ginger Ketchup

Zarzuela

When I used to cook at a restaurant that served only seafood, people constantly asked me how it felt to cook just fish. My answer is that if I were to be confined to just one type of food—fish, poultry, meat, or vegetarian—I would choose fish every time. There's so much variety in the types of fish and shellfish, and this is most apparent when you serve them as a main course.

One great thing about fish and shellfish is how quickly most of them cook, which means that seafood is often just as appropriate for everyday home cooking as it is for entertaining, when you don't want to spend too much time in the kitchen. You can decide what fish dish you want late in the day and, after a quick trip to the market, still have it ready in time for dinner.

When making shellfish the center of attention, I often turn to famous dishes from other countries. For example, the Basque Manila Clams Piperade (page 168), the Spanish Zarzuela (page 230), or the Turkish-inspired Grilled Shrimp Kebabs (page 214). I've also included a few shellfish dishes based on the flavors and traditions I grew up on, such as Mussels Steamed in White Wine (page 205).

To me, lobster is a main-course category all its own because it's so much more luxurious and special than most other shellfish—or fin fish, for that matter. I've included four lobster recipes in this chapter that I hope will open your eyes to the possibility of this grandest of shellfish: Grilled Lobster Tail with Tomato Hollandaise (page 194), Poached Lobster with Ice Wine Nage (page 197), Roasted Lobster and Aromatic Butter (page 198), and Lobster in Coconut and Cilantro Broth (page 193).

When it comes to fin fish, I get a chance to incorporate influences from all of my travels. The United States alone shows up in Tuna "Surf and Turf" with Ginger Ketchup (page 228), a take-off on a dish I saw during my time in Las Vegas; Skate Barbecue with Braised Collard Greens (page 216), Crayfish and Chicken Casserole (page 180), inspired by Louisiana cooking; and two dishes sparked by my time in the South—Grilled Pompano with Vegetable Salsa (page 208), and Grilled Mahi Mahi with Key Lime and Sauternes (page 201). Other countries and cultures are represented in Grouper with Indian-Style Broth (page 185) and Lemon-Curry Flounder with Crispy Cauliflower (page 182). There are even a few dishes that hark back to my home country, such as Salt Cod Auvergnate (page 178) and Walleye Pike with Bacon-Burgundy Sauce (page 206).

As with many other chefs, seafood also puts me in mind of the Mediterranean. So, I make a Tuna Panini (page 226), Poached Cod in Shellfish-Saffron Bouillon (page 174), and Grilled Mackerel with Warm Leek and Potato Salad (page 199). These fish aren't Mediterranean per se, but the ingredients with which I've paired them are.

Because I've had a chance to cook so much fish, I've created a number of signature dishes that combine so much personal experience and taste that they can't be easily categorized. These include Marinated Black Cod with Acacia Honey (page 176), Spicy Moroccan Swordfish (page 220), and Salmon Steak with Ginger-Chile Glaze (page 213).

In addition to the variety of flavors fish can take on, I value the range of techniques that can be used to cook them. Virtually every method of cooking is employed in these pages, from Grilled Hake "Four by Four" (page 187), to Roasted Monkfish with Tomato, Flageolet Beans, and Chorizo (page 202), to Baked Whole Sea Bass with Meyer Lemon (page 164), to Arctic Char and Endive Papillote (page 170), to Broiled Striped Bass with Rosemary-Parmesan Crust (page 166), to Semi-Smoked Salmon with Apple Broth (page 210).

Then there are techniques that actually alter the character of the fish by wrapping or encrusting them. I use this approach in Bacon-Wrapped Hake with Chilled Artichoke Broth (page 188), Red Snapper with Tomato-Ginger Chutney (page 218), Prosciutto-Wrapped Rainbow Trout Stuffed with Herb Butter (page 222), and Mushroom-Crusted Halibut with Truffle Oil Emulsion (page 190).

BAKED WHOLE SEA BASS WITH MEYER LEMON

serves (6) If you're lucky enough to put your hands on a great fresh, whole fish, there's nothing better than simply baking it with olive oil and lemon juice, which allows you to appreciate the flavor of the fish itself. Serve this with Aïoli (recipe follows) and/or pair it with Grilled Summer Vegetable Tart (page 244).

1	**whole black sea bass,** 4 to 5 pounds
	Fine sea salt and freshly ground black pepper to taste
10	**bay leaves**
½	**Meyer lemon,** thinly sliced into 10 pieces, plus juice of 2 lemons, preferably Meyer lemons
¼	**cup olive oil**
5	**garlic cloves,** crushed

PREHEAT THE OVEN to 375°F.

PREPARE THE FISH Season the fish on both sides with salt and pepper. Score the skin 10 times on each side. Place a bay leaf in 1 slit, a lemon slice in the next, and continue in this manner, tucking them into the flesh on both sides of the fish. Lightly grease a baking dish large enough to hold the fish with olive oil, using your fingers to spread it evenly. Put the fish in the dish, drizzle with olive oil and lemon juice, and scatter the garlic cloves around the fish.

BAKE THE FISH Bake the fish in the oven, basting with the pan juices every 10 minutes or so, until the fish appears opaque to the center if you pry apart the flesh at one of the slits, 35 to 40 minutes.

TO SERVE Present the fish whole at the table and remove portions with a knife and fork, being sure to remove and discard the bay leaves.

Wine Suggestion: Jean Dauvissat, Vaillons 2000; Chablis. A lean, elegant French white with touches of minerals and lemons.

AÏOLI

makes about ② cups This Provençal condiment is delicious with most white-fleshed fish, as well as vegetables.

- 1 large head or 2 medium heads roasted garlic (see page 243)
- 2 egg yolks
- ½ cup extra-virgin olive oil
- ¾ cup canola oil
- 3 tablespoons water
  Fine sea salt and freshly ground black pepper to taste

PUT THE GARLIC and egg yolks in the bowl of a food processor fitted with the steel blade. With the machine on, slowly add the olive oil in a thin stream, then add the canola oil in the same fashion to form an emulsified dressing. Beat in the water and season with salt and pepper.

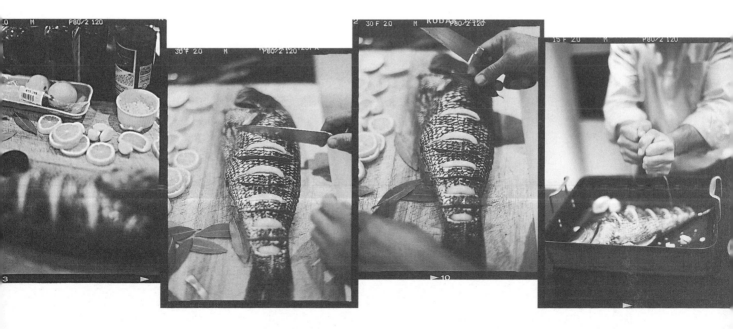

BROILED STRIPED BASS WITH ROSEMARY-PARMESAN CRUST

serves ⑥ The key to making this dish correctly is just barely heating it through on the stove-top so when the broiler is used to crisp the crust, the fish doesn't overcook in the extreme heat. The crust can also be used to coat other fish, such as salmon and halibut.

This is delicious dressed with Spiced Preserved Lemon (page 253), chopped and stirred into olive oil.

½ **cup (1 stick) unsalted butter,** softened at room temperature

1 **cup bread crumbs,** preferably panko (see page 73)

½ **cup grated Parmigiano-Reggiano cheese**

¼ **cup finely chopped onion**

2 **teaspoons chopped fresh rosemary**

Fine sea salt and freshly ground black pepper to taste

2 **tablespoons olive oil**

6 **skinless striped bass fillets,** 6 ounces each

PREHEAT the broiler.

MAKE THE CRUST In a small bowl, stir together the butter, bread crumbs, Parmigiano-Reggiano, onion, and rosemary until blended. Season with salt and pepper and set aside.

SAUTÉ THE FISH Heat the oil in a large sauté pan set over medium-high heat. Season the fillets with salt and pepper. When the oil is hot but not smoking, add the fillets and cook, turning once, until opaque in the center, 3 to 4 minutes per side. Transfer the fish to baking pan or cookie sheet.

COAT THE FISH WITH THE CRUST Use your hands to spread the crumbs over the top of each fish fillet to a thickness of ¼ inch. Set the pan under the broiler, about 4 inches from the heat, and broil just until the crust is golden brown, approximately 3 minutes.

TO SERVE Remove the pan from the oven and place 1 fillet on the center of each of 6 warm plates.

Wine Suggestion: Solaria, Rosso di Montalcino 1998; Tuscany. An Italian red with aromas of dried herbs, cherries, and a touch of earthiness.

MANILA CLAMS PIPERADE

serves (6) This dish is based on a specialty of the Basque region, which is between Spain and the southwest of France. In fact, the mixture of green pepper, white onion, and tomato (the piperade) echo the colors of the Basque flag. Because the clams are cooked right in the serving pot, it's important to clean and scrub them very well. To make this spicier, add more *pimento*.

⅓ cup olive oil

½ cup diced chorizo sausage or Serrano ham (about 2 ounces)

2 medium white onions, sliced

3 garlic cloves, chopped

Pinch *pimento de espelette,* or 1 dried chile, chopped

1 sprig thyme

1 bay leaf

1 tablespoon paprika

2 Cubanelle peppers, sliced

4 vine-ripened tomatoes or canned plum tomatoes, quartered, seeded, and sliced

1 cup dry white wine

6 pounds Manila clams, scrubbed (littlenecks can be substituted)

2 tablespoons chopped parsley leaves

Freshly ground black pepper to taste

MAKE THE PIPERADE SAUCE Warm the olive oil over medium-high heat in a large, attractive flameproof pot suitable for presenting at the table. Add the chorizo and sauté until crisp, approximately 8 minutes. Add the onions and cook until translucent, approximately 4 minutes. Add the garlic, *pimento,* thyme, bay leaf, and paprika; stir for a minute, then add the Cubanelle peppers, tomatoes, and white wine. Raise the heat to high and bring to a boil.

STEAM THE CLAMS Add the clams to the pot, cover, and cook until the clams open, approximately 5 minutes. Remove and discard any that do not open. Scatter the parsley over the top and season with pepper.

TO SERVE Serve the clams right from the pot in the center of the table.

Wine Suggestion: Domaine de Nerleux, Saumur-Champigny 2000; Loire Valley. A simple red from France, with aromas of roses, bell peppers, and cherries.

CUBANELLE PEPPERS are long, slender, pale green peppers, sometimes referred to as Italian frying peppers. They are sweet and not at all spicy and are available from most supermarkets.

PIMENTO DE ESPELETTE is a naturally hot, smoky chile grown in the Basque region of France, specifically in the village of Espelette. It's available by mail order (see page 277).

ARCTIC CHAR AND ENDIVE PAPILLOTE

serves ⑥ I love presenting these fish packets to people at the table and opening them with two forks, then adding a last-second drizzling of lemon juice. (You can also finish it with the "four by four sauce" on page 187, the sauce for Grilled Mahimahi with Key Lime and Sauternes on page 201, or the Sauce Mousseline that follows this recipe.) For a fancier preparation, place a crosswise slice of lemon in the center of each fillet, on top of the endive, before baking. In the spring, you should by all means add some fresh peas or wild asparagus.

This is delicious with boiled fingerling potatoes, a plain or mushroom risotto, or Sage-Potato Gnocchi Gratin (page 236).

½   **cup fava beans,** peeled, or fresh green peas

¼   **cup plus 2 tablespoons olive oil,** plus more for drizzling over fish

6   **skinless arctic char fillets,** 6 ounces each

   Fine sea salt and freshly ground black pepper to taste

¼   **cup plus 2 tablespoons dry vermouth**

¼   **cup plus 2 tablespoons dry white wine**

6   **small button mushrooms,** thinly sliced

3   **tablespoons chopped shallots**

2   **tablespoons chopped fresh tarragon**

20   **leaves Belgian endive (from 3 to 4 endive),** cut lengthwise into very thin julienne (see page 81)

1   **egg white,** lightly beaten, if using parchment paper (see Step 3)

BLANCH THE FAVA BEANS   Bring a pot of salted water to a boil. Fill a large bowl halfway with ice water. Add the fava beans to the boiling water and blanch for 2 minutes. (If using peas, blanch for just 1 minute.) Drain and transfer to the ice water to cool the beans and stop the cooking. Drain and set aside.

PREHEAT THE OVEN to 375°F.

PREPARE THE PAPILLOTE   Cut six 20 by 12-inch squares of parchment paper or aluminum foil. Lay them out before you. Put 1 tablespoon of olive oil on each. Season the char on both sides with salt and pepper, and put 1 fillet on top of the oil on each sheet of foil. Drizzle the fish with 1 tablespoon each of vermouth and white wine. Scatter the mushrooms, shallots, tarragon, and fava beans around the fish. Lay the endive slices crosswise on top of the fish. Season each serving with salt and pepper and drizzle lightly with olive oil. Seal the packets, using egg white as glue if using parchment paper.

BAKE THE PAPILLOTE Arrange the packets on 2 cookie sheets and bake in the oven until they begin to puff up, 10 to 12 minutes.

TO SERVE Put 1 parcel on each of 6 dinner plates and serve the fish in its package.

Wine Suggestion: Marc Colin, "Le Pitangeret" 1999; Saint Aubin. A crisp mineral-driven white from Burgundy with bright lemony acidity.

FAVA BEANS are seasonal spring beans sold in the pod. To cook them, you must first slice the pod open at the seam and remove the beans, which are encased in a thick, white outer shell that must be carefully removed after blanching or cooking them.

SAUCE MOUSSELINE

1½ cups Hollandaise Sauce (page 195)
2 tablespoons freshly squeezed lemon juice
½ cup heavy cream, whipped
Fine sea salt, freshly ground black pepper, and cayenne to taste

IN A BOWL, whisk together the Hollandaise Sauce and lemon juice, then fold in the cream. Season with salt, pepper, and cayenne.

FOIL-BAKED COD

serves ⑥ When I crave a light, simple meal that's also big on flavor, I make myself this dish. It's also delicious with rosemary instead of cumin. I like to serve the fish in the aluminum because of the cool, funky look, but the fish and vegetables can also be transferred to a shallow bowl.

Serve this with Sticky Rice (page 117).

1½ teaspoons grated fresh ginger
   Juice of 1 orange
3 tablespoons olive oil
4 cups spinach, tough stems removed, well rinsed
   Fine sea salt and freshly ground black pepper to taste
6 cod fillets, preferably Atlantic cod, 5 to 6 ounces each
½ teaspoon toasted cumin seeds
¼ teaspoon crushed red pepper flakes

PREHEAT the oven to 375°F.

PREPARE THE PARCELS In a mixing bowl, stir together the ginger, orange juice, and olive oil. Set out six 12 by 20-inch squares of aluminum foil. Put some spinach in the center of each piece and season it with salt and pepper. Season the fish with salt and pepper, and lay 1 piece on each bed of spinach. Drizzle the ginger-orange mixture over the fish. Divide the cumin and red pepper flakes over the fish. Wrap the foil around the fish twice to form a tight package, pressing down on the edges to seal it.

COOK THE FISH Bake the parcels until the fish is firm and opaque, 8 to 10 minutes.

TO SERVE Remove the packages from the oven and place 1 on each of 6 plates. Cut them open with a knife and serve.

Wine Suggestion: Sauvignon Blanc, Cakebread Cellars, 2002; Napa Valley. A fresh, bright white with notes of citrus, spice, and herbs.

POACHED COD IN SHELLFISH-SAFFRON BOUILLON

serves (6) This fish and shellfish chowder features another important ingredient: mushrooms. By using them in the mussel cooking liquid, their flavor infuses the entire dish. If you love clams, intensify their presence by reducing the clam liquid to ½ cup and adding it to the soup at the beginning of Step 5.

Sow hake is a good replacement for the cod. Serve this dish with baked fennel.

1½ pounds white baby creamer potatoes (about 24)

½ cup water

6 pounds cherrystone clams, scrubbed

2 tablespoons unsalted butter

1 cup thinly sliced shallots

4 garlic cloves, chopped

3 sprigs thyme

1 cup dry white wine

½ cup dry vermouth

5 button mushrooms, thinly sliced

2 celery stalks, diced

1 bay leaf

4 pounds blue mussels or Prince Edward Island mussels, debearded and scrubbed

1 cup heavy cream

Pinch saffron threads

Fine sea salt and freshly ground black pepper to taste

6 pieces boneless, skinless cod, 6 ounces each

1 pound small shrimp, peeled (about 18)

1 bunch watercress, bottoms trimmed

BOIL AND SLICE THE POTATOES Put the potatoes in a pot and cover them by 2 inches with cold water. Salt the water and set the pot over high heat. When the water boils, lower the heat until it is just simmering and continue to cook the potatoes until done (a sharp, thin-bladed knife will pierce easily to their center), approximately 8 minutes. Drain the potatoes and let them cool, then halve them. Set aside.

STEAM THE CLAMS Pour the ½ cup water into a large pot with a lid and bring it to a boil over high heat. As soon as the water boils, add the clams, cover, and steam until the clams pop open, approximately 5 minutes. Remove the pot from the heat and strain the contents through a fine-mesh strainer. Discard any clams that have not opened. Set the clams aside to cool. When they are cool enough to handle, reserve 18 clams in their shells and remove the remaining clams from their shells, discarding the empty shells.

COOK THE MUSSELS Put the butter in a large pot and melt it over medium heat. Add the shallots and sauté until softened but not browned, approximately 3 minutes. Add the garlic, thyme, wine, vermouth, mushrooms, celery, and bay leaf. Raise the heat and bring the liquid to a boil. Add the mussels and cover. When the mussels have opened, approximately 5 minutes, carefully turn the contents of the pot out into a fine-mesh strainer set over a pot. Discard any mussels that have not opened. Set the mussels aside and let them cool.

SHELL THE MUSSELS When the mussels have cooled, set aside 18 in their shells. Remove the remaining mussels from their shells, discarding the empty shells.

MAKE THE BOUILLON Set the pot over high heat, bring the liquid to a boil, and continue to boil until reduced by half. Add the cream and saffron, season with salt and pepper, and bring to a boil. Lower the heat so the liquid is simmering and carefully lower the cod pieces into the liquid. Poach the fish until it is opaque in the center, 6 to 8 minutes, depending on the thickness of the fish. After approximately 5 minutes, add the shrimp. During the last minute of cooking, add the clams, mussels, and potatoes and warm them through.

TO SERVE Put some watercress in the center of each of 6 bowls. Spoon a good mixture of fish and shellfish into the bowls, then spoon the bouillon over and around the ingredients.

Wine Suggestion: Domaines Ott, Clair de Noirs 2002; Côtes de Provence. An elegant French rosé with hints of strawberry and Mediterranean herbs.

MARINATED BLACK COD WITH ACACIA HONEY

serves (6) I made this recipe—one of my signature dishes—on Sara Moulton's television show when she invited chefs to cook with six ingredients or fewer. The acacia honey, which has an aroma similar to that of a flower, makes a complex impact, but you can also use other honeys, like wildflower. This is delicious with roasted parsnips, or with the fish served atop a bed of Wilted Spinach or Pea Shoots (recipe follows). Note that the fish marinates overnight, so be sure to plan ahead.

2 cups acacia honey
1 cup reduced-sodium (lite) soy sauce
¾ cup grapeseed oil
¾ cup white wine vinegar
6 black cod fillets, 7 ounces each
Fine sea salt and freshly ground black pepper to taste

MAKE THE MARINADE Combine the honey, soy sauce, grapeseed oil, and vinegar in a bowl. Give a stir and place the fish in the bowl. Cover, top with a weight such as a can, and refrigerate for 24 hours.

COOK THE FISH When ready to proceed, preheat the oven to 450°F. Remove the fish from the marinade and season all over with salt and pepper. Put the fillets on a baking sheet and cook in the oven until they have a golden dark-brown hue and are just cooked through, 7 to 8 minutes.

TO SERVE Put a fillet in the center of each of 6 plates. Spoon some marinade over and around the fish.

Wine Suggestion: Bergstrom, Pinot Noir 1999; Willamette Valley. A red from Oregon with bright red berry fruit.

WILTED SPINACH OR PEA SHOOTS

3 tablespoons unsalted butter

3 garlic cloves, chopped

12 to 15 cups baby spinach, stems removed, or pea shoots (see page 131)

Pinch grated nutmeg

Fine sea salt and freshly ground black pepper to taste

IN A LARGE heavy-bottomed sauté pan, melt the butter with the garlic over medium heat until the butter turns golden brown, 2 to 3 minutes. Add the spinach, turning with tongs as it wilts to make room for more in the pan. Season with nutmeg, salt, and pepper, and cook just until all the spinach is wilted.

SALT COD AUVERGNATE

serves (6) The Auvergne is a region of central France that is so well known for its simple, rustic cuisine that its name has come to signify just that. It was the inspiration for this dish, a rich, golden sauté of potatoes with salt cod that's been poached in milk flavored with peppercorns and thyme. It's as delicious to eat as it is easy to make. It would be even richer topped with a poached egg. Conversely, a simple dandelion salad would offer a pleasing, clean contrast.

Note that the salt cod must be soaked for 24 hours before making this dish.

1½   **pounds skinless salt cod**
2½   **cups whole milk**
2½   **cups water**
 1   **teaspoon black peppercorns**
 1   **sprig thyme**
 1   **bay leaf**
¼   **cup vegetable oil**
½   **cup chopped onion**
 5   **medium Idaho potatoes,** peeled and sliced into ¼-inch rounds
 2   **garlic cloves,** chopped
 3   **tablespoons unsalted butter**
 3   **tablespoons chopped parsley**
    Freshly ground black pepper to taste

SOAK THE SALT COD   Put the cod in a bowl, cover with cold water, cover, and soak in the refrigerator for 24 hours, changing the water 3 times.

POACH THE COD   Drain the cod and put it in a small pot. Pour the milk and water over it; add the peppercorns, thyme, and bay leaf. Set the pot over medium heat and bring the liquid to a simmer. Let simmer until the cod is cooked through, approximately 10 minutes. Remove the pot from the heat and let the fish cool in its cooking liquid.

SAUTÉ THE ONION AND POTATOES   Warm 1 tablespoon of the oil in a large sauté pan set over medium-high heat. Add the onion and sauté until translucent, 3 to 4 minutes. Use a slotted spoon to transfer the onion to a plate. Add half of the remaining olive oil to the sauté pan and half to another large skillet, and set both pans over medium heat. When the oil is hot, add half the potato slices to each pan and sauté, turning occasionally, until golden brown on both sides, 8 to 10 minutes per side.

FINISH THE DISH Remove the cod from its poaching liquid, dry it on a clean kitchen towel, and flake half of it over the potatoes in each pan. Divide the garlic, butter, and reserved onion between the 2 pans and continue to cook until the potatoes are crisp and the ingredients begin to clump together, approximately 5 minutes. Divide the parsley between the 2 pans, season with pepper, and toss.

TO SERVE Transfer the contents of both pans to a large serving bowl and present family-style in the center of the table.

Wine Suggestion: Domaines les Chenets, Crozes-Hermitage 2000; northern Rhône. A French white with aromas of flowers, lime, and minerals.

CRAYFISH AND CHICKEN CASSEROLE

serves ⑥ This is one of the few recipes in the book featuring poultry, but in this vaguely Cajun dish, crayfish and chicken legs seem made for each other. As you might guess from the use of crayfish, this was inspired by my memories of visiting New Orleans, where dishes like jambalaya, red beans and rice, and gumbo are often served family-style from a big casserole. To punch up the Cajun character, add your favorite spice mix.

If you can't put your hands on any crayfish, use head-on shrimp instead.

2 **cups sugar snap peas**
6 **pounds crayfish,** rinsed 3 times, dead ones removed, 6 reserved for garnish
⅓ **cup extra-virgin olive oil**
½ **cup Cognac**
1 **large carrot,** peeled and cut into large dice
1 **medium onion,** cut into large dice
1 **celery stalk,** cut into large dice
1 **head garlic,** halved crosswise
2 **tablespoons tomato paste**
4 **vine-ripened tomatoes,** chopped, or 1½ cups chopped canned tomatoes
1 **sprig thyme**
1 **bay leaf**
10 **parsley stems without their leaves**
1 **tablespoon black peppercorns**
2 **large Idaho potatoes,** peeled and cut into small dice
6 **chicken legs,** separated into drumsticks and thighs
1 **cup heavy cream**
2 **tablespoons chopped tarragon leaves**
Fine sea salt and freshly ground black pepper

BLANCH THE PEAS Bring a pot of lightly salted water to a boil. Fill a large bowl halfway with ice water. Add the sugar snap peas to the boiling water and blanch for 2 minutes. Drain and transfer the peas to the ice water to stop the cooking. Drain and set aside.

COOK THE CRAYFISH Bring a large pot of salted water to a boil over high heat. Fill a large bowl halfway with ice water. Add half the crayfish to the boiling water and cook for 2 minutes. Use tongs or a slotted spoon to transfer the crayfish to the ice water. Cook the remaining crayfish in the boiling water for 2 minutes and add them to the ice water. Drain the crayfish from the water. Separate the bodies from the heads by turning the first 2 knuckles to the left and the tail to the right. Then, pinch the very tip of the tail and, turning the shell and body in opposite directions, remove the meat of the body from its shell; the vein should pull away with the shell. Discard the shell and vein. Rinse the meat, pat it dry with paper towels, and set it aside. Put crayfish heads in a standing mixer fitted with the paddle attachment and paddle until coarsely chopped.

ROAST THE CRAYFISH HEADS Heat 2 tablespoons of the olive oil in a large casserole over high heat. Add the crayfish heads and roast until all moisture has been cooked out and the meat has turned red. Add the Cognac and ignite; cook until the Cognac is evaporated, approximately 2 minutes. Remove the crayfish heads and set aside.

ROAST THE VEGETABLES Add 2 tablespoons olive oil to the casserole and heat. Add the carrot, onion, celery, and garlic, and cook until the onion is translucent, about 4 minutes.

CONTINUE MAKING THE SAUCE Return the crayfish heads to the casserole. Add the tomato paste and stir to coat the vegetables with the paste. Cook 3 to 4 minutes. Add the tomatoes, thyme, bay leaf, parsley, and peppercorns, and cook until the tomatoes break down. Add 14 cups water, raise the heat, bring to a boil, then lower heat and let simmer for at least 45 minutes. Strain the soup through a fine-mesh strainer set over a bowl and return it to the casserole over medium heat. Cook until reduced by half.

COOK THE POTATOES Put the potatoes in a pot, cover with cold water, and set over high heat. Bring to a boil and continue to boil until the potatoes are tender, about 5 minutes. Drain and set aside.

BROWN THE CHICKEN Pour the remaining 1 tablespoon olive oil into a large sauté pan and heat it over high heat. Add the chicken legs and brown all over. Remove the pan from the heat and set aside.

FINISH THE DISH Add the cream to the casserole, bring to a boil, stir in the chicken, cook for 10 minutes to simmer, then add the potatoes, crayfish meat, 6 crayfish in their shells, and sugar snap peas.

TO SERVE Transfer the soup to a serving casserole or individual bowls, stir in the tarragon, and season with salt and pepper.

Wine Suggestion: Alvaro Palacios, Les Terraces 2000; Prioraot. A spicy, jammy Catalan wine with rich berry fruit and a touch of oak.

LEMON-CURRY FLOUNDER WITH CRISPY CAULIFLOWER

serves (6) *Meunière* is a classic fish preparation in which fillets are floured, sautéed, and finished with lemon juice, brown butter, and parsley. (Its name actually refers to the least interesting part of the recipe, the flour—*meunière* means "miller's wife.") Here, a *meunière* is rounded out with the combination of curried cauliflower that's been breaded and fried, so it resembles the fish's texture. Note that the cauliflower is optional; you could serve the fish and sauce with simple steamed rice or boiled potatoes and it would still be immensely satisfying.

6 **tablespoons unsalted butter**

6 **skinless flounder fillets,** 5 ounces each

Fine sea salt and freshly ground black pepper to taste

¾ **teaspoon curry powder**

3 **tablespoons capers,** rinsed and drained

3 **tablespoons chopped parsley leaves**

1 **teaspoon chopped garlic**

3 **tablespoons freshly squeezed lemon juice**

Crispy Cauliflower (optional; recipe follows)

COOK THE FISH Melt the butter in large skillet set over medium heat. Season the fish with salt and pepper. As soon as the butter turns golden, add the fish. Sauté until lightly browned, approximately 2 minutes, then turn the fish over and cook for 1 minute. Transfer 1 fillet to each plate. Add the curry, capers, parsley, garlic, and lemon juice to the pan and sauté for 1 minute to combine the flavors.

TO SERVE Spoon some sauce over and around the fish on each plate. If using, pass the cauliflower alongside in a bowl.

Wine Suggestion: Standing Stone, Gewürztraminer 2001; Finger Lakes. A dry aromatic white from New York State, with hints of lychee and Asian spices.

CRISPY CAULIFLOWER

serves ⑥ as an accompaniment This is a unique way to serve cauliflower by lightly frying it, which alters its texture dramatically.

½ **head cauliflower,** separated into florets
½ **cup grated Parmigiano-Reggiano cheese**
½ **cup panko (see page 73) or dry bread crumbs**
½ **cup all-purpose flour**
1 **egg,** lightly beaten
 Vegetable oil, for frying
 Fine sea salt
 Pinch cayenne

BRING A POT OF SALTED WATER to a boil. Fill a large bowl halfway with ice water. Add the cauliflower to the boiling water and blanch for 2 minutes. Drain and transfer to the ice water to cool it and stop the cooking. Drain and set aside. In a bowl, stir together the Parmigiano-Reggiano and bread crumbs. Dredge the cauliflower in the flour, then in the beaten egg, then the cheese-crumb mixture, shaking off any excess. Pour the oil into a pot to a depth of 2 inches and heat over high heat to a temperature of 375°F. Add the cauliflower and fry until golden brown, then use a slotted spoon to transfer the florets to a paper towel–lined plate and season with salt and cayenne.

ROASTED FLOUNDER WITH CHERRY TOMATOES AND CAPERS

serves (6) This is the kind of dish my grandmother would have cooked for us if we had fresh tomatoes in the garden—a simple dish of white fish cooked with tomatoes, capers, garlic, and thyme. You can serve the entire meal on one plate if you present the fish over a mixed green salad or atop Mashed Fingerling Potatoes (page 242).

30 **cherry tomatoes (about 2½ cups)**

6 **garlic cloves with the skin on,** crushed

3 **tablespoons capers,** rinsed and drained

2 **tablespoons balsamic vinegar**

5 **tablespoons olive oil**
Fine sea salt and freshly ground black pepper to taste

6 **flounder fillets,** 6 ounces each

I **tablespoon thyme leaves**

ROAST THE TOMATOES Preheat the oven to 400°F. In a bowl, combine the tomatoes, garlic, capers, vinegar, and 3 tablespoons olive oil, and season with salt and pepper. Transfer to a large roasting pan in a single layer and roast until the tomatoes begin to shrivel, 20 to 25 minutes.

COOK THE FISH Add the fish to the pan, resting the fillets on the tomatoes. Season with salt and pepper, and drizzle with the remaining 2 tablespoons olive oil. Sprinkle with the thyme leaves, and bake until firm and opaque, approximately 10 minutes.

TO SERVE Place 1 fillet on each of 6 plates. Spoon some vegetables and pan juices over and around the fish.

Wine Suggestion: Vouvray, Pinon, 2002; Loire Valley. A French white with bright acidity and notes of melon and earth.

GROUPER WITH INDIAN-STYLE BROTH

serves (6) Turmeric, a bright yellow powder, is part of just about any curry blend. Here, it flavors an intense broth, to which you can add hot chiles for a spicy result. This recipe calls for a freshly made chicken stock, a staple of Indian cooking, and Cerignola olives, which are large Italian olives shaped like ovals. They are brine-cured with a gently sweet flavor.

¾ cup broken angel hair pasta (¾-inch pieces)
15 chicken wings (about 2 pounds), each wing chopped into 4 pieces
1½ tablespoons turmeric
4 tablespoons olive oil
1 tablespoon toasted cumin seeds
1 medium onion, thinly sliced
8 garlic cloves, crushed, plus ½ teaspoon chopped garlic
3 dried chiles
¼ cup coarsely chopped fresh ginger
   Flesh of 4 Spiced Preserved Lemons (page 253), plus 2 teaspoons chopped
      preserved lemon skin
8 cups water
2 tablespoons vegetable oil
6 skinless grouper fillets, 6 ounces each
⅓ cup green Cerignola olives, pitted and thinly sliced
2 tablespoons chopped cilantro leaves
1 plum tomato, seeded and diced
2 tablespoons freshly squeezed lemon juice

TOAST THE ANGEL HAIR PASTA Preheat the oven to 375°F. Spread the pasta pieces out on a baking sheet in a single layer and toast in the oven until dark brown, 3 to 4 minutes. Remove the pan from the oven and set the pasta aside to cool.

MAKE THE BOUILLON Dust the chicken wings with the turmeric. Heat 2 tablespoons of the olive oil in a wide pot over medium heat. Add the wings and cumin, and stir to coat the wings. Cook, stirring, until the wings are uniformly golden brown, 15 to 20 minutes. Add the onion, crushed garlic, chile, and ginger, and cook, stirring, until the onion starts to brown. Add the Spiced Preserved Lemon flesh and water. Bring to a boil, lower the heat, and let simmer uncovered until 3½ cups liquid remain, 30 to 35 minutes. Strain the contents of the pot through a fine-mesh strainer set over a bowl. Discard the solids. Let the liquid rest for 5 minutes, then skim off any fat that rises to the surface.

COOK THE GROUPER Heat 3 tablespoons of the vegetable oil in a sauté pan set over medium-high heat. Add the fish and cook until golden brown on both sides, approximately 3 minutes per side.

FINISH THE BOUILLON Pour the bouillon into a large pot and bring to a boil over high heat. Lower the heat and add the angel hair pasta. Cook until *al dente,* about 2 minutes. Add the olives, cilantro, preserved lemon skin, tomato, lemon juice, chopped garlic, and remaining 2 tablespoons olive oil. Stir and cook for 30 seconds.

TO SERVE Spoon some pasta and bouillon into the bottom of 6 shallow bowls. Place a grouper fillet on top and serve.

Wine Suggestion: Pockl, Zweigelt 2000, Neusiedlersee. An eclectic Austrian red with nuances of red berries, pepper, and earthiness.

GRILLED HAKE "FOUR BY FOUR"

serves ⑥ This dish is based on one we made when I worked for Jacques Maximin at his Parisian restaurant Ledoyen. Its name comes from a classic dessert, a sly reference to the equal quantities of ingredients in the sauce and garnish. There is one ingredient that may exceed the indicated quantity: if the lemon is very acidic, you'll need to add a bit more butter to sweeten the sauce.

Hake is my favorite fish, but if you can't find it, this would also be delicious with cod or halibut. Pair this with gnocchi (page 236) or Broccoli Rabe with Garlic (page 250).

- **6 tablespoons bottled clam juice or water**
- **6 tablespoons extra-virgin olive oil**
- **6 tablespoons (¾ stick) unsalted butter,** cut into 6 pieces
- **6 tablespoons freshly squeezed lemon juice**
  - **Fine sea salt and freshly ground black pepper to taste**
- ¼ **cup olive oil**
- ¼ **cup thinly sliced sun-dried tomatoes**
- ¼ **cup Niçoise olives,** pitted and thinly sliced
- ¼ **cup thinly sliced scallions,** green part only
- **6 hake fillets,** 6 ounces each

MAKE THE SAUCE: Bring the clam juice to a boil in a small pot set over medium-high heat. Whisk in the extra-virgin olive oil, then the butter, one piece at a time. Stir in the lemon juice, season with salt and pepper, and set aside, covered, to keep it warm.

COOK THE VEGETABLES Warm 2 tablespoons of the olive oil in a small pot set over medium-high heat. Add the sun-dried tomatoes, olives, and scallions. Season with salt and pepper. Warm the vegetables, stirring, until they soften, 3 to 4 minutes. Set aside, covered, to keep warm.

SAUTÉ THE FISH Warm the remaining 2 tablespoons of olive oil in a large sauté pan over medium high heat. Season the fillets with salt and pepper. Add the fillets to the pan without crowding. Cook for 4 minutes on one side, then turn over and cook on the other side for 3 minutes, or until the fish is opaque in the center.

TO SERVE Put 1 fillet on the center of each of 6 dinner plates. Spoon some vegetables over each serving and spoon some sauce around the plate.

Wine Suggestion: Kollwentz, "Steinmuhle" Sauvignon Blanc 2001; Burgenland. A mouthwatering, citrus-laden white from Austria.

BACON-WRAPPED HAKE WITH CHILLED ARTICHOKE BROTH

serves (6) This dish is unusual and compelling because the hot fish with its crispy bacon "shell" is served in a cool broth. The contrast makes it especially appropriate for late spring and early summer, when the weather fluctuates between hot and cold.

To add even more flavor to the bacon-wrapped hake, throw a few crushed garlic cloves and a sprig or two of thyme into the sauté pan along with the fish. For an appropriate side dish, I recommend Potato Louisette (page 238).

 2 **ounces bacon,** diced (about ½ cup)
 4 **garlic cloves,** halved lengthwise
 ½ **cup finely diced onion**
 1 **sprig fresh thyme**
 1 **teaspoon black peppercorns**
18 **small cipolline onions (see page 47) or pearl onions,** peeled (about 6 ounces)
 6 **medium artichoke hearts,** cut into sixths
 1 **bay leaf**
 3 **cups dry white wine**
 2 **cups water**
 1 **small carrot,** sliced into ⅛-inch rounds
 ¼ **cup olive oil**
   Juice of ½ lemon
10 **large basil leaves,** chopped
   Fine sea salt and freshly ground black pepper to taste
 6 **hake fillets,** 6 ounces each
24 **paper-thin slices smoked bacon,** preferably apple-smoked
 2 **tablespoons unsalted butter**

MAKE THE ARITICHOKE BROTH   Put the bacon in a pot and cook over medium heat until it turns golden brown and renders enough fat to coat the bottom of the pan, approximately 5 minutes. Add the garlic, diced onion, thyme, peppercorns, cipolline onions, artichoke hearts, and bay leaf. Cook, stirring, for 2 to 3 minutes. Pour in the wine, raise the heat to high, and bring to a boil, then add the water. As soon as the liquid returns to a simmer, lower the heat and simmer, covered, until the artichokes are tender but still firm in the center, approximately 35 minutes, adding the carrot after 20 minutes. Remove the pot from the heat and let the liquid cool. Remove and discard the bay leaf, and stir in 2 tablespoons of the olive oil, the lemon juice, and the basil. Taste and season with salt and pepper. (The broth can be covered and refrigerated for a few hours, but no longer or it will turn black.)

WRAP THE FISH IN BACON Season the fish with salt and pepper. Lay 4 strips of bacon, slightly overlapping, on a work surface and lay a piece of hake across the narrow edge of the slices closest to you. Holding the fish and bacon firmly, roll away from yourself to tightly wrap the fish in the bacon. Repeat with the remaining fillets and bacon.

COOK THE FISH Heat the remaining 2 tablespoons olive oil in a large sauté pan. Add the butter and when the butter begins to foam, add the fish to the pan, seam side down. Cook to brown the bacon all over, approximately 4 minutes per side. To test for doneness, slide a sharp thin-bladed knife into the center of 1 fillet; remove it and touch it to your lips. If the knife is warm, the fish is done. You may need to do this in batches, or in 2 pans simultaneously.

TO SERVE Divide the cool broth among 6 shallow bowls, being sure to include 6 artichoke pieces in each bowl. Rest a bacon-wrapped fillet on top of the artichokes in each bowl and serve.

Wine Suggestion: Robert Jasmin, Côte Rôtie 1998; northern Rhône. A spicy French red with aromas of smoked bacon, plums, and olives.

MUSHROOM-CRUSTED HALIBUT WITH TRUFFLE OIL EMULSION

serves (6) Flaky white halibut is very receptive to the other flavors. Here it becomes a wonderful vehicle for mushrooms and truffle. To make this richer, serve it with a simple sauté of peas, bacon, and—if you're feeling decadent—diced black truffle.

When I lived in Las Vegas, I organized a dinner at Caesar's Palace at which the late, great French chef Jean-Louis Palladin cooked this dish. I offer it here as an homage to him.

2   tablespoons unsalted butter
2   **shallots,** finely chopped
2   **garlic cloves,** chopped
4   cups finely chopped button mushrooms
    Fine sea salt and freshly ground black pepper to taste
2   tablespoons olive oil
6   **skinless halibut fillets,** 7 ounces each
1   cup heavy cream
½   cup grated Parmigiano-Reggiano cheese
    Truffle oil, to taste

MAKE THE MUSHROOM CRUST Melt the butter in a wide, deep sauté pan set over medium-high heat. Add the shallots and sauté until softened but not browned, about 3 minutes. Add the garlic and sauté for 1 minute. Add the mushrooms, season with salt and pepper, and sauté until dry, 10 to 15 minutes. Remove the pan from the heat and let the mushrooms cool.

PREHEAT the broiler.

SAUTÉ THE FISH Heat the olive oil in a large sauté pan set over medium-high heat. Season the fillets with salt and pepper. When the oil is hot, add the fillets and cook until opaque in the center, 3 to 4 minutes per side. Transfer the fish to a baking sheet.

MAKE THE CREAM Warm the cream in a saucepan set over medium heat. Add the Parmigiano-Reggiano. Season with salt, pepper, and truffle oil, bearing in mind that the cheese may be salty enough.

CRUST AND REHEAT THE FISH Spread the mushrooms over the top of the fillets, covering them completely to a thickness of ¼ inch. Place under the broiler and broil until warmed, approximately 1 minute.

TO SERVE Spoon some sauce onto 6 warm plates. Top each with a fillet and serve at once.

Wine Suggestion: Parent, Pommard 1998; Burgundy. A hearty Pinot from France with nuances of mushrooms, earth, and red berries.

MUSTARD-CRUSTED HALIBUT

serves (6) This is such a simple recipe that there's really just one thing to remember: halibut cooks very fast and can dry out if overcooked even slightly.

For more flavor, finish the sauce by stirring in one-quarter of a Spiced Preserved Lemon (page 253), chopped, plus the juice of half a lemon. Serve it with Broccoli Rabe with Garlic (page 250) or Mashed Fingerling Potatoes (page 242).

6   **center-cut halibut steaks,** 6 ounces each
    Fine sea salt and freshly ground black pepper to taste
2   **tablespoons whole-grain mustard**
2   **teaspoons rosemary leaves**
½   **cup dry white wine**
1   **large shallot,** chopped
1   **garlic clove,** halved
½   **cup heavy cream**

PREHEAT THE OVEN to 375°F.

PREPARE THE FISH AND COOKING LIQUID Season the fish with salt and pepper. Spread the mustard and rosemary on 1 side of each steak. Put the wine, shallot, and garlic in a flameproof casserole. Add the fish in a single layer and bring the liquid to a boil over high heat.

BAKE THE FISH Transfer to the oven and bake until the fish is firm and opaque, approximately 10 minutes.

TO SERVE Transfer the fish to a platter. Stir the cream into the sauce, season with salt and pepper, and serve the sauce alongside the fish.

Wine Suggestion: Chardonnay, Forman, 2002; Napa Valley. An American Chardonnay that is clean and crisp, with integrated oak notes.

LOBSTER IN COCONUT AND CILANTRO BROTH

serves (6) This recipe is based on one I learned from Claude Troisgros, at C.T. restaurant in New York; that recipe in turn was based on a sauce from Bahia, Brazil, where they make it with palm oil. The use of sweet and unsweetened coconut milk and hot and sweet peppers creates a perfect balance. Serve this with Basmati Rice Galette (page 239) or Sticky Rice (page 117).

- 2 tablespoons olive oil
- ½ cup finely diced onion
- ½ **red bell pepper,** stem and seeds removed, diced
- ½ **green bell pepper,** stem and seeds removed, diced
- 1 **dried chile**
- 2 **garlic cloves,** chopped
- 3 **vine-ripened medium tomatoes,** seeded and diced
- 1 teaspoon Thai red curry paste (optional)
- 2 cups unsweetened coconut milk
- 3 tablespoons sweetened coconut milk
- 1 cup canned low-sodium chicken broth or water
  Juice of 1 lime
- 3 tablespoons chopped cilantro leaves
  Fine sea salt and freshly ground black pepper to taste
- 6 **lobsters,** 1¼ pounds each, poached in court bouillon (see page 274),
      all meat removed and reserved

MAKE THE SAUCE Warm the olive oil in a saucepan set over medium-high heat. Add the onion and red and green peppers, and cook until translucent, approximately 4 minutes. Add the chile and garlic, and sauté for another minute. Add the tomatoes and cook for 2 minutes. Add the curry paste, both coconut milks, and the broth. Raise the heat to high, bring to a boil, then lower the heat and let simmer for 4 minutes. Add the lime juice and cilantro. Season the sauce with salt and pepper. Add the lobster meat to the sauce and gently warm it through, covered, for 3 to 4 minutes.

TO SERVE Transfer the lobster and sauce to a large serving bowl and serve family-style from the center of the table. Or divide among 6 individual plates.

Wine Suggestion: Paul Blanck, "Schlossberg" Pinot Gris 1999; Alsace. A white from France with ripe tropical aromas and a touch of Asian spices.

GRILLED LOBSTER TAIL WITH TOMATO HOLLANDAISE

serves ⑥ The simple pleasures of this dish make it one of my favorites. It's based on *sauce choron*, a Béarnaise (or, less commonly, Hollandaise) sauce with tomato puree stirred into it, a perfect complement to the luxurious flavor and texture of lobster.

½ cup white wine vinegar

¼ cup dry white wine

3 tablespoons chopped shallots

5 tarragon stems, chopped, plus 2 tablespoons chopped leaves

1½ teaspoons cracked black peppercorns

5 egg yolks

1 pound unsalted butter, clarified (1¼ cups), warm (see page 275)

½ cup Oven-Roasted Tomatoes, warm (recipe follows)

Fine sea salt and freshly ground black pepper to taste

3 tablespoons olive oil

6 spiny lobster tails, 10 to 12 ounces each, halved lengthwise and deveined

Pinch cayenne

MAKE THE SAUCE Put the vinegar, wine, shallots, tarragon stems, and peppercorns in a pot and bring to a boil over high heat. Continue to boil until reduced by one-third, approximately 4 minutes. Set aside and let cool for a few minutes.

Whisk the yolks into the mixture, one at a time. Set the pot over another pot half full of simmering water and whisk, moving the bowl on and off the heat as necessary to avoid cooking the eggs. Continue whisking until the sauce is emulsified. (If the emulsion doesn't take, it's easy to fix; see page 275.) Remove the pot from the heat and let cool to the same temperature as the butter, then add the butter, slowly, whisking it in. Add the chopped tarragon leaves and warm Oven-Roasted Tomatoes, and season with salt and pepper.

GRILL THE LOBSTERS Prepare an outdoor grill for grilling or preheat the broiler. Spread the olive oil over the open face of the lobster tails and season them with salt, pepper, and cayenne. Grill the lobsters over indirect heat, or broil them, until firm and opaque.

TO SERVE Put 1 lobster tail on each of 6 plates and pass the sauce on the side.

Wine Suggestion: Château Rayas, La Pialade 1999; Côtes-du-Rhône. A medium-bodied, spicy French red with red berry and peppery aromas.

BÉARNAISE AND HOLLANDAISE SAUCES

makes about 1½ cups Classically, Hollandaise sauce is made with egg yolks, lemon juice, and butter. Béarnaise is a variation with chervil and tarragon added. Here's a basic Hollandaise recipe:

5 egg yolks
1 pound unsalted butter, clarified (1¼ cups), warm (see page 275)
2 tablespoons freshly squeezed lemon juice
  Fine sea salt and freshly ground black pepper to taste

PUT THE EGG YOLKS in a pot and set the pot over another pot half full of simmering water. Whisk the yolks, one at a time, moving the bowl on and off the heat as necessary to avoid cooking the eggs. Whisk in the lemon juice and remove the pot from the heat. Let the mixture cool to the same temperature as the butter, then add the butter, slowly, whisking it in. Season with salt and pepper.

OVEN-ROASTED TOMATOES

serves (6) as a garnish   These are a fine accompaniment to grilled fish and pasta dishes.

- **6 ripe plum tomatoes,** halved lengthwise
- **4 garlic cloves,** halved
- **Leaves from 3 thyme sprigs**
- **¼ cup extra-virgin olive oil**
- **1 teaspoon sugar**
- **Fine sea salt and freshly ground black pepper to taste**

PREHEAT THE OVEN to 375°F. Put all the ingredients in a bowl and gently toss. Remove the tomatoes from the bowl and place in a single layer in a cast-iron pan. Roast in the oven until the tomatoes dry and just begin to shrivel, approximately 2 hours. Remove the pan from the oven; remove the tomatoes from the pan, letting any excess oil run off, then pick out the garlic and coarsely chop while still hot. Serve alongside grilled fish, pasta, or other dishes.

POACHED LOBSTER WITH ICE WINE NAGE

serves (6) A *nage* is an aromatic broth served with seafood. Ice wine, made from late-harvest grapes picked during a frost and swiftly processed, is an unusual choice for a nage, but surprisingly pleasant. Some of the best ice wines come from Long Island, so use one from there for this dish.
Serve this with Horseradish Mashed Potatoes (see page 242).

12 tablespoons (1½ sticks) unsalted butter

 7 cipolline onions (see page 43) or pearl onions, sliced

 2 Belgian endive, cut into thin julienne strips

 2 carrots, peeled and cut crosswise into thin rounds

1½ cups white ice wine

   Juice of 1 orange

   Juiceof 1 lemon

¼ teaspoon saffron threads

   Fine sea salt and freshly ground black pepper to taste

 6 lobsters, 1½ pounds each, poached in court bouillon (see page 274), tail, claw, and knuckle meat removed from shell

 2 tablespoons chopped parsley leaves

MAKE THE SAUCE Melt 2 tablespoons of the butter in a sauté pan set over medium heat. Add the onions and sauté until translucent, approximately 4 minutes. Add the endive and carrots, and sauté for 2 minutes. Remove the pan from the heat, add the wine, and carefully ignite with a match. When the flames subside, add the orange juice, lemon juice, and saffron; bring to a boil over high heat. Strain the sauce over a bowl; reserve the liquid and vegetables. Whisk in the remaining butter or use an immersion blender to incorporate it. Season with salt and pepper. Return the vegetables to the pot with the sauce.

REHEAT THE LOBSTER Reheat the lobster meat very gently in the sauce over low heat so the butter doesn't separate and the lobster doesn't toughen.

TO SERVE Use a slotted spoon to put the pieces of the lobster and some vegetables in the center of each of 6 plates. (For a more striking presentation, spoon the meat into the shell.) Spoon some sauce and vegetables over and around each serving, and garnish with parsley.

Wine Suggestion: Cuilleron, Condrieu 2001; northern Rhône. An unctuous, aromatic French white with layers of apricot, honey, and wild flowers.

ROASTED LOBSTER AND AROMATIC BUTTER

serves (6) This visually stunning dish presents the whole lobsters on a platter. If you want to serve the lobster out of the shell, poach it rather than roasting it, following the instructions on page 274. Remove the meat from the lobster tails and claws in single, large pieces.

Serve this with sautéed Swiss chard or Creamy Rosemary Polenta (page 235).

6 **lobsters,** 1½ pounds each
  Fine sea salt and freshly ground black pepper to taste
3 **tablespoons olive oil**
⅓ **cup heavy cream**
½ **cup (1 stick) unsalted butter**
1½ **teaspoons chopped garlic**
1 **tablespoon chopped shallot**
3 **tablespoons reduced-sodium (lite) soy sauce**
2 **tablespoons freshly squeezed lime juice**
2 **tablespoons chopped cilantro leaves**
1 **tablespoon chopped tarragon leaves**
1 **teaspoon chopped parsley leaves**
1 **teaspoon chopped chives**

ROAST THE LOBSTER Preheat the broiler. Cut the lobsters in half through the head and all the way through to the tail, which will kill them instantly. Remove the eye sockets, devein the lobsters, and crack the claws. Season the insides with salt and pepper, and drizzle with olive oil. Put the lobsters in a roasting pan or two and broil until cooked through (test by piercing one lobster with a sharp, thin-bladed knife at the center and peering inside), 12 to 14 minutes.

MAKE THE AROMATIC BUTTER SAUCE In a small pot, combine the cream and butter, and set the pot over medium heat. Cook until the butter melts and turns brown, stirring to prevent scorching. Add the remaining garlic, shallot, soy sauce, and lime juice, and cook in the sauce for 1 minute. Stir in the cilantro, tarragon, parsley, and chives.

TO SERVE Arrange the lobsters on a large, oval platter. Spoon some sauce over and around the lobsters, and serve the remaining sauce on the side.

Wine Suggestion: Kistler, "Les Noisetières" Chardonnay 2001; Russian River Valley. A rich white from California, with aromas of pears, quince, lees, and toast.

GRILLED MACKEREL WITH WARM LEEK AND POTATO SALAD

serves ⑥ The potato salad in this recipe isn't the cold, mayonnaise-dressed version you probably associate with picnics and barbecues. Rather, it's a warm combination of fingerling potatoes and leeks tossed with mustard vinaigrette. Timing is essential to getting this dish right; you want the potatoes to be warm but not hot.

I think you'll find mackerel a very forgiving fish to work with. Because of its relatively high fat content, it stays moist even after grilling, meaning that it doesn't overcook as easily as many other fish.

Serve this with Endive Salad with Blue Cheese and Walnuts (recipe follows) or Roasted Red Onions with Honey and Balsamic Vinegar (page 248).

I **medium shallot,** finely chopped

I **garlic clove,** finely chopped

2 **tablespoons dry white wine**

I **tablespoon white wine vinegar**

I **tablespoon whole-grain mustard**

I **tablespoon Dijon mustard**

    Fine sea salt and freshly ground black pepper to taste

6 **pounds medium fingerling potatoes (about 48)**

3 **leeks,** well rinsed

6 **skin-on mackerel fillets,** 4 to 5 ounces each, skin scored

3 **tablespoons extra-virgin olive oil**

2 **tablespoons coarsely chopped fresh rosemary**

PREPARE AN OUTDOOR GRILL for cooking, letting the coals burn until covered with white ash, or preheat an indoor grill.

MAKE THE VINAIGRETTE Put the shallot, garlic, white wine, vinegar, mustards, and olive oil in a bowl and whisk together. Season with salt and pepper. Set aside.

COOK THE POTATOES Put the potatoes in a large pot and cover by a few inches with cold water. Set the pot over high heat, bring to a boil, then lower the heat and simmer until the potatoes are done (a sharp, thin-bladed knife will pierce easily to the center of a potato), 20 to 30 minutes. Drain them and, when cool enough to handle but still warm, cut them crosswise into ½-inch rounds.

COOK THE LEEKS AND FINISH THE SALAD Fill another pot with salted water and bring it to a boil over high heat. Fill a bowl halfway with ice water. Add the leeks to the boiling water and cook until tender, 10 to 12 minutes. Use tongs or a slotted spoon to transfer them to the ice water to shock them and set the color. Drain them, pat them dry, and slice them crosswise into ½-inch pieces. Gently toss the leeks and warm potatoes with the vinaigrette.

GRILL THE FISH Season the fish with salt and pepper. Drizzle with the olive oil and scatter some rosemary on both sides. Grill the fish, skin side up, pressing down with tongs or a spatula to keep it from curling. Cook for approximately 2 minutes on each side, depending on the thickness of the fish.

TO SERVE Mound some warm potato salad in the center of each of 6 warm dinner plates. Lean a mackerel fillet against the salad on each plate and serve at once.

Wine Suggestion: Clos Floridene, Graves 1998; Bordeaux. A white from France with citrus and melon notes and a hint of grassiness.

ENDIVE SALAD WITH BLUE CHEESE AND WALNUTS

serves ⑥ as an accompaniment This is a perfect, simple fall salad that can be eaten on its own or as a side dish.

3 large Belgian endive, thinly sliced crosswise on the bias
1 cup walnut halves, lightly toasted
¾ cup crumbled Stilton cheese, or other mild blue cheese (about 3 ounces)
5 small button mushrooms, thinly sliced
2 tablespoons chopped chives
2 tablespoons Banyuls or sherry vinegar
3 tablespoons walnut oil
   Fine sea salt and freshly ground black pepper to taste

PUT THE ENDIVE, walnuts, cheese, mushrooms, and chives in a bowl. Drizzle the vinegar and oil over the salad and season it with salt and pepper. Toss and serve.

GRILLED MAHI MAHI WITH KEY LIME AND SAUTERNES

serves (6) The unusual sauce that tops the fish here, combining Key lime and Sauternes, tastes like sweet-and-sour candy. Use the best butter you can find for this—it's essential to keeping the other flavors in balance. To add complexity, season the fish with caraway seeds as well as salt and pepper before grilling. Serve this with Watercress and Cucumber Salad (page 46) or Basmati Rice Galette (page 239).

> **Grated zest of 5 Key limes,** or regular limes (about 1 tablespoon),
>   plus the juice of ½ lime
> ½ **cup Sauternes or other sweet white wine**
> ¼ **cup water**
> 1 **cup (2 sticks) cold unsalted butter,** diced
>   **Fine sea salt and freshly ground black pepper to taste**
> 6 **skinless mahi mahi fillets,** about 6 ounces each
>   **Olive oil,** for grilling

PREPARE an outdoor or indoor grill for grilling.

BLANCH THE LIME ZEST   Bring a small pot of lightly salted water to a boil. Add the lime zest and blanch it for 20 seconds. Strain through a fine-mesh strainer and set aside.

MAKE THE SAUCE   Put the Sauternes and water in a saucepan and bring to a boil over high heat. Add the butter, one piece at a time, whisking or blending it in with an immersion blender. Add the lime zest and season with salt and pepper.

GRILL THE FISH   Season the fish with salt and pepper. Oil the grill grate and grill the fish until nicely browned on both sides, 3 to 4 minutes per side (Time will vary depending on thickness of the fish, heat of the grill, and proximity of the grate to the flame.)

TO SERVE   Put 1 fillet on each of 6 plates and spoon some sauce over the top.

Wine Suggestion: Domaine Cauhape, Jurançon Sec 1998; Jurançon. A southwestern French white with aromas of melon and lime zest.

ROASTED MONKFISH WITH TOMATO, FLAGEOLET BEANS, AND CHORIZO

serves (6) This is a great winter stew that I recommend for serving to family or friends, right from the center of the table with bread alongside for soaking up the sauce. For a more dramatic osso buco–like presentation, ask your fishmonger to leave the bone in the monkfish and cut the pieces right through the bone.

Bear in mind that the beans need to be soaked overnight before you can begin the recipe.

2 cups dried *flageolet* beans
2 large portobello mushrooms, stems removed
¼ cup olive oil
Fine sea salt and freshly ground black pepper to taste
8 ounces chorizo (2 links), thinly sliced
2 tablespoons diced bacon
¼ cup chopped onion
5 garlic cloves, chopped
1 bay leaf
2 sprigs thyme
1 teaspoon dried oregano
1 dried chile
2 sage leaves, chopped
4 medium vine-ripened tomatoes, chopped
1 cup dry white wine
5 cups canned low-sodium chicken broth
6 monkfish tails (the ends, which look like a shank, or osso buco, with a bone down the middle), 6 ounces each, tied

SOAK THE BEANS Soak the beans overnight in enough cold water to cover them by at least 2 inches. Drain.

ROAST THE MUSHROOMS Preheat the oven to 375°F. Brush the mushrooms with 1 tablespoon of the olive oil, season with salt and pepper, put on a baking sheet, and roast in the oven until lightly browned and fragrant, 15 to 20 minutes. Let the mushrooms cool, then dice them and set aside.

SAUTÉ THE CHORIZO Put the chorizo in a sauté pan and set over low heat. Cook over medium heat until crisp, approximately 10 minutes. Remove to a paper towel–lined plate, but keep the fat in the pan.

MAKE THE STEW Sauté the bacon with the remaining 3 tablespoons olive oil in a large pot set over medium-high heat until crisp, approximately 5 minutes. Add the onion, garlic, bay leaf, thyme, oregano, chile, and sage, and sauté until the onion is translucent, approximately 4 minutes. Add the tomatoes, beans, and white wine, and bring to a boil. Add the chicken broth and bring to a boil. Lower the heat and simmer until the beans are tender, approximately 45 minutes.

Pick out and discard the bay leaf. Add the mushrooms and chorizo to the pot.

SAUTÉ THE FISH Heat the chorizo's oil in its sauté pan over medium heat. Season the monkfish with salt and pepper. Put the fish in the pan and cook on both sides until lightly browned, 4 to 5 minutes per side. Transfer the fish to the pot with the beans and gently warm over medium heat to finish cooking. Taste and adjust seasoning with salt and pepper.

TO SERVE Present the stew from its pot family style, from the center of the table.

Wine Suggestion: Heredad Corinda, Rioja Reserva 1998; Rioja. A medium-bodied Spanish red with aromas of stewed tomatoes, red cherries, and herbs.

MOUCLADE

serves (6) A *mouclade* is a regional French mussel dish in which the mussels are cooked just as they are for *moules marinière*, or mussels steamed in white wine with shallots, garlic, and herbs. (My version of that dish is on the facing page). To make a mouclade, the cooking liquid is thickened with cream and the mussels are served on the half-shell, topped with a spoonful of the sauce.

I make my mouclade with curry powder, and an addition of cornstarch makes the thickening process foolproof. The presentation here is more user-friendly than in the original: You simply return the mussels to the pot and serve them family-style from the center of the table.

This is delicious with Corn and Scallion Pancakes (page 249).

2 **cups dry white wine**
4 **medium shallots,** sliced
2 **garlic cloves**
1 **tablespoon curry powder,** or more to taste
6 **pounds mussels,** scrubbed and debearded
½ **cup coarsely chopped parsley**
1 **cup heavy cream**
1 **tablespoon cornstarch mixed with 2 tablespoons water**
Fine sea salt and freshly ground black pepper to taste

COOK THE MUSSELS Put the wine, shallots, garlic, and curry powder in a saucepan and bring to a boil over high heat. Add the mussels and parsley, cover, and cook until the mussels open, approximately 3 minutes. Drain the mussels in a fine-mesh strainer set over a pot. Discard any mussels that have not opened.

MAKE THE SAUCE Reheat the strained liquid over medium heat. Stir in the cream and cornstarch, and season with salt and pepper.

TO SERVE Return the mussels to the pot and bring the pot to the table.

Wine Suggestion: Gewurztraminer, Standing Stone, 2002; Finger Lakes. An aromatic white to complement the curry with spice and tropical notes.

MUSSELS STEAMED IN WHITE WINE

serves (6) This is the mussel dish my mother used to make for me at home. She made hers with flour to thicken the cooking liquid and make it more of a soup; I've removed the flour, but don't tell her. I sometimes add a slice of rye bread to each bowl before it's served; the bread soaks up the broth and becomes incredibly flavorful. Splurge for the best mussels you can find because they are the centerpiece of this dish.

French fries and beer are the perfect accompaniments to these mussels.

4 **medium shallots,** chopped

3 **tablespoons unsalted butter**

½ **small bunch parsley,** stems removed and reserved, 3 tablespoons chopped
   leaves set aside

2 **garlic cloves,** chopped

1 **sprig thyme**

1 **bay leaf**

2 **cups dry white wine**
   Few grinds black pepper

6 **pounds blue mussels or Prince Edward Island mussels,** cleaned and debearded
   Country bread, sliced

COOK THE MUSSELS Put the shallots, butter, parsley stems, garlic, thyme, bay leaf, white wine, and pepper in a stockpot and set over high heat. Bring to a boil, add the mussels, cover, and cook until they open, approximately 5 minutes. Remove the cover, then remove and discard any mussels that have not opened.

TO SERVE Transfer the mussels and liquid to a large bowl, scatter the chopped parsley over the bowl, and serve from the center of the table. Give each person a soup bowl, a spoon for eating the broth, and country bread for soaking up every last drop. Pass an empty bowl for collecting the shells.

Wine Suggestion: Bisci, Verdicchio di Matelica 2001; Marches. An Italian white with hints of sea salt and lemon.

WALLEYE PIKE WITH BACON-BURGUNDY SAUCE

serves ⑥ A *meurette* is a classic Burgundian dish, in which a river fish is cooked in red wine. This recipe is based on that method, with bacon, mushrooms, and croutons added. Pearl onions are another classic addition, but I prefer to accompany the dish with Caramelized Cipolline Onions and Brussels Sprouts (page 252). This is also delicious with Sage-Potato Gnocchi Gratin (page 236), which is a great vehicle for soaking up the extra sauce. Classically, a *meurette* is topped with a poached egg, but I've made that optional here since the combination isn't for all tastes.

> 1 cup chopped bacon (in ¾-inch lardons; see page 276)
> 10 medium button mushrooms, trimmed and sliced ¾ inch thick
> Fine sea salt and freshly ground black pepper to taste
> 1 large shallot, finely chopped
> 1 garlic clove, chopped
> 4 cups red wine
> Leaves from 2 thyme sprigs
> 1 cup (2 sticks) unsalted butter, cut into about 16 pieces
> 2 tablespoons vegetable oil
> 6 skinless walleye pike fillets, 6 ounces each
> 6 slices country bread, ½ inch thick, grilled or toasted
> 6 eggs, poached (optional)

SAUTÉ THE BACON Put the bacon in a sauté pan and set over low heat. Cook, stirring, until golden brown and crisp, 5 to 7 minutes. Transfer the bacon to a paper towel–lined plate and set aside. Add the mushrooms to the pan with the bacon fat and sauté until they give off their liquid and the liquid evaporates, approximately 8 minutes. Season with salt and pepper and set aside.

MAKE THE SAUCE Put the shallot, garlic, red wine, and thyme in a medium saucepan and set over high heat. Bring to a boil and continue to boil until reduced to 1 to 2 tablespoons of syrupy liquid, 20 to 25 minutes. Remove the pan from the heat and add the butter, one piece at a time, whisking it into the shallot and wine. If the sauce cools too much to accept more butter, return it to low heat briefly, taking care to not let it become too hot and separate. Season with salt and pepper. Add the mushrooms and bacon to the sauce.

COOK THE FISH Pour the vegetable oil into a sauté pan and set it over medium-high heat. Add the fish and cook until golden brown on both sides and opaque in the center, approximately 3 minutes per side.

TO SERVE Put a slice of grilled bread in the center of each of 6 warm plates. Top with a fish fillet and a poached egg, if you like. Spoon the sauce over and around the fish and serve at once.

Wine Suggestion: Domaine Forey, Pinot Noir 2000; Vosne-Romanée. A red from Burgundy, with good structure and aromas of wild berries.

GRILLED POMPANO WITH VEGETABLE SALSA

serves (6) This is a very simple summertime dish, a logical use for pompano, which comes from the waters around southern Florida. The accompanying Vegetable Salsa (recipe follows) is really more of a chopped vegetable salad featuring tomatoes, avocado, pepper, and onion. Serve this with Corn and Scallion Pancakes (page 249) or Creamy Rosemary Polenta (page 235).

6 medium artichoke bottoms, sliced paper-thin, ideally with a mandoline
Juice of 1 lemon
Olive oil, for brushing
Fine sea salt and freshly ground black pepper to taste
6 pompano fillets, 5 ounces each
Vegetable Salsa (recipe follows)

PREPARE AN OUTDOOR GRILL for grilling, letting the coals burn down until covered with white ash, or preheat an indoor grill.

PREPARE THE ARTICHOKES Dress the artichoke slices with lemon juice and olive oil, and season them with salt and pepper.

GRILL THE FISH Season the pompano with salt and pepper, and brush with olive oil. Put on the grill skin side down and grill for 2 to 3 minutes on each side, depending on the thickness of the fish.

TO SERVE Mound some salsa in the center of each of 6 plates and arrange a fillet on top of each mound. Top each serving with artichoke slices.

Wine Suggestion: Luigi Maffini, "Kratos" Fiano 2001; Campania. A southern Italian white with aromas of acacia and pineapple.

VEGETABLE SALSA

serves ⑥ as an accompaniment Pair this salsa with Baked Whole Sea Bass with Meyer Lemon (page 164) or Grilled Hake "Four by Four" (page 187).

- 2 **medium vine-ripened tomatoes,** diced
- 1 **avocado,** diced
- 1 **yellow bell pepper,** finely diced
- ½ **red onion,** finely diced
- 1 **garlic clove,** chopped
- ⅓ **cucumber,** finely diced
- 1 **jalapeño pepper,** finely diced
- **Juice of 2 limes**
- ½ **cup olive oil**
- 2 **tablespoons chopped cilantro leaves**
- **Fine sea salt and freshly ground black pepper to taste**

IN A BOWL, stir together the tomatoes, avocado, bell pepper, red onion, garlic, cucumber, jalapeño, lime juice, olive oil, and cilantro. Season with salt and pepper. Cover and let marinate for at least 1 hour in the refrigerator.

SEMI-SMOKED SALMON WITH APPLE BROTH

serves (6) In this dish, the refreshing broth, with its clean flavor and garnish, bring apple, pea shoots, and radish sprouts to the plate, all offering a pronounced contrast to the smoky fish. It's especially delicious and beautiful with white Alaskan King salmon, if you can find it, but any variety works well. Note that the fish is first smoked lightly to perk up the flavors, then sautéed to finish cooking.

You can also cook this in a covered, outdoor grill.

1 **cup hardwood chips,** preferably applewood

2 **Granny Smith apples,** cut into large wedges, plus ¼ apple cut into very thin julienne
strips and tossed with lemon juice

5 **tablespoons unsalted butter**

½ **teaspoon Dijon mustard**

Fine sea salt and freshly ground white pepper to taste

1 **garlic clove,** minced

7 **ounces pea shoots (see page 131) or well-trimmed watercress sprigs**

Pinch nutmeg

6 **skinless center-cut salmon fillets,** 6 ounces each

½ **Red Delicious apple,** cut into very thin julienne strips and tossed with lemon juice

¼ **cup daikon radish or red radish sprouts**

SOAK THE WOOD CHIPS in warm water for about 20 minutes. Start a smoker with the chips inside.

MAKE THE APPLE BROTH Juice the apple wedges in a juicer. (If you don't have a juicer, puree the apples in a food processor fitted with the steel blade and strain the puree through a fine-mesh strainer, pressing down on the solids to extract as much liquid as possible.) Put the apple juice in a saucepan set over medium heat. Blend in 4 tablespoons of the butter and the mustard with an immersion blender, or by whisking vigorously by hand, until incorporated. Season with salt and pepper and strain through a fine-mesh strainer set over a bowl.

WILT THE GREENS In a pan, melt the remaining 1 tablespoon butter and continue to cook until it turns brown. Add the garlic and pea shoots, and cook over high heat, tossing, until wilted, 2 to 3 minutes. Season with salt, pepper, and nutmeg, and set aside.

SMOKE THE SALMON Cook the salmon in the smoker until fragrant but still rare in the center, approximately 10 minutes. (The salmon and sauce can be made to this point, cooled, covered, and refrigerated separately for up to 24 hours. Let come to room temperature before proceeding.)

SAUTÉ THE SALMON Warm a large nonstick skillet over medium-high heat. Add the salmon and cook until lightly golden brown, approximately 2 minutes per side. Remove from the heat.

TO SERVE Divide the pea shoots among 6 warm dinner plates. Top each serving with 1 fillet. Scatter the julienned red and green apple around the plates with the radish sprouts. Reheat the apple broth over high heat, again blending with an immersion blender or whisking until foamy, and spoon it over the fish. Serve at once.

Wine Suggestion: Bernard Moreau, Les Chenevottes 2000; Chassagne-Montrachet. A white Burgundy with nuances of apple, smoke, and slight toast.

SALT-CRUSTED SALMON

serves (6) This age-old and simply brilliant method of cooking salmon keeps all the moisture inside, resulting in a succulent cooked fish whose silky texture is perfectly matched by the salt crust. Since the salmon can't be removed from the salt after cooking (the meat fuses to the salt), consider presenting the fish on the same tray on which it's been cooked.

Serve with olive oil or Sauce Mousseline (page 172). For an accompaniment, try this with the Grilled Summer Vegetable Tart (page 244) alongside.

Zest of 2 lemons
2 tablespoons chopped fresh dill
1 tablespoon olive oil
5 cups coarse sea salt
2½ to 3 pounds salmon fillet, center cut

MARINATE THE SALMON In a bowl, stir together the lemon zest, dill, and olive oil. Rub the salmon with the mixture and let marinate, refrigerated, for 1 hour.

BAKE THE SALMON Preheat the oven to 350°F. Mound about 2 cups of the salt on a baking tray. Lay the salmon on top and mound the remaining salt over the fish, completely encasing it. Bake in the oven 15 to 20 minutes for medium rare to medium, or longer if desired.

TO SERVE Present the salmon at the table right away. Remove the salt with a knife or spoon, and cut the fish into 6 portions.

Wine Suggestion: Chablis, Bernard Defaix, 2002; Burgundy. A fresh, crisp white with aromas of lemon and minerals.

SALMON STEAK WITH GINGER-CHILE GLAZE

serves ⑥ When I serve this dish in my restaurants, I use galangal, in place of the ginger. Galangal is a popular root in Asian cooking because of its gingery, peppery flavor. If there's an Asian market in your city or town, you can probably find it frozen and use it in this dish. Serve this with Sticky Rice (page 117), Corn and Scallion Pancakes (page 249), or Broccoli Rabe with Garlic (page 250).

4 fresh red chiles, chopped
2 tablespoons grated fresh ginger or galangal
2 cups orange juice
⅔ cup reduced-sodium (lite) soy sauce
½ cup white wine vinegar
⅔ cup sugar
2 tablespoons olive oil
   Fine sea salt and freshly ground black pepper to taste
6 center-cut salmon steaks, 1 inch thick, 6 to 7 ounces each
2 limes, halved
⅓ cup chopped cilantro leaves

MAKE THE SAUCE Put the chiles, ginger, orange juice, soy sauce, vinegar, and sugar in a pot. Bring to a boil over high heat and let boil, stirring occasionally, until reduced to 1 cup, approximately 12 minutes. Remove the pot from the heat and let the contents cool.

MARINATE THE SALMON Put the salmon steaks in a bowl. Pour the sauce over them and turn gently to coat the steaks with the sauce. Cover with plastic wrap and let marinate for 1 hour in the refrigerator.

COOK THE SALMON Heat the olive oil in a nonstick pan set over medium-high heat. Season the salmon on both sides with salt and pepper. When the oil is hot but not smoking, add the salmon steaks to the pan and cook until pink in the center, approximately 3 minutes per side. Pour the remaining marinade over the fish in the pan. Squeeze the limes over the fish, catching any seeds with your hands. Scatter the cilantro over the fish.

TO SERVE Divide the steaks among 4 dinner plates and serve at once.

Wine Suggestion: Kunin, "French Camp" Syrah 2000; Paso Robles. A spicy California red with jammy blackberry and raspberry notes.

GRILLED SHRIMP KEBABS

serves (6) Kebabs, in which fish, meat, and/or vegetables are skewered and grilled over an open flame, are real crowd-pleasers; diners in restaurants and home settings alike love pushing the ingredients off the skewer and eating them in whatever order they please. So I recommend this to you for large gatherings.

For this dish, you'll need 6 wooden skewers, soaked in water.

1 **pound large shrimp (about 30),** preferably head-on, peeled and deveined
1 **tablespoon Chinese chile sauce**
¾ **cup reduced-sodium (lite) soy sauce**
1 **bunch cilantro,** stems removed, leaves chopped
3 **scallions,** green part only, sliced
½ **cup chopped salted roasted peanuts**
2 **tablespoons honey**
1 **tablespoon Asian sesame oil**
2 **tablespoons olive oil**
2 **garlic cloves,** chopped
Fine sea salt and freshly ground black pepper to taste

PREPARE A HOT FIRE in an outdoor grill or preheat a grill pan.

MARINATE THE SHRIMP Put the shrimp in a bowl, add the remaining ingredients, and toss well to combine and coat the shrimp. Cover and let marinate in the refrigerator for 45 minutes. (If you prefer to serve shrimp in their shells, marinate them for 2 hours.)

GRILL THE SHRIMP Remove the shrimp from the bowl, shaking off any excess marinade. Impale 5 shrimp on each skewer and place on the grill. Cook, turning, until firm and pink on all sides, approximately 5 minutes, basting with the marinade.

TO SERVE Arrange the skewers on a platter and serve hot from the grill.

Wine Suggestion: Peachy Canyon, "Westside" Zinfandel 2000; Paso Robles. A spicy and jammy red from California, perfect for barbecued food.

SHRIMP OMELET

serves ⑥ Because it features shellfish, this omelet is a perfect, surprising dish for lunch or even dinner. The Vietnamese make sandwiches with this omelet, chiles, cucumber, and cream cheese. If you decide to do the same, enjoy it with reduced-sodium soy sauce and a watercress salad.

> 2 **ounces bacon,** diced (about ½ cup)
> 5 **medium shiitake mushrooms,** thinly sliced
> 1 **large shallot,** chopped
> **Fine sea salt and freshly ground black pepper to taste**
> 12 **eggs**
> 1 **medium carrot,** shredded
> ½ **cup chopped scallions,** green and white parts
> ½ **cup chopped cilantro leaves**
> 2 **tablespoons Vietnamese fish sauce** (*nuoc mam*)
> 1½ **pounds medium shrimp,** peeled and deveined
> 2 **tablespoons sesame oil**

PREHEAT THE OVEN to 375°F.

COOK THE BACON AND VEGETABLES Sauté the bacon in a deep-sided heavy-bottomed ovenproof sauté pan set over medium heat until it renders enough fat to coat the bottom of the pan, approximately 8 minutes. Add the mushrooms and shallot, and season with salt and pepper. Cook, stirring, until the shallot and mushrooms are golden brown, approximately 8 minutes. Remove the pan from the heat.

COOK THE OMELET Beat the eggs in a mixing bowl. Stir in the bacon and mushrooms, carrot, scallions, cilantro, fish sauce, and shrimp. Season with salt and pepper. Heat the sesame oil in the same sauté pan over medium heat. Add the egg mixture, transfer the pan to the oven, and bake until the eggs are set, the shrimp are firm and pink, and the top of the omelet is lightly golden, 30 to 35 minutes.

TO SERVE Unmold the omelet onto a plate, slice into 6 equal portions, and serve warm or at room temperature.

Wine Suggestion: Pinot Gris, King Estate, 2002; Willamette Valley. An American white with tropical, spice, and mineral notes.

SKATE BARBECUE WITH BRAISED COLLARD GREENS

serves (6) Early in my career, I took a year off and traveled all over the United States. One of the types of foods I most enjoyed discovering was barbecue, which most people here think of as simple. While it's true that barbecue is easy to cook, I think the flavors are actually quite complex. This is my version of a fish with barbecue flavors using skate, a homemade sauce, and one of the most popular accompaniments for real Southern barbecue—braised collard greens. Serve this with Fried Baked Potato (page 251), an easy-to-make side that includes ingredients found in many popular barbecue pairings, such as fried potatoes, cheese, and bacon.

¾ cup ketchup

¼ cup honey

2 tablespoons reduced-sodium (lite) soy sauce

½ cup canned low-sodium chicken broth

1 tablespoon chopped fresh ginger

1½ teaspoons chopped garlic

1 dried chile

2 tablespoons red wine vinegar

1 tablespoon chopped mint leaves

1 tablespoon Liquid Smoke (optional)

3 tablespoons unsalted butter

Fine sea salt and freshly ground black pepper to taste

6 boneless skate wings, 6 ounces each

½ cup Wondra flour (see page 53)

2 tablespoons vegetable oil

Braised Collard Greens (recipe follows)

MAKE THE BARBECUE SAUCE Put the ketchup and honey in a small pot and cook until the mixture turns a dark caramelized color. Add the soy sauce, bring to a boil over high heat, and let boil for 2 minutes. Add the broth, bring to a boil, then lower the heat and let simmer for 5 minutes. Add the ginger, garlic, and chile, and cook until the mixture coats the back of a spoon. Add the vinegar, mint, Liquid Smoke (if using), and butter. Season with salt and pepper. Set the sauce aside.

COOK THE FISH Season the skate wings with salt and pepper and dredge them in the flour, shaking off any excess. Heat the vegetable oil in a sauté pan set over medium-high heat. Add the skate wings and cook until golden brown on both sides, approximately 3 minutes per side.

TO SERVE Mound some Braised Collard Greens in the center of each of 6 plates. Lean a skate wing against the greens, and spoon some sauce around the plate.

Wine Suggestion: Vina Sastre, Roble 2000; Ribera del Duero. An earthy Spanish red with hints of spice cabinet and blackberries.

BRAISED COLLARD GREENS

serves ⑥ as an accompaniment Serve these alongside barbecue and other Southern-style cooking.

    Fine sea salt
2 **large bunches collard greens,** leaves only
2 **ounces bacon,** finely diced (about ½ cup)
2 **large garlic cloves,** smashed
10 **tablespoons (1 stick plus 2 tablespoons) unsalted butter**

BRING A LARGE POT of salted water to a boil over high heat. Fill a large bowl halfway with ice water. When the water comes to a boil, add the collard greens and blanch for 6 to 8 minutes. Drain and transfer the greens to the ice water to stop the cooking and preserve their color. Remove from the water and squeeze out any excess liquid. Coarsely chop the greens and set them aside.

IN A MEDIUM POT, sauté the bacon over medium heat until golden brown, 4 to 5 minutes. Add the garlic and sauté for 1 minute, then pour off the fat. Add the collard greens and cook, stirring, just until wilted. Add the butter, one piece at a time, stirring so the greens absorb the butter as it softens and taking care to not let the butter separate.

RED SNAPPER WITH TOMATO-GINGER CHUTNEY

serves ⑥ In this unusual preparation, the scales are left on the fish fillets for a stunning effect that I first learned from Claude Troisgros, at C.T. restaurant in New York. When the scales meet hot oil, they puff up like popcorn and become edible. To obtain red snapper with scales you will probably have to visit a fish store or gourmet market, and it wouldn't be a bad idea to call ahead to make sure they can accommodate the request. The crunchy scales call for a softer accompaniment; serve this with *haricot verts,* plain polenta (see page 235), or Wilted Spinach (page 177).

As compelling as this presentation is, you can make this dish without the scales and the snapper and chutney will still carry the day. By the way, if you've always thought of chutney as an Indian condiment, it might surprise you to know that it's actually British in origin.

6 **skin and scale-on red snapper fillets,** 6 ounces each, at least 1 inch thick
Fine sea salt and freshly ground black pepper to taste
About 1/4 cup vegetable oil
Tomato-Ginger Chutney (recipe follows)
Extra-virgin olive oil, for drizzling (optional)

PREPARE THE FISH Remove about a quarter of the scales by gently running the tines of a fork or your fingertips across them, being careful not to break the fish. Season the fish on both sides with salt and pepper.

COOK THE FISH Pour the vegetable oil into a nonstick frying pan to a depth of 1/4 inch. Set the pan over high heat. When the oil is hot, carefully put the fillets in the oil without crowding and press down on them with a spatula to keep them from curling. The scales will absorb the hot oil and swell up like popcorn—this will take 8 to 10 minutes. Turn the fillets over and cook on the other side for 2 to 3 minutes.

TO SERVE Mound some Tomato-Ginger Chutney in the center of each of 6 plates. Top with a fillet and drizzle some extra-virgin olive oil over and around the fish, if desired.

Wine Suggestion: Capiaux, Pinot Noir 2000; Russian River Valley. A California red with exotic red berry aromas and slight earthy, soy notes.

TOMATO-GINGER CHUTNEY

serves ⑥ as an accompaniment Serve this chutney alongside grilled fish, particularly those seasoned with hot or exotic spices; as in Indian food, the chutney will refresh the palate between bites.

- ¼ cup light brown sugar
- ¼ cup rice wine vinegar
- 1 cinnamon stick
- 5 vine-ripened medium tomatoes, quartered, seeded, and diced
- 2 tablespoons chopped fresh ginger
- 1 teaspoon cracked coriander seeds
- 2 tablespoons chopped mint leaves
- Fine sea salt and freshly ground black pepper to taste

IN A SMALL NONREACTIVE SAUCEPAN, cook the brown sugar, vinegar, and cinnamon over high heat until the vinegar boils and the sugar dissolves. Reduce the heat to low. Add the tomatoes, ginger, and coriander, and cook slowly over low heat, stirring occasionally, until the ingredients soften into a compote, approximately 20 minutes. Discard the cinnamon stick, stir in the mint, season with salt and pepper, and set aside.

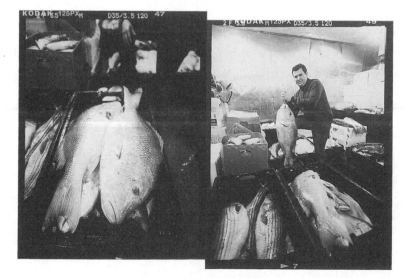

SPICY MOROCCAN SWORDFISH

serves (6) Because of its meaty texture, swordfish—one of the best fish for sport fishing—is one of the few fish that can stand up to an intense blend of Moroccan flavors. (The same is true of its variant, pink swordfish.) This recipe has them all: cumin, coriander, harissa, cilantro, turmeric, and lemon. As delicious as the marinade is, the key to this recipe is to cook the fish just right: too much time on the grill and it becomes tough; underdone and it doesn't taste good at all. The fish needs to marinate several hours, so plan ahead.

Serve this with Fennel Salad with aged pecorino Toscano, Fried Green Tomatoes (page 238), and/or Aïoli (page 165) on the side.

- 2 tablespoons toasted cumin seeds
- 2 tablespoons toasted cracked coriander seeds
- 1 teaspoon turmeric
- 1 tablespoon harissa (see page 91)
- ½ cup olive oil, plus more for serving
- ¼ cup chopped cilantro leaves
- 2 garlic cloves, chopped
  Fine sea salt and freshly ground black pepper to taste
- 6 skinless swordfish steaks, 6 ounces each (ideally 1¼ inches thick)
  Juice of 2 lemons, preferably Meyer lemons
  Lemon slices, for garnish (optional)

MAKE THE MARINADE In a bowl, stir together the cumin, coriander, turmeric, harissa, olive oil, cilantro, and garlic. Set the fish in a single layer in a glass baking dish. Cover with the marinade, cover, and let marinate in the refrigerator for 6 to 12 hours.

COOK THE FISH Prepare an outdoor grill for cooking, letting the coals burn until covered with white ash, or preheat an indoor grill or the broiler. Remove the fish from the marinade and shake gently to release any excess oil but leave the spices more or less intact. Season with salt and pepper. Grill or broil the fish for 8 to 10 minutes, turning once.

TO SERVE Serve the steaks family style from a platter in the center of the table, finishing them with lemon juice and a drizzle of olive oil. Garnish with lemon slices, if you like.

Wine Suggestion: Sanford and Benedict, Cold Heaven Viognier 2000; Santa Barbara. A white from California with floral, Asian spice, and apricot aromas.

FENNEL SALAD WITH AGED PECORINO TOSCANO

serves ⑥ **as an accompaniment** If you love fennel, here's a quick way to enjoy it without the trouble of cooking it. Fresh fennel, with its bright licorice flavor, provides a refreshing contrast to oily or spicy fish.

2 **large fennel bulbs,** shaved paper-thin
¼ **small red onion,** sliced paper-thin
1 **cup coarsely grated aged pecorino Toscano or Parmigiano-Reggiano cheese**
½ **cup croutons (see page 275)**
3 **tablespoons extra-virgin olive oil**
2 **tablespoons freshly squeezed lemon juice**
Fine sea salt and freshly ground black pepper to taste

CHILL THE FENNEL in ice water for 1 hour before serving. Drain and pat it dry. Put the fennel in a bowl with the red onion, cheese, and croutons. Drizzle the oil and lemon juice over the top and season with salt and pepper. Toss.

PROSCIUTTO-WRAPPED RAINBOW TROUT STUFFED WITH HERB BUTTER

serves (6) Bacon-wrapping fish is a rustic way to add flavor and texture without a lot of work. Here, I use prosciutto, a cousin of bacon with a finer taste that doesn't overpower the trout. Serve this with roasted garlic mashed potatoes (see page 243) or Potato Louisette (page 240).

- 8 **tablespoons (1 stick) unsalted butter,** 5 tablespoons softened at room temperature and 3 tablespoons cold butter
- 2 **tablespoons chopped tarragon leaves**
- 7 **garlic cloves,** 6 crushed and 1 chopped
- 2 **tablespoons chopped chives**
  Fine sea salt and freshly ground black pepper to taste
- 12 **boneless skin-on rainbow trout fillets,** with the tail intact
- 3 **Portobello mushrooms,** grilled and sliced
- 18 **thin slices prosciutto di Parma or San Daniele**
- 6 **sprigs thyme**
- 1 **cup dry white wine**
  Juice of ½ **lemon**
- ½ **Spiced Preserved Lemon (page 253) or fresh lemon,** skinned, rinsed, and chopped

MAKE THE HERBED BUTTER In a small bowl, stir together the 5 tablespoons softened butter with the tarragon, 1 chopped garlic, and the chopped chives. Season with salt and pepper and set aside.

PREPARE THE TROUT Lay the 12 fillets out on your work surface and season them with salt and pepper. Spread some of the remaining butter over each fillet. Top 6 fillets with a layer of mushroom slices and top each one by inverting a remaining fillet on top of it, so the fillets are head-to-head and tail-to-tail.

WRAP THE TROUT Lay a sheet of plastic wrap about 18 inches long in front of you. Put 3 slices of prosciutto, slightly overlapping them, in the center of the sheet. Put 1 trout "sandwich" at the end of the prosciutto and carefully roll the trout away from you, wrapping it tightly in the prosciutto. Roll the trout in the plastic wrap to encase it tightly. Gather one end of the plastic wrap in each hand and twist the ends over and over until they will turn no more and the trout is firmly sealed in the plastic. Repeat with the remaining prosciutto and trout, and refrigerate them for at least 2 hours, or overnight.

COOK THE TROUT AND MAKE THE SAUCE Take the trout out of the refrigerator and unwrap them. Melt 2 tablespoons of the butter in a sauté pan set over medium-high heat. Add the crushed garlic and the thyme. Put the trout in the pan and cook, turning it as each side turns golden brown, approximately 3 minutes per side. Remove the trout, garlic, and thyme from the pan, reserving all of them. Pour off and discard the fat from the pan. Pour the wine into the pan, raise the heat to high, bring the wine to a boil, and let boil until reduced by half. Add the remaining 1 tablespoon of butter, whisking it into the sauce. Add the lemon juice and Spiced Preserved Lemon. Season the sauce with salt and pepper.

TO SERVE Cut each trout "sandwich" crosswise into 3 or 5 pieces, depending on the length of the fillets. Divide the pieces evenly among 6 warm plates, spoon some sauce over each serving, and garnish with garlic and thyme.

Wine Suggestion: Morassino, Barbaresco 1998; Piedmont. A soulful Italian red with aromas of dried roses, Bing cherries, and smoky notes.

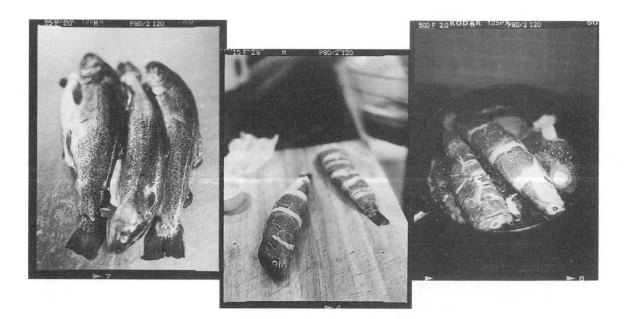

TUNA BURGER

serves (6) There's nothing like a tuna burger to make great seafood into an all-American event. I like to serve tuna burgers on a bun with a selection of garnishes such as sliced beefsteak tomatoes, pickled cucumbers, mayonnaise, sliced red onion, and more tuna-appropriate choices such as avocado and cilantro. Put out as many options as possible and let everyone make his or her own favorite combination.

2	**pounds sushi-grade tuna,** finely chopped
2	**scallions,** green part only, finely chopped
1	**large shallot,** minced
1	**garlic clove,** minced
1½	teaspoons **Worcestershire sauce**
¼	cup **olive oil**
	Fine sea salt, freshly ground black pepper, and Tabasco sauce to taste
6	**hamburger-style buns**

PREPARE THE TUNA Put the tuna, scallions, shallot, garlic, Worcestershire sauce, and 2 tablespoons olive oil in a bowl and knead together. Season to taste with salt, pepper, and Tabasco. Divide the tuna into 6 portions and form each portion into a burger.

COOK THE BURGERS Pour the remaining 2 tablespoons olive oil in a wide heavy-bottomed sauté pan, skillet, or grill pan over medium-high heat. Cook the burgers, in batches if necessary, for 2 minutes on each side for rare, or longer for more well done.

TO SERVE Put each burger on a bun and present with garnishes.

Wine Suggestion: Côtes du Rhône, Mont-Redon, 2001; Southern Rhone. A light red that has aromas of berries, spice, and smoke.

TUNA-SWORDFISH SKEWERS

serves (6) Although associated with the grill, skewers can also be successfully cooked indoors on a grill pan. In this case, the marinade caramelizes to produce a grilled result. You could, of course, cook these on a grill, and add diced or small vegetables like cherry tomatoes, onions, zucchini, eggplant, and bell pepper between the fish cubes.

Serve this with Corn and Scallion Pancakes (page 249).

3 tablespoons balsamic vinegar
1 tablespoon grated fresh ginger
1 dried hot chile, chopped
3 tablespoons chopped cilantro leaves
¼ cup olive oil
1½ pounds tuna, cut into 1¼-inch cubes
1½ pounds swordfish, cut into 1¼-inch cubes
Fine sea salt and freshly ground black pepper to taste
Lemon wedges

MAKE THE MARINADE In a baking dish, stir together the vinegar, ginger, chile, cilantro, and 2 tablespoons olive oil.

MARINATE THE FISH Put the fish in the dish, roll in the marinade, cover, and refrigerate for 1 hour.

SKEWER THE FISH Remove the fish from the marinade and divide among six 8-inch skewers. Season with salt and pepper.

COOK THE FISH Heat the remaining 2 tablespoons olive oil in a pan and heat over medium-high heat. Add the skewers to the pan without crowding and cook until the marinade caramelizes on all 4 sides, 2 to 3 minutes per side. (If you like, you can grill the skewers on an outdoor grill.)

TO SERVE Put 1 skewer on each of 6 plates and serve with lemon wedges alongside.

Wine Suggestion: Côtes du Roussillon, Domaine des Chenes, 2001; Roussillon. A simple French white from the Languedoc-Roussillon with aromas nuts, blossoms, and honey.

TUNA PANINI

serves (6) A *pan bagna* (literally means "wet bread") is a sandwich that essentially features the same ingredients as a *salade Niçoise*. Its name refers to the fact that it's practically dripping with olive oil. This recipe makes a *pan bagna* in the tradition of a grilled Italian panini.

Obviously, this dish lends itself to Mediterranean expansion: you could add salted anchovies or sun-dried tomato paste, spread on Tapenade or Hummus (recipe follows), or pair it with Roasted Red Onions with Honey and Balsamic Vinegar (page 248).

6 **individual ciabatta rolls,** about 4 by 4 inches each
6 **slices sushi-grade tuna,** 3 ounces each, cut 4 by 4 inches
3 **tablespoons extra-virgin olive oil,** plus more for serving
   Fine sea salt and freshly ground black pepper to taste
2 **garlic cloves,** finely chopped
6 **tablespoons Tapenade (olive paste; page 27)**
2 **large beefsteak tomatoes,** thinly sliced
¼ **cup finely diced red onion**
18 **large basil leaves**
1 **avocado,** thinly sliced lengthwise
6 **hard-boiled eggs,** peeled and sliced
6 **thin slices Parmigiano-Reggiano cheese,** cut with a vegetable peeler
1 **bunch arugula,** stems discarded
6 **tablespoons mayonnaise or pesto mayonnaise (see Step 1, page 26)**

PREPARE THE GRILL Prepare a hot fire in a barbecue grill or preheat an indoor grill.

GRILL THE BREAD Cut each roll in half lengthwise and grill the cut side until crisp. Remove from grill and set aside.

GRILL THE TUNA Season the tuna with olive oil, salt, and pepper, and scatter with the garlic. Grill the tuna until the outside is cooked but still a bit red at the center, approximately 2 minutes each side. Remove from the grill and set aside.

BUILD THE SANDWICHES Lay out the 6 roll bottoms before you. Spread 1 tablespoon of the tapenade on each bottom. Top with a few slices of tomato, onion, basil leaves, avocado, eggs, Parmigiano-Reggiano, 1 slice of tuna, and some arugula. Spread 1 tablespoon of mayonnaise on the cut side of each roll top and place 1 top on each sandwich.

GRILL THE SANDWICHES Place the sandwiches on the grill and press down on them with a cast-iron pan to keep them together and help form nice grill marks, 1 to 2 minutes per side. Or, if you have a panini press or George Forman–type grill, use it to achieve the same effect.

TO SERVE Cut each sandwich in half. For a decadent touch, serve a shallow dish of extra-virgin olive oil and invite your guests to dip their sandwiches in the oil.

Wine Suggestion: Illuminati "Daniele" Trebbiano d'Abruzzo, 2002; Abruzzi. A simple Italian white with hints of apple, mineral, and nuts.

HUMMUS

serves ⑥ as an accompaniment My version of the Middle Eastern chickpea puree. It's great for snacking as a dip for pita bread or vegetables.

- ½ **cup chickpeas,** soaked for 12 hours in cold water
- 2 **to 3 tablespoons lemon juice**
- 2 **garlic cloves,** left whole
- 2 **tablespoons sesame oil**
- 2 **tablespoons olive oil**
- ¼ **teaspoon ground cumin**
  Fine sea salt and freshly ground black pepper to taste
  Crushed red pepper flakes (optional)

DRAIN THE CHICKPEAS, transfer them to a pot, cover with salted water, and cook at a simmer for 2 hours, or until tender. Drain and let cool. Transfer to a food processor fitted with the metal blade, add the remaining ingredients except red pepper flakes, and process until smooth. Transfer to a bowl. Add red pepper flakes if you like and let rest for 24 hours. Serve with warm Indian or pita bread.

TUNA "SURF AND TURF" WITH GINGER KETCHUP

serves ⑥ When I worked in Las Vegas, I saw the term "surf and turf" on a lot of signs advertising inexpensive dinners of lobster and steak. The phrase here is a bit of a joke because, where those dinners usually served poor-quality fish and meat, this one calls for the best sushi-grade tuna (ideally Yellowfin), pancetta, and foie gras. It's very important that you ask your fishmonger to cut the fish as specified in the recipe. For a decadent side dish, sauté porcini or portobello mushrooms in the fat given off by the foie gras. This would also be terrific with horseradish mashed potatoes (see page 242), or Braised Collard Greens (page 217).

  6 tablespoons ketchup
  6 tablespoons reduced-sodium (lite) soy sauce
  ¼ cup balsamic vinegar
4½ sticks (1 pound plus 4 tablespoons) unsalted butter, cut into pieces
  3 tablespoons ginger juice (page 51)
      Fine sea salt and freshly ground black pepper
  6 sushi-grade tuna fillets, preferably Yellowfin, 5 ounces each, cut 4 inches long and
         1½ inches thick
 24 paper-thin slices pancetta, or bacon (about 2 ounces)
  6 (2-ounce) slices foie gras, at room temperature

MAKE THE GINGER-KETCHUP EMULSION   Put the ketchup in a pot and set over high heat. Cook, stirring, until caramelized. Add the soy sauce and vinegar, bring to a boil, then add the butter, one piece at a time, whisking it in. Add the ginger juice and season with salt and pepper. If the sauce is thicker than you prefer, add a few drops of warm tap water. Set aside, covered, to keep it warm.

WRAP THE FISH IN PANCETTA   Season the fish with salt and pepper. Lay 4 strips of pancetta, slightly overlapping, on a work surface and lay a piece of tuna across the narrow edge of the slices closest to you. Holding the fish and pancetta firmly, roll away from yourself to wrap the fish in the pancetta. Repeat with the remaining fillets and pancetta. Set aside.

(Note: If not using foie gras, skip Step 3 and begin Step 4 by warming 2 tablespoons of olive oil in the pan.)

SAUTÉ THE FOIE GRAS Season the foie gras with salt and pepper. Warm a sauté pan over medium heat and add the foie gras to the pan. Cook just until browned on both sides, about 1 minute per side. Carefully remove the foie gras slices with a spatula and set aside on a plate, covered to keep them warm.

SAUTÉ THE TUNA Pour off all but 2 tablespoons of fat from the pan. Add the fish to the pan, seam side down. Cook, turning the fillets to brown the pancetta all over, rolling the fillets as soon as each side is browned, 8 to 10 minutes total cooking time. (To check for doneness, cut the end off 1 fillet; it should be raw at the center.) Slice each fillet in half crosswise.

TO SERVE Put 1 slice of foie gras on each of 6 plates. Arrange 2 tuna pieces next to or on top of the foie gras. Spoon some of the emulsion around the tuna.

Wine Suggestion: Mas Jullien, Coteaux du Languedoc 1999; Languedoc. A spicy, juicy red from southern France.

PANCETTA, also referred to as Italian bacon, is unsmoked pork belly that has been cured with salt, spices, and pepper. It's often used as the source of fat in a dish to infuse the other ingredients with its flavors. Look for it in the deli section of your supermarket and in Italian food shops.

ZARZUELA

serves ⑥ I learned to cook this variation of the Spanish bouillabaisse from the Catalonian region at one of my first jobs. It was taught to me by Jean Carrascosa, at Don Quichotte. Some original recipes use almond power as a binding element and add ham to the sauce, but I don't find that either is essential. This is a very adaptable dish that also can be made with larger shrimp (called *gambas* in Spain) and langoustine, or other shellfish of your choosing. It's traditionally served in the dish in which it is cooked.

This dish is noteworthy for its use of *picada,* a traditional Spanish fried bread mixture. For a more interesting presentation, serve the picada on the side and instruct guests to add as much as desired to their servings.

This would be delicious with Rouille (page 112).

½ **cup olive oil**

2 **medium onions,** sliced

1 **green bell pepper,** sliced

Pinch saffron

2 **tablespoons tomato paste**

1 **cup dry white wine**

8 **vine-ripened medium tomatoes,** diced

2 **cups water**

Fine sea salt and freshly ground black pepper to taste

3 **slices country bread**

⅓ **cup chopped parsley**

5 **garlic cloves,** chopped

1¼ **pounds cod fillets,** cut crosswise into 6 pieces

1 **pound medium shrimp (about 18)**

1 **lobster,** 2 pounds, sliced at each joint (optional)

4 **medium squid,** cleaned and sliced (about 4 pounds total)

6 **sea scallops (about** ⅓ **pound)**

¾ **pound cockles or small clams**

¾ **pound mussels,** scrubbed and debearded

6 **razor clams,** cleaned (optional)

MAKE THE SAUCE Put ¼ cup of the olive oil in a stockpot. Add the onions and green pepper, and sauté over high heat until softened but not browned, approximately 3 minutes. Add the saffron and tomato paste, and stir. Pour in the white wine and bring to a boil over medium heat. Add the tomatoes and water, and cook until the tomatoes break down and the mixture begins to thicken. Season with salt and pepper. Keep warm.

MAKE THE PICADA Pound the bread by hand and knead together with the parsley and garlic. Set aside.

SAUTÉ THE FISH AND SHELLFISH Warm the remaining ¼ cup olive oil in a large sauté pan, letting it get very hot. Season the cod, shrimp, lobster, squid, and scallops with salt and pepper and sauté each of them individually in the pan, leaving each a bit underdone because they will finish cooking in the sauce—approximately 3 minutes for the cod, 2 minutes for the lobster (if using), 2 minutes for the shrimp, 1 minute for the squid, and 2 minutes for the scallops. As they are cooked, reserve the fish and shellfish on a plate.

STEAM THE MOLLUSKS Put the cooked fish and shellfish in the stockpot with the sauce. Add the cockles, mussels, and clams, cover, and cook until all have opened, approximately 5 minutes. Discard any that do not open.

TO SERVE Stir in the bread mixture and serve the zarzuela family style from the center of the table.

Wine Suggestion: Muga, Rosé 2002; Rioja. A bright Spanish rosé with aromas of fresh picked strawberries.

VEGETABLES AND SIDE DISHES

Creamy Rosemary Polenta

Sage-Potato Gnocchi Gratin

Fried Green Tomatoes

Basmati Rice Galette

Potato Louisette

Mashed Fingerling Potatoes

Grilled Summer Vegetable Tart

Louise's Potato Pie

Roasted Red Onions with Honey and
Balsamic Vinegar

Corn and Scallion Pancakes

Broccoli Rabe with Garlic

Fried Baked Potato

Caramelized Cipolline Onions and
Brussels Sprouts

Spiced Preserved Lemon

Many of the fish recipes in this book feature vegetables, but I always try to serve a vegetable side dish with my main courses as well. It reminds me of the way my grandmother cooked with the vegetables from our garden. It's also a way to hammer home the seasonality of a dish by including of-the-moment ingredients, and to make the experience of the meal more aromatic with the addition of herbs.

One of the most exciting aspects of contemporary cooking is the way vegetables and side dishes have been reimagined as compelling creations in their own right. Generations ago, a fish dish would most likely be paired with a simply cooked vegetable and one of a standard repertoire of potato dishes or rice.

Today, side dishes can be as interesting as the main course. I try to create compelling side dishes on my restaurant menus, and I am delighted to share some of my favorites here. I even take a fresh look at potatoes, using them in sides like Potato Louisette (page 246), Louise's Potato Pie (page 246), Mashed Fingerling Potatoes (page 242), Sage-Potato Gnocchi Gratin (page 236), and Fried Baked Potato (page 251). When I'm not in the mood for potatoes, I turn to other starches like Creamy Rosemary Polenta (page 235) or Basmati Rice Galette (page 239).

One of the ways you can make sure your meals have a noteworthy flourish is to keep some ready-made side dishes on hand. One of the recipes in this chapter, Spiced Preserved Lemon (page 253), while not a side dish per se, can be made months in advance and kept in the refrigerator. So, even at the last second, you have a way to add something special to a dinner.

When it comes to vegetables themselves, one of the most important pieces of advice I can give you has nothing to do with the actual cooking. Rather, it's about shopping: Search out the freshest produce you get, whether from a farm stand or local farmers' market, a greengrocer, or even a supermarket that buys with care. And, whenever you can, buy organic. I can't tell you how much difference it makes to eat the most healthful, natural vegetables possible. When they aren't touched by pesticides or chemicals, they're as good as can be, even though they might not always look as pretty as mass-produced varieties.

Buying the freshest, locally grown, purest ingredients will help you get the most out of recipes for Fried Green Tomatoes (page 238), Grilled Summer Vegetable Tart (page 244), Roasted Red Onions with Honey and Balsamic Vinegar (page 248), Corn and Scallion Pancakes (page 249), Broccoli Rabe with Garlic (page 250), and Caramelized Cipolline Onions and Brussels Sprouts (page 252).

CREAMY ROSEMARY POLENTA

serves (6) My version of the Italian side dish polenta (cooked cornmeal) is flavored with rosemary and hearty with a mixture of milk, cream, and butter. Depending on the fineness of the grain, you may want to add a bit more cream just before serving to lighten the polenta; it has a tendency to firm up when resting. Serve this with Grilled Pompano with Vegetable Salsa (page 208) or Roasted Lobster and Aromatic Butter (page 198).

For a more substantial side dish, transfer the cooked polenta to a baking dish, top with the grated Parmigiano-Reggiano cheese, dot it with butter, and pass it under the broiler until the cheese melts and turns golden brown. Place in the center of the table and scoop out individual portions.

1 quart milk
3 tablespoons chopped fresh rosemary leaves
1½ cups quick-cooking polenta
3 tablespoons unsalted butter
1½ cups heavy cream
Fine sea salt and freshly ground black pepper to taste
1 cup grated Parmigiano-Reggiano cheese

INFUSE THE MILK Bring the milk to a boil in a pot set over medium-high heat. Turn off the heat, add the rosemary, cover, and let infuse for 5 minutes. Strain the liquid through a fine-mesh strainer set over a bowl.

MAKE THE POLENTA Return the milk to the pot and set it over medium heat. Add the polenta and cook, whisking constantly, for 3 minutes. Add the butter and cream, and season with salt and pepper. Just before serving, whisk in the Parmigiano-Reggiano.

TO SERVE Transfer servings of polenta to each plate, or present it in a bowl from the center of the table.

To Make Plain Polenta: Skip Step 1, leaving out the rosemary.

To Make Flavored Polenta: Make Plain Polenta (see above), then stir in your favorite herbs or spices.

SAGE-POTATO GNOCCHI GRATIN

serves (6) This rich gratin, infused with the flavor of sage, is a hearty accompaniment for grilled or poached fish such as Skate Barbecue with Braised Collard Greens (page 216) and Walleye Pike with Bacon-Burgundy Sauce (page 206), as well as those cooked *en papillote* (see page 170).

You can simplify the dish by grating some Parmigiano-Reggiano over the gnocchi while sautéing them in Step 3 and serving them right after that step. (Note: Don't be frightened by the amount of salt called for at the beginning of this recipe; it's used as a bed to cook the potatoes.)

2 cups coarse sea salt, plus more to taste
2¼ pounds Idaho potatoes
½ cup plus 3 tablespoons all-purpose flour
¼ cup plus 1 tablespoon olive oil
1 egg
2 pinches grated nutmeg
Fine sea salt and freshly ground black pepper to taste
1 tablespoon unsalted butter
2 ounces bacon, finely diced (about ½ cup)
1 tablespoon chopped sage leaves
2 tablespoons chopped garlic
1 cup heavy cream
½ cup milk
⅔ cup grated Parmigiano-Reggiano cheese

MAKE THE GNOCCHI DOUGH Preheat the oven to 375°F. Mound the salt in the center of a baking sheet. Put the potatoes on the salt and bake in the oven until a sharp thin-bladed knife easily pierces to the center of a potato. Remove the baking sheet from the oven and let the potatoes cool. When cool enough to handle, peel the potatoes and pass them through a food mill or ricer or mash thoroughly with a masher. Add the flour, 2 tablespoons of the olive oil, the egg, and a pinch of nutmeg. Season dough with salt and pepper.

SHAPE AND BOIL THE GNOCCHI Divide the dough into 5 or 6 batches and roll each one out into a rope length about ¾ inch in diameter. Cut each length into 1-inch segments and set aside. Bring a pot of salted water to a boil and add the gnocchi in batches. Cook until they float to the surface, then remove them with a slotted spoon and set aside on a clean kitchen towel.

BEGIN ASSEMBLING THE GRATIN Grease a large gratin dish with the butter and preheat the broiler. Heat the remaining 3 tablespoons of the olive oil in a large sauté pan and sauté the gnocchi in batches until golden brown, removing them to the gratin dish.

MAKE THE SAUCE In another pan, cook the bacon over medium-high heat with the sage and garlic until the bacon is crisp and enough fat has rendered to coat the other ingredients, 5 to 7 minutes. Add the cream, milk, and remaining pinch of nutmeg; bring to a boil. Stir in the Parmigiano-Reggiano and remove the pot from the heat. Season with salt and pepper and pour the liquid over the gnocchi. Place the gratin dish under the broiler and broil until browned on top, approximately 2 minutes.

TO SERVE Present the gratin dish family style from the center of the table.

Wine Suggestion: Enzo Boglietti, Dolcetto d'Alba 2001; Piedmont. A light Italian red with aromas of red berries, earth, and soft tannis.

FRIED GREEN TOMATOES

serves (6) Green tomatoes are tomatoes that have not yet fully ripened; they have a tart, almost lemony flavor that is a perfect pairing with many fish dishes. Frying them, which is a beloved tradition in the Southern United States, gives them a crispy exterior that is the perfect contrast with the soft, flavorful fruit within.

I enjoy this summery side dish with Spicy Moroccan Swordfish (page 220) or Poached Skate with Spicy Lime-Yogurt Vinaigrette (page 90). It's also delicious passed as an hors d'oeuvre with Aïoli (page 165) or added to a shrimp salad. If you can't find young green tomatoes, don't use red ones; substitute Mexican tomatillos—a relative of the gooseberry that happens to be green.

6 **medium green tomatoes or 12 husked tomatillos,** sliced ½ inch thick
Fine sea salt and freshly ground black pepper to taste
⅔ **cup dry bread crumbs**
⅓ **cup grated Parmigiano-Reggiano cheese**
3 **tablespoons all-purpose flour**
2 **eggs,** lightly beaten
¼ **cup olive oil**
Pinch Old Bay Seasoning (see page 69)
A few shakes of Tabasco sauce

SEASON AND COAT THE TOMATOES Season the green tomatoes with salt and pepper. Mix the bread crumbs and cheese. Dredge the tomato slices in the flour, then the beaten eggs, then the bread crumb–Parmigiano-Reggiano mixture to coat on both sides. Run your finger around the circumference of each slice to remove the coatings and show the green tomato skin underneath.

FRY THE TOMATOES Heat the olive oil in a sauté pan set over medium-high heat. Add the tomatoes and cook until golden brown on both sides, approximately 2 minutes per side. Use a slotted spoon to transfer the tomatoes to paper towels to drain. Season them lightly with Old Bay Seasoning and Tabasco sauce.

TO SERVE Present the tomatoes alongside the dish of your choice or pass them from a platter or basket.

Wine Suggestion: Domaine de Chantenoy, Ménétou-Salon 2001; Loire Valley. A simple French white with good acidity and slight herbaceous notes.

PROSCIUTTO-WRAPPED RAINBOW TROUT STUFFED WITH HERB BUTTER, SERVED WITH POTATO LOUISETTE AND PRESERVED LEMONS   pages 222, 249, 253

BITTER ALMOND CHOCOLATE SOUFFLÉ ADELYNN page 260

BASMATI RICE GALETTE

serves (6) Basmati rice is an Indian rice that has an enticing aroma when cooked. (It actually belongs to a family of rice known as aromatic rice.) In case you're wondering, I use a combination of oil and butter here because they each have a property that is useful in this recipe: the butter causes the outside of the galette to brown, while the oil—which has a higher smoking point so it takes longer to burn—keeps it from scorching.

These galettes would be an ideal accompaniment to Lobster in Coconut and Cilantro Broth (page 193).

2 **tablespoons cornstarch**
⅔ **cup heavy cream**
2 **scallions,** green parts only, chopped
⅔ **cup cooked and cooled basmati rice (from about**
    ¼ **cup raw rice cooked in** ¾ **cup water)**
  Fine sea salt and freshly ground black pepper to taste
2 **tablespoons vegetable oil**
1 **tablespoon unsalted butter**

MAKE THE BATTER In a bowl, stir together the cornstarch and heavy cream. Add the scallions and rice, and season with salt and pepper. Cover and refrigerate for 2 hours.

COOK THE GALETTE Warm the oil in a sauté pan set over medium heat. Add the butter and let it melt, tilting the pan to coat it. Divide the batter into 6 small mounds by hand, shaping each mound into a patty about ¾ inch thick. Place the patties in the sauté pan, in batches if necessary to avoid crowding, and sauté until golden brown on both sides, approximately 2 minutes per side. Transfer to paper towels to drain.

TO SERVE Present the cakes on a linen napkin–lined plate to soak up any lingering grease.

POTATO LOUISETTE

serves (6) My grandmother Louisette, who is a wonderful home cook, taught me to make this gigantic potato pancake, regionally referred to as a *millassou*, which has a consistency similar to sticky rice. The original recipe calls for topping it with slices of cheese and cooking it over an open wood fire. If you like, you can top this recipe with a silky cheese like St. Nectaire, Chamberat, or Cantal, and melt it under the broiler just before serving.

I like this this with Prosciutto-Wrapped Rainbow Trout Stuffed with Herb Butter (page 222) or Bacon-Wrapped Hake with Chilled Artichoke Broth (page 188). It's also a great meal with a simple Caesar salad; see my recipe for Caesar Dressing below.

1 **small leek,** white and tender green parts, well washed and chopped
4 **large Idaho potatoes,** peeled
1 **garlic clove,** chopped
1 **tablespoon chopped parsley**
Fine sea salt and freshly ground black pepper to taste
¼ **cup canola oil**

BLANCH THE LEEK Bring a pot of salted water to a boil. Fill a large bowl halfway with ice water. Add the leek to the boiling water and blanch for 2 minutes. Drain and transfer to the ice water to cool and stop the cooking. Drain and set aside.

MAKE THE POTATO MIXURE Grate the potatoes through the finest holes of a box grater to make a raw puree, collecting it in a bowl. Add the leek, garlic, and parsley; season with salt and pepper, and stir until well incorporated. Work quickly to keep the potato from oxidizing.

COOK THE PANCAKE Heat 2 tablespoons of the canola oil in a large nonstick pan over medium heat. Mound the potato mixture in the center of the pan and use a spatula to flatten it into a single large "pancake" about 1 inch thick. Cook slowly until golden brown on the bottom, 15 to 20 minutes. Carefully slide the pancake off the pan onto a plate as you would an omelet. Add the remaining oil to the pan and coat the surface evenly. Carefully invert the potato cake and slip it back into the pan. Return the pan to the stovetop and cook until golden brown, approximately 15 minutes.

TO SERVE Slide the pancake out of the pan onto a large, clean plate. Season with salt and cut into wedges.

CAESAR DRESSING

makes about ① cup   Here's my version of the classic Caesar dressing. Like my Soft-Boiled Egg Mayonnaise (page 41), it uses a cooked rather than a raw egg.

 1 soft-boiled egg (see page 275)
 3 **salted anchovy fillets,** rinsed and patted dry
 1 **garlic clove**
 1 **tablespoon Dijon mustard**
 ⅓ **cup olive oil**
 2 **tablespoons freshly squeezed lemon juice**
 6 **tablespoons grated Parmigiano-Reggiano cheese**
    Fine sea salt and freshly ground black pepper to taste

PUT THE EGG, anchovies, garlic, and mustard in a blender and process until well blended. With the motor running slowly, add the olive oil in a thin stream to form an emulsified dressing, then add the lemon juice and Parmigiano-Reggiano. Transfer the dressing to a bowl and season with salt and pepper.

MASHED FINGERLING POTATOES

serves (6) This is my basic recipe for mashed potatoes. I prefer fingerling potatoes to Idaho, rus-set, or Yukon Gold because they have a more distinct flavor and a useful starchiness that helps bind them together when mashed. But, of course, you can use your favorite.

Obviously, mashed potatoes go well with almost anything, but I especially like them with Tuna "Surf and Turf" with Ginger Ketchup (page 228) or Arctic Char and Endive Papillote (page 170).

You can personalize these potatoes by adding roasted garlic puree (recipe follows), lemon and olive oil, horseradish, wasabi, or mixed spices. For a classic French side dish, make *aligot* by adding smashed garlic to the hot milk and a large quantity of cheese, ideally Cantal or Tomme, stir-ring it in until the potatoes are creamy and the cheese becomes stringy. You can also flambé the potatoes with *eau de vie*, which will infuse them with an elegant flavor.

2 pounds yellow fingerling or Yukon Gold potatoes
Coarse sea salt
1¼ cups hot milk
10 tablespoons (1 stick plus 2 tablespoons) unsalted butter, cut into 10 pieces
Fine sea salt and freshly ground black pepper to taste

PUT THE POTATOES in a pot, cover them with cold water, and add a pinch of salt. Set the pot over high heat and bring the water to a boil. Continue to cook until you can easily piece a pota-to with the tip of a sharp, thin-bladed knife. Drain the potatoes and peel while hot by using a clean, dry towel to protect your hands.

PASS THE POTATOES through a food mill, or mash with a masher, and transfer them to a pot set over medium heat. Add the hot milk and the butter, and stir until incorporated. Season with salt and pepper.

ROASTED GARLIC MASHED POTATOES

1 **head elephant garlic,** or 2 heads regular garlic, top ¼ inch cut off
2 **tablespoons extra-virgin olive oil**
   Fine sea salt and freshly ground black pepper to taste

PREHEAT THE OVEN to 375°F. Place the garlic on a sheet of foil, drizzle with the oil, season with salt and pepper, and bake until the cloves are soft, about 1 hour. Test by inserting a sharp thin-bladed knife. When cool, squeeze the garlic from the cloves and mash with the back of a spoon. Stir into Mashed Fingerling Potatoes to taste.

GRILLED SUMMER VEGETABLE TART

serves ⑥ Classically, this dish would be called a *feuilletée,* a French word that means "in leaves," a reference to the way the vegetables are layered between puff pastry. This is a perfect complement to summery fish dishes like Baked Whole Sea Bass with Meyer Lemon (page 164), or pair it with an arugula salad for an appetizer or light lunch. You can also serve this with Tapenade (page 27) and a simple goat cheese salad, or as an accompaniment to grilled sardines. If you like, add anchovies to this dish by layering them in after the tomatoes.

¼ **cup olive oil**

2 **garlic cloves,** chopped

1 **teaspoon chopped fresh rosemary leaves**

1 **medium eggplant,** cut crosswise into ⅜-inch slices

1 **medium zucchini,** cut crosswise into ⅜-inch slices

1 **medium onion,** cut into ⅜-inch slices

1½ **red bell peppers,** stems and seeds removed, quartered

2 **medium tomatoes,** cut into ⅜-inch slices

Fine sea salt and freshly ground black pepper to taste

2 **sheets puff pastry,** each cut into a 5 by 15-inch rectangle (from a 17¼-ounce package)

6 **tablespoons grated Parmigiano-Reggiano cheese,** or 6 (¼-inch-thick) slices provolone cheese

20 **basil leaves**

1 **egg yolk,** beaten with 1 tablespoon cold water to make an egg wash

PREPARE AND GRILL THE VEGETABLES Prepare an outdoor or indoor grill for cooking. Mix the olive oil with the garlic and rosemary, and brush the eggplant, zucchini, onion, bell peppers, and tomato slices with the seasoned oil. Season the vegetables with salt and pepper, and grill until cooked through. (Times will vary based on the moisture content of each vegetable and the heat of your grill.)

PREHEAT THE OVEN to 375°F.

START BUILDING THE DISH Arrange one puff pastry sheet on a cookie sheet. Arrange a layer of overlapping eggplant slices on top of the pastry, leaving a 1-inch border all around. Top with a layer of overlapping zucchini slices and a layer of cheese. Top the cheese with a layer of overlapping onion slices, followed by tomatoes. Top the tomatoes with a layer of basil and end with a layer of peppers.

COMPLETE THE DISH Brush the pastry border with egg wash and lay the other pastry sheet on top. Score the top with a sharp thin-bladed knife and paint the top with egg wash. Bake until cooked through (a sharp thin-bladed knife inserted into the center of the tart will come out hot) and golden on top, 20 to 25 minutes.

TO SERVE Remove the cookie sheet from the oven, let the dish cool slightly, transfer it to a serving platter, cut it into individual portions with a serrated knife, and present warm.

Wine Suggestion: Terra do Gargola, Monterrei 2001; Spain. A fresh, simple white from Spain, with slight, fruity nuances.

LOUISE'S POTATO PIE

serves (6) My great-grandmother Louise taught me how to make this Bourbonnais-style *pâte aux patates,* which she used to bake for me in a wood oven. Her original recipe calls for a short pastry; I substitute puff pastry, which you can buy. This is the kind of dish you would enjoy during Sunday brunch with an escarole salad with mustard vinaigrette, and finish it cold on Monday, or in my case, at three in the morning after the last guest has left a party. For a luxurious variation, place a layer of sliced truffles in the center of the potatoes.

This is delicious with Walleye Pike with Bacon-Burgundy Sauce (page 206), especially if you make it with the optional poached egg.

4	**large Idaho potatoes**
1	**small onion,** sliced
1	**garlic clove,** chopped
2	**tablespoons chopped parsley**
	Fine sea salt and freshly ground black pepper to taste
1	**package (17.25 ounces) puff pastry**
1½	**cups heavy cream or crème fraîche**
1	**egg yolk,** beaten with 1 tablespoon water to make an egg wash
¼	**cup all-purpose flour,** for dusting work surface

PREPARE THE POTATOES Peel the potatoes and slice them into ⅛-inch rounds, preferably on a mandoline. Put them in a large bowl and add the onion, garlic, and parsley. Season generously with salt and pepper and set aside.

PREHEAT THE OVEN to 375°F.

PREPARE THE DISH Shape 1 sheet of the puff pastry to an 11-inch metallic pie dish. Add the potatoes. Cut around the perimeter of the pie dish, removing the excess pastry but leaving about 1 inch of dough hanging over the side. Discard the scrap pastry and fold the portion hanging over the side so it encloses the potatoes. Brush the upward-facing dough with egg wash. Place another sheet of puff pastry on top of the pie dish and cut it so it conforms to the top of the pie dish. Brush the top with egg wash.

BAKE THE PIE Put the dish on a baking sheet on the oven's center rack and bake until cooked through (a sharp thin-bladed knife inserted to the center of the tart will come out hot),

45 to 50 minutes. Remove the dish from the oven and cut around the perimeter of the top, removing the puff pastry from the top. Set the pastry cover aside. Pour the cream into the pie and jiggle the potatoes with a spoon to let the cream seep into the deepest part of the pie. Season with salt and pepper, return the cover, and let the cream infuse for 15 to 20 minutes, covered with a clean, dry cloth.

TO SERVE Present the pie in its dish from the center of the table.

Wine Suggestion: Producteurs Plaimont, Côtes de Saint-Mont "Les Vignes Retrouvees" 2002; Madiran. A simple French country white with crisp acidity and soft stone fruits.

ROASTED RED ONIONS WITH HONEY AND BALSAMIC VINEGAR

serves (6) This side dish is easy to prepare, but complex in flavor: roasting the onions mellows their sharp flavor, and the reduction of honey and balsamic vinegar provides a sweet, tart glaze.

I serve this with Tuna Panini (page 226) and Grilled Mackerel with Warm Leek and Potato Salad (page 199).

6 medium red onions, peeled
Fine sea salt and freshly ground black pepper to taste
About 2 tablespoons olive oil
⅓ cup wildflower honey
¼ cup balsamic vinegar

PREHEAT THE OVEN to 325°F.

BROWN THE ONIONS Cut the red onions in half lengthwise through the stem end and season the cut sides with salt and pepper. Heat the olive oil in a large sauté pan over medium heat. Add the onion halves, cut sides down, to the pan and sauté until golden brown, about 4 minutes. You may have to do this in batches; if necessary, add more oil to the pan between batches. Put the onion halves, cut side up, in a baking dish just large enough to hold them snugly in a single layer.

DRESS AND ROAST THE ONIONS In a bowl, stir together the honey and vinegar. Drizzle the honey-vinegar mixture over the onions and roast the onions in the oven for 1 hour to 1 hour and 30 minutes. Every 10 to 15 minutes, baste the onions with the juice from the bottom of the pan.

MAKE THE GLAZE Remove the pan from the oven, remove the onions from the pan, and set them aside. Pour the pan juice into a pot and set over medium-high heat. Boil until reduced to a glaze.

TO SERVE Brush the cut side of each onion with the glaze, and serve from a platter or alongside a main course.

CORN AND SCALLION PANCAKES

serves (6) These Southwestern-style pancakes are small in size, but they pack big flavor thanks to the use of fresh corn and curry powder. Be sure to make these in the late summer, when corn is at the height of its flavor. The pancakes are perfect with Roasted Lobster and Aromatic Butter (page 198), and a fine accompaniment to many soups and stews.

1 teaspoon active dry yeast
2 tablespoons lukewarm (110° to 115°F) water
1 cup milk
4 tablespoons (½ stick) butter, melted
1 egg, lightly beaten
1 cup all-purpose flour
1½ teaspoons curry powder
¼ cup chopped scallions, green part only
2 cups cooked corn kernels
Fine sea salt, freshly ground black pepper, and cayenne to taste
Vegetable oil, for frying

MAKE THE BATTER In a bowl, stir together the yeast and warm water. Let sit for 3 minutes. Add the milk, butter, and egg, and stir to combine. Add the flour, curry powder, scallions, and corn. Season with salt, pepper, and cayenne.

MAKE THE PANCAKES Heat 1 tablespoon oil in a sauté pan set over medium-high heat. Add 2 table-spoons of batter, letting it spread into a circle in the middle of the pan. When the batter begins to bubble and looks golden brown at the edges, carefully turn and cook on the other side until golden brown, about 1 minute. Remove the pancake to a paper towel–lined plate and continue in this manner until you have used up all the batter.

TO SERVE Present the pancakes alongside the dish of your choosing, or in a linen napkin–lined basket or plate.

BROCCOLI RABE WITH GARLIC

serves (6) A popular Italian alternative to plain old broccoli, broccoli rabe is pleasingly bitter, with a nice, firm bite. I recommend this as an accompaniment to Grilled Hake "Four by Four" (page 187) and Salmon Steak with Ginger-Chile Glaze (page 213).

2 **to 3 large bunches broccoli rabe,** separated into smaller bunches
4 **tablespoons (½ stick) unsalted butter**
3 **garlic cloves,** chopped
   Fine sea salt and freshly ground black pepper to taste
   Pinch grated nutmeg

BLANCH THE BROCCOLI RABE Bring a pot of salted water to a boil. Fill a large bowl halfway with ice water. Add the broccoli rabe to the boiling water and blanch until *al dente*, 2 to 3 minutes. Drain and transfer to the ice water to cool and stop the cooking. Drain and set aside.

SAUTÉ THE BROCCOLI RABE AND GARLIC Melt the butter in a wide, deep sauté pan set over medium heat. Add the garlic and sauté until golden brown and the butter is light brown. Add the broccoli rabe and sauté until warmed through. Season with salt, pepper, and nutmeg, transfer to a bowl, and serve.

FRIED BAKED POTATO

serves (6) This is a sophisticated version of potato skins, the incredibly popular and decadent American pub snack of the 1980s that topped carved-out potato skins with cheese, bacon, and scallions. Only here, I use the whole potato instead of just what remains in the skins. Serve this with dishes that have enough flavor to stand up to the combination of thrice-cooked potatoes and cheese, like Skate Barbecue with Braised Collard Greens (page 216) and Tuna Burger (page 224).

Canola oil, for frying

6 **medium Idaho potatoes,** baked, cooled, peeled, and broken into large chunks

½ **cup diced bacon (about 2 ounces)**

2 **garlic cloves,** chopped

¾ **cup diced Vermont Cheddar or Emmental cheese (about 3 ounces)**

¼ **cup chopped scallions,** green part only

Fine sea salt and freshly ground black pepper to taste

FRY THE POTATOES Pour oil into a large pot to a depth of 5 inches and heat to 375°F. Carefully add the potatoes in batches and fry until golden brown, about 1 to 2 minutes. Remove with a slotted spoon and drain on paper towels.

SAUTÉ THE BACON Sauté the bacon in a sauté pan over medium heat until crisp. Add the garlic, potatoes, cheese, and scallions. Toss well, then season with salt and pepper.

TO SERVE Turn the contents of the pan out into a serving dish or bowl.

CARAMELIZED CIPOLLINE ONIONS AND BRUSSELS SPROUTS

serves (6) Cipolline onions and Brussels sprouts are both very sweet, making this a perfect balancing side dish to powerfully flavored dishes like Walleye Pike with Bacon-Burgundy Sauce (page 206).

1½ **cups Brussels sprouts,** trimmed
1 **tablespoon unsalted butter**
½ **cup diced bacon (about 2 ounces)**
5 **cipolline onions (see page 47),** or 12 pearl onions, peeled and sliced
1 **garlic clove,** chopped
1 **tablespoon sugar**
   Fine sea salt and freshly ground black pepper to taste

BLANCH THE BRUSSELS SPROUTS Bring a pot of salted water to a boil. Fill a large bowl halfway with ice water. Add the Brussels sprouts to the boiling water and blanch for 10 to 12 minutes. Drain and transfer to the ice water to cool it and stop the cooking. Drain, halve them, and set aside.

SAUTÉ THE VEGETABLES Melt the butter in a large sauté pan. Add the bacon, onions, garlic, sugar, and Brussels sprouts. Sauté until the vegetables are golden brown, about 5 minutes. Season with salt and pepper.

TO SERVE Spoon the vegetables alongside the dish of your choosing, or turn them out into a serving bowl and pass family style from the center of the table.

SPICED PRESERVED LEMON

makes ② quarts Preserved lemon, one of the staples of Moroccan cooking, can be used both in whole form and chopped in a relish or as a salad seasoning. It is a condiment employed to flavor everything from fish to stews to frog's legs, poultry, and meat dishes. You can adapt this recipe to preserve up to 15 kumquats, which will look beautiful displayed in your refrigerator.

6 large or 7 medium Meyer lemons or regular lemons, preferably organic
¾ cup coarse sea salt
3½ cups water
⅓ cup sugar
⅓ cup olive oil
Pinch saffron
3 cardamom pods
½ teaspoon ground cumin
2 star anise
1 teaspoon black peppercorns
1 dried chile
1 bay leaf

PREPARE THE LEMONS Rinse the lemons well, scrubbing them with a vegetable brush, and pat dry. Quarter the lemons, leaving the quarters attached at the stem end. Stuff each lemon with about 2 tablespoons sea salt and put them in a 2-quart jar. Set aside.

PREPARE THE SEASONED LIQUID Pour the water into a pot and bring to a boil over high heat. Remove the pot from the heat and add the sugar, olive oil, saffron, cardamom, cumin, star anise, black peppercorns, chile, and bay leaf. Stir to combine. Pour the hot mixture over the lemons. Immediately put the lid on the jar, let cool to room temperature, then refrigerate for at least 4 weeks or up to 6 months.

TO SERVE Use the lemons as a flavoring or condiment.

DESSERTS A Gift from the Chef

Coffee-Cointreau Crème Brûlée

Strawberry Cheesecake

Bitter Almond Chocolate Soufflé Adeline

Gateau of Pancake Bourbonnaise

Coconut Bread Pudding

Steamed Banana Baba with Rum Syrup

Chocolate Cup with Condensed Milk Cappuccino

Orange Blossom Water Glazed Doughnuts

Raspberry-Rhubarb Soup with Lemongrass Tapioca

When there's an extra-special guest in one of my restaurants, I often send the person a little something from the kitchen, usually an additional dish between the appetizer and main course. But sometimes I send out a whole table full of desserts for the party to share. I love sneaking a look at their joyful reaction when the waiter says, "Here's a little gift from the chef."

Well, now that we've spent some time together, I feel I can share a secret with you: I, too, love dessert. In fact, I love making dessert even more than cooking fish. Maybe it's because my grandmother was such a great dessert maker at home. Maybe it's because I appreciate the precision of the recipes. Or maybe it's because I treasure that moment when you finish making a dessert and you get to take a taste for yourself in the kitchen.

So, here you go: a gift from the chef, a little something extra before you close this book—some of my favorite desserts, selected for how well they complement a seafood meal.

A lot of people say that desserts should always recall a childhood memory. Well, maybe I've never grown up because a lot of my desserts are based on sweets I discovered here in the United States, like the Orange Blossom Water Glazed Doughnuts (page 270), which grew out of my love for Krispy Kreme doughnuts.

I also enjoy making my own version of classic desserts. Examples include my Coffee-Cointreau Crème Brûlée (page 256), Strawberry Cheesecake (page 258), Coconut Bread Pudding (page 264), and Steamed Banana Baba with Rum Syrup (page 266).

I have a lot of strong feelings about desserts. One that might surprise you is that I don't find the combination of fruit and chocolate appealing. But I do like sweet, simple compositions of fruit like Raspberry-Rhubarb Soup with Lemongrass Tapioca (page 272).

I also think desserts should be fun, so I offer two here that are visually amusing: the Gateau of Pancake Bourbonnaise (page 262), which is a cake made from pancakes, and the Chocolate Cup with Condensed Milk Cappuccino (page 268), which might just trick your friends into thinking coffee's been served.

But my favorite dessert of all is Bitter Almond Chocolate Soufflé Adelynn (page 260). Not because it's my favorite to eat, but because of who I made it for—my daughter Adelynn, who loves Jordan almonds with chocolate. There's no greater pleasure for a chef than cooking for someone he loves, and I love making this for her.

COFFEE-COINTREAU CRÈME BRÛLÉE

serves (6) *Crème brûlée,* or "burnt cream," is a cold custard topped with a caramelized sugar crust. Most people make the crust with dark brown sugar, but—in the case of this crème brûlée— you would lose the fine flavor of the coffee and orange-flavored liqueur inside. For a more interesting version, place a layer of thinly sliced banana in the bottom of the ramekin; you'll be surprised at how well the coffee and this fruit get along.

Serve this with a Financier (recipe follows) or sugar cookies, if desired.

6 egg yolks
¾ cup plus 6 to 8 tablespoons sugar
1 cup milk
2 cups heavy cream
2 tablespoons coarsely cracked coffee beans
2 tablespoons Cointreau liqueur

MAKE THE CUSTARD Combine the egg yolks and ¾ cup of the sugar in a standing mixer. Beat until smooth and white. Pour the milk and cream into a pot and bring to a boil over high heat. Immediately remove from the heat, stir in the coffee beans, and set aside to infuse for 10 minutes. Gently whisk the coffee cream into the egg and sugar mixture. Whisk to cool slightly. Cover and refrigerate for approximately 3 hours, then strain. Stir in the Cointreau.

PREHEAT THE OVEN to 325°F.

PREPARE AND BAKE THE INDIVIDUAL SERVINGS Divide the mixture among six 6-ounce ramekins. Set in a roasting pan and pour warm water into the pan to come halfway up the sides of the ramekins. Bake in the oven until the custards are set (a toothpick inserted to the center of a custard should come out clean), 50 to 55 minutes. Remove the pan from the oven. Remove the ramekins from the pan and let cool for a few minutes at room temperature. Cover them with plastic wrap and chill in the refrigerator for at least 4 hours or overnight.

CARAMELIZE THE TOPS When ready to serve, sprinkle the remaining 6 to 8 tablespoons of sugar over the tops of the cold custards. Caramelize the sugar into a hard crust with a small propane blowtorch (see page 275), or preheat the broiler, put the ramekins on a baking sheet, and broil 3 to 4 inches from the heat until caramelized, 1 to 2 minutes.

TO SERVE Put each ramekin on its own small plate and serve immediately.

Wine Suggestion: Blandy's 10-year Madeira. A fortified wine with aromas of caramel, roasted nuts, and figs.

FINANCIERS

serves ⑥ as an accompaniment These moist little almond cakes can be embellished with marinated fruit dice, like banana with rum, pineapple with Malibu, or raspberry with kirsch. Marinate the fruit in the alcohol, then spoon them over the batter. They'll sink in a bit and cook in the financier as it bakes.

4 egg whites
½ cup sugar
1 teaspoon vanilla extract
¼ teaspoon almond extract
⅓ cup all-purpose flour
½ cup almond flour or finely ground almonds
1 tablespoon cornstarch
9 tablespoons (1 stick plus 1 tablespoon) butter, browned (see page 83)

IN A BOWL, stir together the egg whites, sugar, vanilla, and almond extract. Sift the flour, almond flour, and cornstarch into this mixture. Add the brown butter and stir to incorporate. Refrigerate the batter for at least 2 hours. Preheat the oven to 375°F. Divide among the wells of a mini-muffin mold and bake for 6 to 7 minutes.

STRAWBERRY CHEESECAKE

serves ⑥ My technique for making cheesecake is fairly traditional, but it yields a very light cake with a creamy texture. And the method I use for cooking strawberries in a covered double-boiler is worth noting because it keeps all of the flavor in the pot. You can add other fruits to the mix; blueberries, raspberries, and blackberries would be especially delicious. If you don't feel like making the berries, caramelize the top as you would a crème brûlée (see page 256) and serve it warm with passionfruit pulp on the side.

2½ **cups strawberries,** trimmed and cleaned, larger ones halved

1¼ **cups sugar**

1½ **teaspoons (½ envelope) unflavored powdered gelatin,** softened in a few tablespoons water

1¼ **cups honey graham cracker crumbs**

8 **tablespoons (1 stick) unsalted butter,** melted

8 **ounces cream cheese**

Seeds from 1 vanilla bean

2 **eggs**

¼ **cup heavy cream**

¾ **cup sour cream**

Juice of ½ lemon

MAKE THE STRAWBERRIES Put the strawberries and ½ cup of the sugar in the pot of a double-boiler and cover with plastic wrap. Place over simmering water. Cook for 30 to 40 minutes, then stir in the softened gelatin. Chill in the refrigerator for 3 hours.

MAKE THE CRUST Preheat the oven to 350°F. Stir together the graham cracker crumbs, ¼ cup of the sugar, and the melted butter. Press into the bottom and 1½ inches up the sides of a 10-inch Springform pan (2 to 3 inches high). Bake for 10 minutes. If the crust has fallen from the top of the mold, push it back up the sides. Let cool.

MAKE THE CHEESE FILLING Put the cream cheese and the vanilla seeds in the bowl of a standing mixer with the whisk attachment or food processor using the plastic blade. Begin mixing on medium speed. Add the eggs and the remaining ½ cup sugar. Add the heavy cream and sour cream. Add the lemon juice and continue whisking until smooth. Strain the mixture and pour into the crust. Wrap the pan with aluminum foil and bake for 25 to 30 minutes in a water bath. Remove from the water bath and let cool, then chill for at least 2 hours and up to 24 hours.

TO SERVE Unmold, top with the strawberries and strawberry gel, and serve.

Wine Suggestion: Marion, Passito Bianco 2000; Veneto. A passito (raisinated)-style wine from Italy, with aromas of dried apricot and vanilla.

BITTER ALMOND CHOCOLATE SOUFFLÉ ADELYNN

serves ⑥ This dessert is named for my daughter, who loves the simply perfect combination of chocolate and Jordan almonds—the large Spanish almonds that are often sold with a pastel candy shell. If you don't have soufflé molds, this can be made in ovenproof soup bowls. In fact, it will be even more attractive that way.

Serve this with pistachio ice cream or chocolate sorbet.

4 **tablespoons unsalted butter,** plus more melted for mold
½ **cup granulated sugar,** plus more for mold
1 **cup milk**
5 **egg yolks**
¼ **cup plus 3 tablespoons all-purpose flour**
About 2 **teaspoons almond extract**
6 **egg whites**
24 **extra-large chocolate chips** (about ⅓ cup)
15 **Jordan almonds,** cracked
2 **tablespoons confectioners' sugar**

PREPARE THE SOUFFLÉ MOLDS Brush the insides of 6 individual soufflé cups (2 inches tall and 3 inches in diameter) with butter and coat with sugar. Set in the refrigerator.

MAKE THE SOUFFLÉ BASE Combine the milk and 4 tablespoons butter in a heavy-bottomed medium saucepan and bring to a boil. Remove from the heat and set aside. In a large bowl, combine the egg yolks and ¼ cup of the sugar, and beat with an electric mixture until the mixture becomes thick and lighter in color. Stir in the flour. Very slowly, in a thin stream, whisk the milk and butter into the yolk mixture. Return to the pan and cook over low heat, whisking contantly, until it becomes very thick. Remove from heat, add the almond extract, and return to a large bowl. Taste the mixture; if you can't quite taste the almond, add a few more drops of extract. Set aside. (The base can be made up to this point as much as 1 hour in advance. Cover and keep in a warm place until ready to proceed.)

PREHEAT THE OVEN to 375°F.

BAKE THE SOUFFLÉ With an electric mixer, beat the egg whites and remaining ¼ cup sugar until soft peaks form. Using a rubber spatula, fold half of the beaten egg whites into the soufflé base. Repeat with the other half. Divide enough of the soufflé mixture among the molds to fill about one-third up the sides. Place 3 chocolate chips in each cup. Fill the cup the rest of the way with the remaining soufflé mixture. Run a spatula over the top to level it off. Place 1 chocolate chip in the center of each cup and sprinkle the tops with almonds. Place the molds on a baking sheet and bake in the oven until the soufflés are golden brown on top, 15 to 18 minutes.

TO SERVE Remove from the oven. Dust with confectioners' sugar. Serve immediately with ice cream on the side or prepare individual portions at the table, placing a scoop of ice cream right on top of each serving.

Wine Suggestion: Ramos Pinto, 10-Year Tawny Port. A nutty tawny port with aromas of dried berries.

GÂTEAU OF PANCAKE BOURBONNAISE

serves (6) This recipe, based on a dessert served by the Troisgros brothers, is named for the region where I grew up in France, le Bourbonnais. Other jams, like raspberry or bitter orange, or Nutella, can be substituted for the apricot. This could be a holiday dessert, perhaps for Thanksgiving, using cranberry jam. It can be made ahead of time (on the morning of the day you will serve it). For an extra dimension of flavor and texture, caramelize the top.

> 2 **cups milk**
> 9 **tablespoons (1 stick plus 1 tablespoon) unsalted butter,** cut into 9 pieces, at room temperature
> 1 **vanilla bean,** split lengthwise
> 8 **eggs,** separated
> ⅔ **cup sugar**
> ½ **cup plus 2 tablespoons all-purpose flour**
> **Pinch fine sea salt**
> **Juice of ¼ lemon**
> 1 **cup bitter orange marmalade or apricot jam**
> **Store-bought maple ice cream or orange sorbet**

PREHEAT THE OVEN to 375°F.

MAKE THE BATTER   In a small saucepan, warm the milk, 5 tablespoons of the butter, and the vanilla bean over medium-high heat. As soon as it boils, remove from heat and let infuse for 10 minutes. Remove and discard the vanilla bean. In a mixing bowl, whisk together the egg yolks, 3 tablespoons of the sugar, and the flour until creamy and paler in color. Slowly add the cooled milk, stirring with a wooden spoon. In another bowl, beat the egg whites with a pinch of salt and a few drops of lemon juice. When soft peaks have formed, slowly beat in the remaining ¼ cup sugar. Add the beaten egg whites to the egg yolk mixture, slowly folding from the bottom to the top with a rubber spatula until just blended.

MAKE THE FIRST PANCAKE   Warm a 10-inch ovenproof sauté pan or any metal skillet with 1 teaspoon butter over medium heat. Ladle some batter into the sauté pan and cook for 10 seconds, then transfer the pan to the oven for 3 minutes. Carefully transfer the pancake to the center of a large plate and top with 3 to 4 tablespoons of jam.

MAKE THE REMAINING PANCAKES   Repeat Step 3 with most of the remaining butter (as needed), batter, and jam until 5 more pancakes are formed and stacked. Make the last pancake a bit wider than the others and put it on top, but do *not* cover the final pancake with jam.

TO SERVE   Slice into individual servings as you would a cake, and serve with ice cream and maple syrup.

Wine Suggestion: Jaboulet, Muscat Beaumes de Venise 2001; southern Rhône. An aromatic, sweet white from France, with aromas of blossoms and orange.

COCONUT BREAD PUDDING

serves ⑥ This is a truly outrageous version of bread pudding that's made rich with coconut milk and caramelized before serving, almost like a crème brûlée. Take care not to burn the brioche while caramelizing the top, and be careful—you might eat the whole thing yourself! (Or, in my case, your co-author might do the same. When I offered Andrew Friedman a taste, he couldn't stop eating it. I left to take a phone call and when I returned he was standing there over an empty mold.)
Serve this with Madeleines (recipe follows).

 6 eggs
 1 cup plus 2 tablespoons granulated sugar, plus more for topping dish
 2 cups heavy cream
 2 cups unsweetened coconut milk
 1 tablespoon dark rum
10 slices brioche or other fluffy bread such as challah, ⅜ inch thick
    Confectioners' sugar, for serving

MAKE THE CUSTARD In a large bowl, whisk together the eggs and granulated sugar until smooth and pale in color. Bring the cream to a boil and gradually whisk into the egg mixture, a little at a time. Whisk in the coconut milk and rum and let sit for 1 hour.

PREHEAT THE OVEN to 350°F.

PREPARE THE DISH FOR BAKING Arrange the brioche slices overlapping in 2 rows in a baking pan 10 by 12 by 3 inches deep. Pour the custard over the top. Set in a larger pan half filled with hot water and bake until set but not too firm, 30 to 35 minutes. Top with confectioners' sugar and caramelize it using a small propane blowtorch (see page 275) or by passing under the broiler for 1 to 3 minutes.

TO SERVE Serve the dish from the middle of the table, scooping out individual portions.

Wine Suggestion: Chateau Pajzos, Tokay Azsú 1993, 5 *puttonyos*; Tokay. An ancient dessert wine from Hungary, with honey and custard aromas.

MADELEINES

serves (6) These are delicious on their own, or as an accompaniment to fruit-based desserts. They're also perfect as a snack with coffee or tea.

4 eggs
1 cup granulated sugar
Grated zest of 1 lemon
Grated zest of 1 orange
Seeds of 1 vanilla bean, scraped out
14 tablespoons (1¾ sticks) butter, melted
2 tablespoons orange blossom water
1¾ cups all-purpose flour
1 teaspoon baking powder
Confectioners' sugar, for dusting

IN A MIXING BOWL, whisk together the eggs, sugar, lemon and orange zests, and vanilla seeds until the mixture is homogenous and fluffy. Add the butter and orange blossom water. Sift the flour and baking powder into the bowl, stir to combine, and let the batter rest for 30 minutes. Preheat the oven to 400°F. Butter and flour small madeleine molds and divide the dough among the compartments. Bake for 6 to 7 minutes. Remove the madeleines from the mold, dust with confectioners' sugar, and serve hot.

STEAMED BANANA BABA WITH RUM SYRUP

serves (6) I strongly recommend that you serve this dessert, a simplified version of the classic baba, which is traditionally made with yeast, with whipped cream or Crème Diplomat (recipe follows). You can make it the morning of the day you plan to eat it, and reheat it later in a microwave to prevent it from drying out.

13½	tablespoons unsalted butter, at room temperature
½	cup self-rising flour (Presto)
1	teaspoon baking soda
⅔	cup packed light brown sugar
2	large eggs
3	large ripe bananas, mashed (about 1⅓ cups)
½	cup granulated sugar
¼	cup dark rum
¼	cup water
1½	cups chopped roasted pecans, preferably caramelized

PREHEAT THE OVEN to 350°F. Generously butter six 3-ounce baba molds or muffin tins with 2 tablespoons of the butter.

MAKE THE BATTER In a small bowl, mix the flour and baking soda. In another bowl, using an electric mixer, beat 4½ tablespoons of butter until creamy. Add the brown sugar and beat until fluffy. Add the eggs, one at a time, and beat until just incorporated. Add the banana and beat to mix in. Using a large spatula, fold the flour mixture into the banana mixture until incorporated. Spoon the batter into the ramekins and set in a baking pan. Carefully pour enough hot water into the pan to reach halfway up the sides of the ramekins.

BAKE THE CAKES Bake for 40 to 50 minutes, or until the cakes are firm but spring back when pressed lightly with your finger. Remove the pan from the oven and transfer the ramekins to a rack with tongs. Let cool slightly. Run a knife around the side of the cakes, then invert onto a rack to cool.

MAKE THE SAUCE In a medium saucepan, combine the remaining 7 tablespoons butter with the sugar, rum, and water. Bring to a boil, stirring to dissolve the sugar. Remove the sauce from the heat.

TO SERVE   Spoon 2 to 3 tablespoons some of the rum sauce onto each of 6 plates. Top each with
a warm cake, and garnish the cakes with a few pecans.

Wine Suggestion: Lustau, Pedro Ximenez, "San Emilio" Jerez. A sweet sherry with rich
toasted, roasted aromas and nuances of nuts, figs, and dates.

PASTRY CREAM AND CRÈME DIPLOMAT

makes ③ **cups** This is a very useful recipe for a basic pastry cream. Crème Diplomat is a pastry cream with liqueur and whipped cream added. The one here uses kirsch, but it can be made
for other uses with Grand Marnier, rum, Cointreau, amaretto, or another liqueur.

- 2 **cups milk**
- 1 **vanilla bean,** split in half
- 4 **egg yolks**
- ¼ **cup sugar**
- 2 **tablespoons all-purpose flour**
- 2 **tablespoons cornstarch**

IN A POT, combine the milk and vanilla bean, and bring it to a boil. Meanwhile in a bowl, mix the
yolks, sugar, flour, and cornstarch. Slowly pour the hot milk over the mixture and combine.
Return to the pot and set over high heat. Stir constantly with a whisk and cook for 4 minutes after it comes to a boil. Use tongs or a slotted spoon to remove and discard the
vanilla bean. Place the pastry cream in a bowl and refrigerate until completely cold.

For *Crème Diplomat,* make the pastry cream as described above. Stir 2 to 3
tablespoons of kirsch into the cooled pastry cream and whip in 1 cup heavy cream.

CHOCOLATE CUP WITH CONDENSED MILK CAPPUCCINO

serves ⑥ With this amusing presentation, chocolate cake is baked in an espresso cup and topped with a foam of milk and condensed milk, which looks like—cappuccino! It's a great dessert to make ahead for a dinner party. This would be amazing with coffee or caramel ice cream, or the Rice Crispy (recipe follows).

1¼ **cups whole milk**
¾ **cup sweetened condensed milk**
4 **ounces bittersweet chocolate,** such as Valrhona
3 **tablespoons unsalted butter,** plus more for greasing the cups
3 **eggs,** separated
¼ **cup sugar**
1 **tablespoon almond flour or flour ground in a food processor**
2½ **tablespoons all-purpose flour**
Ground cinnamon

PREHEAT THE OVEN to 425°F and generously butter and flour 6 espresso cups.

MAKE THE SAUCE In a medium saucepan, warm 1 cup of the whole milk and all the condensed milk in a double boiler. Remove from the heat and cover to keep warm.

MAKE THE CAKES Melt the chocolate, butter, and remaining ¼ cup milk in a double boiler set over simmering water. Put the egg yolks and sugar in a mixer and whisk until light and fluffy. Add the almond flour and all-purpose flour. Beat in the chocolate mixture.

IN A CLEAN BOWL, beat the egg whites until soft peaks form. Add to the batter and fold just until no streaks remain. Fill the espresso cups three-fourths of the way with the batter. Place on a baking sheet and bake until the cakes puffs up but are still slightly runny in the center, 8 to 9 minutes. Serve immediately in the cup or let rest for 2 minutes and unmold.

TO SERVE Place 1 cake on each of 6 plates. Blend the sauce with an immersion blender or whisk until foamy. Spoon some sauce over each serving. Dust with cinnamon and serve.

Wine Suggestion: Dr. Parce, Banyuls 1998; Rousillon. A fortified red sweet wine from southern France, with aromas of crushed wild berries.

RICE CRISPY

serves (6) I see no reason to tinker with this basic recipe for a delicious American treat.

      3 tablespoons unsalted butter
    40 large marshmallows
      6 cups Rice Crispies cereal

MELT THE BUTTER in a pot set over medium heat. Add the marshmallows and let them melt. Add the cereal and stir together. Pour the mixture out onto a waxed paper–lined tray. Let cool and slice.

ORANGE BLOSSOM WATER GLAZED DOUGHNUTS

serves (6) I love doughnuts so much that I once applied for a job at Krispy Kreme so I could learn how they make theirs so delicious. They didn't hire me, but I've spent a lot of time learning to make doughnuts, nonetheless.

You've never tasted doughnuts as light and airy or as gently flavored as these. You can sprinkle them with a mixture of cinnamon and sugar, or turn them into jelly doughnuts, fill them with orange or raspberry jam, lemon curd, apricot jam, or flavored honey.

Serve these with Chocolate Truffles (recipe follows) or creamy vanilla ice cream.

2 cups confectioners' sugar
⅓ cup light corn syrup
  Juice of ½ lime
2½ tablespoons orange blossom water
  Grated zest of 1 orange
½ cup warm milk
2 teaspoons active dry yeast
2½ cups all-purpose flour
½ teaspoon fine sea salt
⅓ cup sugar
1 egg
⅓ cup water
4 tablespoons butter, melted
  Vegetable oil, for frying

MAKE THE GLAZE Mix the confectioners' sugar, corn syrup, lime juice, orange blossom water, and orange zest. Set aside.

MAKE THE DOUGH Warm the milk in a pot with the yeast. Set aside for 10 minutes to let the yeast bloom. Mix the flour, salt, and sugar. Beat the egg and add it to the milk mixture. Add the water and butter. Add the milk mixture to the flour mixture. Paddle until all ingredients are well incorporated. Switch to the hook attachment and mix on medium speed for 20 minutes. Cover and refrigerate for at least 8 hours.

MAKE THE DOUGHNUTS   Roll out the dough to a thickness of ¼ inch. Cut 1¼-inch circles out of the dough with a round cutter. Place them on a parchment paper–lined cookie sheet. Let rise for 30 minutes in a warm place, such as an open oven door.

FRY THE DOUGHNUTS   Pour the vegetable oil into a wide, deep pot to a depth of 3 inches. Heat the oil to 375°F. Lower the doughnuts into the oil and fry until golden brown, 1 or 2 minutes. Place on a paper towel to drain, roll them in the glaze, and place on a rack.

TO SERVE   Reheat the doughnuts in a microwave for just a few seconds, if necessary, and present the warm doughnuts in a linen-lined basket as an accompaniment to coffee or tea.

Wine Suggestion: Paolo Sarocco, Moscato d'Asti 2002; Piedmont. A slightly sparkling sweet wine from Italy with nuances of peaches and flowers.

CHOCOLATE TRUFFLES

makes (40) truffles   Once you make these indulgent chocolate confections, you might find yourself making them all the time. They're as easy as they are delicious, and addictive.

10 ounces bittersweet Valrhona chocolate, coarsely chopped
 1 cup heavy cream
 2 tablespoons unsalted butter
¼ cup sugar
 2 tablespoons Grand Marnier liqueur
 2 tablespoons amaretto liqueur
½ cup unsweetened cocoa powder

MELT THE CHOCOLATE   in a double boiler. In a pot, bring the cream to a boil with the butter and sugar. Stir together with the chocolate, then add the Grand Marnier and amaretto. Cool on a tray in refrigerator overnight. Scoop with a melon baller, dipping the scoop in hot water between truffles, and roll in cocoa powder.

RASPBERRY-RHUBARB SOUP WITH LEMONGRASS TAPIOCA

serves (6) This soup offers a number of options: you can serve the "broth" on its own as a refreshing dessert or pre-dessert course, and the tapioca can be presented on its own as well. And you can replace the fruits with strawberry, pineapple, or kiwi. Serve this with the Spiced Conversation (recipe follows).

2 water plus 2 cups water
1¼ cups plus ⅓ cup sugar
½ stalk lemongrass, finely chopped, plus 2 stalks, coarsely chopped (see page 153)
½ vanilla bean, split and scraped
4 branches rhubarb, thinly sliced (about 3 cups slices)
1½ cups raspberries
1½ cups milk
¼ cup heavy cream
1 cup tapioca pearls (medium)
1½ cups unsweetened coconut milk
3 ripe passionfruit, halved, pulp extracted and reserved

MAKE THE RASPBERRY-RHUBARB SOUP In a pot, combine 2 cups of water, ¾ cup of the sugar, the finely chopped lemongrass, and the vanilla bean half. Bring to a boil, cover, remove from the heat, and let infuse for 30 minutes. Strain the syrup and transfer it to a large saucepan. Bring it to a boil over high heat. Add the rhubarb, remove the pot from the heat, cover, and let cool to room temperature. Fold in the raspberries and refrigerate the fruit mixture for at least 4 hours or overnight, until chilled.

MAKE THE COCONUT MIXTURE Put the coconut milk, milk, coarsely chopped lemongrass, ⅓ cup of the sugar, and the cream in a pot. Bring to a boil over high heat, then remove the pot from the heat and let stand, covered, for 30 minutes. Strain the mixture and refrigerate it.

MAKE THE TAPIOCA Bring the 2 quarts of water and the remaining ½ cup of sugar to a boil in a pot set over high heat. Add the tapioca, lower the heat to medium, and stir until the tapioca is clear, 20 to 25 minutes. Strain the tapioca and rinse under warm water to remove the starch. In a bowl, combine the coconut milk and tapioca.

TO SERVE Present the soup and tapioca side by side in 2 separate small bowls for each person, or
in 2 large bowls from the center of the table. Top the rhubarb soup with the passionfruit.

Wine Suggestion: Giacomo Bologna, Brachetto d'Acqui 2002; Piedmont. A slightly
sparkling sweet red wine from Italy, with aromas of rose petals and raspberries.

SPICED CONVERSATION

serves ⑥ I enjoy these warm, but still a bit undercooked when they come out of the oven.
Ironically, the more you eat them, the less conversation you'll have.

- **3 tablespoons egg whites,** from 2 to 3 eggs
- 2½ **cups confectioners' sugar**
- ¼ **teaspoon ground ginger**
- ¼ **teaspoon ground cinnamon**
- ¼ **teaspoon ground star anise**
- ¼ **teaspoon ground cardamom**
- ¼ **teaspoon freshly ground white pepper**
- **2 puff pastry sheets,** 8 by 12 inches each (from a 17¼-ounce package)

STIR ALL INGREDIENTS except the puff pastry together in a bowl. Set the pastry sheets on a cookie sheet and use a spatula to spread the mixture over the surface. Freeze on the sheet,
then cut into ¾ by 8-inch strips. Set a wire rack over the frozen sheets to keep them from
falling when they puff. Bake at 385°F for about 15 minutes.

TECHNIQUES

Here's how to perform certain steps called for throughout the book:

TO POACH LOBSTERS IN COURT BOUILLON

Lobsters should be poached in batches, 2 at a time, in a large lobster or stock pot. I generally poach them in a court bouillion, but sometimes use just water. Here is the court bouillon recipe:

2	cups dry white wine	1	tablespoon coarse salt
1	carrot, sliced	10	black peppercorns
1	small leek, green part only, sliced	3	sprigs thyme
1	stalk celery, sliced	2	bay leaves
½	onion, cut into large dice		

POUR THE WINE and 5 quarts of water into a large stockpot. Add the carrot, leek, celery, onion, salt, peppercorns, thyme, and bay leaves. Bring to a boil over high heat. Add the lobsters to the pot in batches of 2 and cook for 10 to 12 minutes. Use tongs to remove the lobsters from the pot; set aside to cool over ice.

Follow as much of the instructions below as each recipe calls for:

When the lobster is cool enough to handle, take the head in one hand and the tail in the other and twist them in opposite directions until the upper and lower halves come apart. Remove the meat from the tail in 1 piece and slice it in half lengthwise. Remove the dark intestine. Remove the lobster meat. Crack the claws and knuckles with a cracker or the back of a heavy chef's knife and remove the meat from within. Cut the meat into desired-size dice and set it aside. The lobster meat can be wrapped and refrigerated for up to 8 hours.

Remove the gray-green tomalley (liver) and red roe, if any, from the lobster shells and set the shells aside separately.

TO SOFT-BOIL AN EGG

Put an egg in a heavy-bottomed pot and gently cover with cold water. Add 1 tablespoon of distilled white vinegar to keep the egg from leaking out if the shell cracks while cooking. Bring the water to a boil over medium heat, then lower the heat and let simmer for 3 minutes. Remove the egg from the water with a slotted spoon and set aside in ice water.

For Hard-Boiled Eggs, cook the egg for 12 to 15 minutes (depending on size), then transfer to a bowl of ice water to stop the cooking.

TO MAKE BAGUETTE CROUTONS

Slice a baguette into 1-inch bias cuts or ½-inch cubes, discarding the ends. If desired, arrange on a baking sheet, drizzle with olive oil, and bake in an oven preheated to 325°F until crispy and golden-brown, about 8 minutes. Remove from oven and let cool.

TO FLAMBÉ

Flambéing is a way of quickly reducing liqueur or wine in a pan so that it evaporates almost instantly, intensifying and fusing its flavor to that of the pan's contents. *It is something that should only be attempted by experienced home cooks using great caution.* To flambé, add the liqueur or wine to the pan, grasp the pan firmly by the end of the handle, lean away from the stove, tip the pan away and carefully ignite the liqueur with a match. Immediately remove the pan from the heat and keep it off heat until the flame goes out.

TO CARAMELIZE USING A BLOW TORCH

First of all, a clarification: When I say "blow torch," I'm talking about a small torch meant for cooking. To caramelize, simply ignite the torch and hold it at a right angle 6 to 8 inches above the area to be cooked. Work your way around the surface of the food, from the outside in, moving inward as soon as the surface is golden brown, taking care not to blacken it.

MAKING CLARIFIED BUTTER

To make clarified butter, also known as "drawn butter," put the butter in a pan and melt it over low heat until the fat separates out into a thick layer. Remove the pan from the heat and spoon the foam from the top. Then, pour the milk from the pan into a heatproof container, being careful not to include the milky residue at the bottom, which should be discarded.

FIXING A BROKEN EMULSION

If an emulsion doesn't hold together, pour a few tablespoons of it into a new bowl and add some hot water, whisking to start the emulsion anew. Slowly add the remaining portion of the broken emulsion to the new one, whisking as you do. The hot water will help incorporate the ingredients more easily.

TO CUT BACON INTO LARDONS

Beginning with a ½-inch-thick slice of slab bacon, cut ½-inch-wide and 1-inch long pieces, slicing across the width of the bacon so that each lardon contains both meat and fat.

TO POACH AN EGG

Fill a small pot ⅔ with water and add a tablespoon or so of white vinegar. (Do not add salt, which will cause the white to separate from the yolk.) Fill a large bowl halfway with ice water. Bring the water to a simmer, not a boil, over medium heat. While the water is coming to a simmer, carefully crack the egg onto a small plate or saucer. When the water simmers, tip the plate over the water to slide the egg into it. It will cook on the surface. When the egg is firm and white, 3 minutes, remove it with a slotted spoon, letting any excess water run off, and transfer it to the ice water to cool it and stop the cooking. When ready to add it to a dish, remove it with a slotted spoon.

TO TRIM ARTICHOKES

Pull off the tough outer leaves. Use a heavy knife to remove the stem, if any, then cut the choke just above the heart, about 1½ inches from the stem end. Use a paring knife to trim away the excess until you get to the yellow portion, which is where the heart begins. Put the heart in acidulated water to keep it from discoloring.

TO SCORE FISH

The skin of fish is often scored to prevent it from curling when cooked. To score a fish, make crosshatch patterns on the skin using a single-edged razor blade or very sharp, very thin-bladed knife. Cut into the skin, but take care not to puncture the flesh.

TO BLANCH VEGETABLES

Blanching vegetables pre- or par-cooks them so they can be quickly sautéed or added to sauces or soups at the last minute and simply warmed through. To blanch vegetables, cook them in boiling, salted water for the time indicated in each recipe. Usually, the vegetables are then "shocked" in ice water, which stops the cooking process and keeps them nicely al dente until they are finished at the end of the recipe.

TO SHUCK AN OYSTER

Using a towel to protect your hand, grasp the oyster in one hand. Force a paring knife or other small knife into the oyster and move it around inside until the shell "pops" open. If you want to separate the oyster from the shell, cut it where the muscle meets the shell. Store oysters in an airtight container in their liquid.

MAIL-ORDER SOURCES

FISH AND SHELLFISH

Browne Trading Company
800-944-7848
www.browne-trading.com
Rod Mitchell's Browne Trading Company is one of the most revered fish purveyors in the country, and supplies many three- and four-star restaurants with hard-to-find fish and shellfish.

In my opinion, these are the two finest fish purveyors in New York City:

Pisacane
212-758-1525

F. Rozzo & Sons
212-242-6100

OTHER

The Chef's Garden
419-433-4947
222.chefs-garden.com
As its name indicates, this Ohio-based operation is a source for hard-to-find fruits and vegetables, as well as micro-greens, exotic mushrooms, and dried and fresh fruits and beans.

D'Artagnan, Inc.
800-DARTAGN
www.dartagnan.com
This near-legendary company, named for one of the Three Musketeers, sells decadent foods like foie gras, as well as other duck and game products, wild mushrooms, demi-glace, and wild mushrooms.

De Bragga and Spitler
212-924-1311
A New York City operation specializing in beef, lamb, and pork.

Hudson Valley Foie Gras
845-292-2500
www.hudsonvalleyfoiegras.com
The name says it all: American foie gras and other duck products.

J.B. Prince
212-683-3553
www.jbprince.com
This is a great source of kitchen equipment like knives, mixers, and hand blenders.

Kalustyans
212-685-3451
www.kalustyans.com
If you're looking for a source for gourmet and Middle Eastern food products, look no further than this store, which a lot of New York chefs, myself included, love visiting.

Kitchen Arts and Letters
212-876-5550
This New York institution sells rare and out-of-print culinary books and cookbooks.

Murray's Cheese Shop
888-692-4339
www.murrayscheese.com
This New York institution sells a breathtaking assortment of domestic and imported cheeses.

Urbani Truffles USA
215-699-8780
www.urbaniusa.com
The American offshoot of the Italian purveyor sells sublime truffles and caviar.

CONVERSIONS

Liquid Measures

½ fluid ounce = 3 teaspoons = 1 tablespoon

1 fluid ounce = 2 tablespoons

2 fluid ounces = 4 tablespoons = ¼ cup

4 fluid ounces = 8 tablespoons = ½ cup

6 fluid ounces = ¾ cup

8 fluid ounces = 1 cup

10 fluid ounces = 1¼ cups

12 fluid ounces = 1½ cups

16 fluid ounces = 2 cups = 1 pint

24 fluid ounces = 3 cups = 1½ pints

32 fluid ounces = 4 cups = 2 pints = 1 quart

Solid Measures

16 ounces = 1 pound

20 ounces = 1¼ pounds

24 ounces = 1½ pounds

28 ounces = 1¾ pounds

32 ounces = 2 pounds

36 ounces = 2¼ pounds

40 ounces = 2½ pounds

48 ounces = 3 pounds

Oven Temperature Equivalents

Fahrenheit	Celsius	Gas Mark
225	110	¼
250	130	½
275	140	1
300	150	2
325	170	3
350	180	4
375	190	5
400	200	6
425	220	7
450	230	8
475	240	9
500	250	10

INDEX